"In taking us straight to t[...]
us magnificently. We so [...]
Scriptures get into us. The [...]
such submission to Biblical revelation means that we are genuinely
helped to be shaped by the Bible's teaching."

– Terry Virgo

"Phil makes the deep truths of Scripture alive and accessible. If you
want to grow in your understanding of each book of the Bible, then
buy these books and let them change your life!"

– PJ Smyth – GodFirst Church, Johannesburg, South Africa

"Most commentaries are dull. These are alive. Most commentaries are
for scholars. These are for you!"

– Canon Michael Green

"These notes are amazingly good. Lots of content and depth of
research, yet packed in a Big Breakfast that leaves the reader well fed
and full. Bible notes often say too little, yet larger commentaries can
be dull - missing the wood for the trees. Phil's insights are striking,
original, and fresh, going straight to the heart of the text and the
reader! Substantial yet succinct, they bristle with amazing insights
and life applications, compelling us to read more. Bible reading
will become enriched and informed with such a scintillating guide.
Teachers and preachers will find nuggets of pure gold here!"

– Greg Haslam – Westminster Chapel, London, UK

"The Bible is living and dangerous. The ones who teach it best are
those who bear that in mind – and let the author do the talking. Phil
has written these studies with a sharp mind and a combination of
creative application and reverence."

– Joel Virgo – Leader of Newday Youth Festival

"Phil Moore's new commentaries are outstanding: biblical and
passionate, clear and well-illustrated, simple and profound. God's
Word comes to life as you read them, and the wonder of God shines
through every page."

– Andrew Wilson – Author of Incomparable and GodStories

"Want to understand the Bible better? Don't have the time or energy to read complicated commentaries? The book you have in your hand could be the answer. Allow Phil Moore to explain and then apply God's message to your life. Think of this book as the Bible's message distilled for everyone."

– Adrian Warnock – *Christian blogger*

"Phil Moore presents Scripture in a dynamic, accessible and relevant way. The bite-size chunks – set in context and grounded in contemporary life – really make the Word become flesh and dwell among us."

– Dr David Landrum – *The Bible Society*

"Through a relevant, very readable, up to date storying approach, Phil Moore sets the big picture, relates God's Word to today and gives us fresh insights to increase our vision, deepen our worship, know our identity and fire our imagination. Highly recommended!"

– Geoff Knott – *former CEO of Wycliffe Bible Translators UK*

"What an exciting project Phil has embarked upon! These accessible and insightful books will ignite the hearts of believers, inspire the minds of preachers and help shape a new generation of men and women who are seeking to learn from God's Word."

– David Stroud – *Newfrontiers and ChristChurch London*

For more information about the Straight to the Heart series, please go to **www.philmoorebooks.com**.

STRAIGHT TO
THE HEART OF

Romans

60 BITE-SIZED INSIGHTS

Phil Moore

MONARCH
BOOKS

Oxford, UK & Grand Rapids, Michigan, USA

First published in the UK in 2011 by Monarch Books
(a publishing imprint of Lion Hudson plc)
Wilkinson House, Jordan Hill Road, Oxford OX2 8DR, England
Tel: +44 (0)1865 302750 Fax: +44 (0)1865 302757
Email: monarch@lionhudson.com
www.lionhudson.com

ISBN 978 0 85721 057 9 (print)
ISBN 978 0 85721 184 2 (epub)
ISBN 978 0 85721 183 5 (Kindle)
ISBN 978 0 85721 185 9 (PDF)

Distributed by:
UK: Marston Book Services, PO Box 269, Abingdon, Oxon, OX14 4YN
USA: Kregel Publications, PO Box 2607, Grand Rapids, Michigan 49501

The text paper used in this book has been made from wood independently certified as having come from sustainable forests.

British Library Cataloguing Data
A catalogue record for this book is available from the British Library.

Printed and bound in Great Britain by Clays Ltd, St Ives plc.

This book is for my brother, Jonathan.
I first studied Romans because your changed life
convinced me that there must be
a new King in town.

CONTENTS

ROMANS 9–11: THE NEW KING HAS A PLAN

ROMANS 12:1–15:13: THE NEW KING IS LORD

ROMANS 15:14–16:27: THE NEW KING IS ADVANCING

About the *Straight to the Heart* Series

On his eightieth birthday, Sir Winston Churchill dismissed the compliment that he was the "lion" who had defeated Nazi Germany in World War Two. He told the Houses of Parliament that *"It was a nation and race dwelling all around the globe that had the lion's heart. I had the luck to be called upon to give the roar."*

I hope that God speaks to you very powerfully through the "roar" of the books in the *Straight to the Heart* series. I hope they help you to understand the books of the Bible and the message which the Holy Spirit inspired their authors to write. I hope that they help you to hear God's voice challenging you, and that they provide you with a springboard for further journeys into each book of Scripture for yourself.

But when you hear my "roar", I want you to know that it comes from the heart of a much bigger "lion" than me. I have been shaped by a whole host of great Christian thinkers and preachers from around the world, and I want to give due credit to at least some of them here:

Terry Virgo, David Stroud, John Hosier, Adrian Holloway, Greg Haslam, Lex Loizides and all those who lead the Newfrontiers family of churches. Friends and encouragers, such as Stef Liston, Joel Virgo, Stuart Gibbs, Scott Taylor, Nick Sharp, Nick Derbridge, Phil Whittall, and Kevin and Sarah Aires. Tony Collins, Jenny Ward and Simon Cox at Monarch Books. Malcolm Kayes and all the elders of The Coign Church, Woking. My fellow elders and church members here at Queens Road Church, Wimbledon.

My great friend Andrew Wilson – without your friendship, encouragement and example, this series would never have happened.

I would like to thank my parents, my brother Jonathan, and my in-laws, Clive and Sue Jackson. Dad – your example birthed in my heart the passion that brought this series into being. I didn't listen to all you said when I was a child, but I couldn't ignore the way you got up at five o'clock every morning to pray, read the Bible and worship, because of your radical love for God and for his Word. I'd like to thank my children – Isaac, Noah and Esther – for keeping me sane when publishing deadlines were looming. But most of all, I'm grateful to my incredible wife, Ruth – my friend, encourager, corrector and helper.

You all have the lion's heart, and you have all developed the lion's heart in me. I count it an enormous privilege to be the one who was chosen to sound the lion's roar.

So welcome to the *Straight to the Heart* series. My prayer is that you will let this roar grip your own heart too – for the glory of the great Lion of the Tribe of Judah, the Lord Jesus Christ!

Introduction: There's a New King in Town

Paul, a servant of…Jesus Christ our Lord.

(Romans 1:1, 4)

Paul's letter to the Romans is not just the longest surviving letter from the ancient world. It was also the most dangerous. It was written to a city where a murderer built his reign on the corpses of his rivals. Ten years later, because of the message of Romans, Paul's own corpse would be added to his ever-growing pile.

The Emperor Nero had come to the throne in October 54 AD when his mother assassinated his stepfather, the Emperor Claudius. She had heard rumours that Claudius was about to disinherit Nero in favour of his son from a previous marriage, so she persuaded court officials to poison him before he could. Nothing must stand in the way of her sixteen-year-old son's aspirations to the throne.

Nero quickly followed his mother's example and made murder the hallmark of his insecure reign. Only weeks after becoming the most powerful ruler in the world, he consolidated his position by poisoning his stepbrother. In the years that followed, he murdered his mother, two of his wives and any nobleman who posed a threat. The Roman historian Suetonius tells us that Nero *"showed neither discrimination nor moderation in putting to death whoever he pleased on any pretext whatever."*[1] That's why when Paul wrote from Corinth to the Christians at

---

[1] Suetonius, writing in c.120 AD in his *Life of Nero* (37). Nero did not kill his mother until two years after Paul wrote Romans, but he murdered his stepbrother and many noblemen almost straightaway.

Rome in the spring of 57 AD, his letter was as dangerous as throwing a flaming torch into a room filled with gunpowder.[2]

Paul claimed that there was one true King and that it wasn't Nero. Many of us miss this because we skim over Paul's choice of words in his opening verses, but three key words cannot have failed to capture the attention of his original Roman readers.

First, he used the Greek word *euangelion*, which means *gospel*. This was a technical word used by the Caesars themselves to proclaim the news that they had fathered an heir or had won a great victory on the battlefield. An inscription in the ruins of the Greek city Priene which dates back to 9 BC declares that *"When Caesar appeared he exceeded the hopes of all who received the gospel... The birthday of the god Augustus was the beginning of the gospel regarding him for the world."* Paul therefore uses the word *euangelion* as a deliberate challenge to Caesar's vain boast. The real Gospel was not the good news of Rome regarding Nero, but *"the gospel of God...regarding his Son"*.

Second, Paul used the word *kurios*, or *Lord*. This was the word used by the translators of the Old Testament into Greek to translate God's name *Yahweh*, but it was also a title that the Roman emperors used of themselves. One of Nero's officials illustrates this by referring to him as the *Kurios* in Acts 25:26, so Paul's letter told the Romans a dangerously different story. He announced the reign of *"Jesus Christ our Lord"* and promised in Romans 10:9 that *"If you confess with your mouth, 'Jesus is Kurios,' and believe in your heart that God raised him from the dead, you will be saved."*

Third, Paul used the word *christos*, meaning *Christ* or *Messiah*. This was the word used in the Greek Old Testament to refer to King David's heir who would one day take his throne and establish God's Kingdom which would last forever. Daniel 7 had even prophesied that this Messiah would face up to

14

[2] The context of 15:25–26 links this letter to Acts 20:2–3, as does Paul's mention in 16:1, 23 of Phoebe from nearby Cenchrea and the Corinthians Gaius and Erastus (1 Corinthians 1:14; 2 Timothy 4:20).

the iron-toothed Roman Empire and destroy it along with its boastful ruler.[3] Now Paul claimed that this Messiah had come: Jesus of Nazareth. He was telling the Romans there was a new King in town.[4]

Stop for a moment and think how risky that was. Jesus had been dragged before a Roman judge under the charge that *"he opposes payment of taxes to Caesar and claims to be Christ, a king."* When the Roman judge hesitated, Jesus' enemies reminded him that *"If you let this man go, you are no friend of Caesar. Anyone who claims to be a king opposes Caesar."* The judge had therefore ordered that Jesus be crucified by a team of Roman soldiers, wearing a mocking crown of thorns and under a sign which told everyone what Rome thought of his claim to be *"the King of the Jews".*[5] Now Paul was claiming that God had raised this same Jesus to life, and in doing so had revealed him as the true Lord and King of the universe.[6]

Nero was emperor because the Praetorian Guard had supported him when he stood over the dead body of his adoptive father. Paul responded that Jesus was the true King because God had supported him when he raised his dead body back to life. Nero's first act as emperor had been to deify Claudius and claim to be *divi filius*, Latin for *the son of a god*. Paul responded that it was actually Jesus who *"through the Spirit of holiness was declared with power to be the Son of God."*[7] This threat was not

---

[3] The four empires of Daniel 7:1–7 belong in turn to Babylon, Medo-Persia, Macedon and Rome.

[4] Paul never actually uses the word "king" in Romans, since first-century Romans used it to describe their puppet rulers. To clarify the kind of king Jesus is, he uses the far more dangerous word *kurios* over forty times.

[5] Luke 23:2; John 19:12; Matthew 27:27–31, 37.

[6] The Greek word *horizō* in 1:4 means either *to appoint* or *to mark out*. Since Jesus is God's eternal Son, Paul must be telling us that God marked him out to the entire world as his Son when he raised him from the dead.

[7] *"The Spirit of holiness"* is simply a Jewish way of saying *"the Holy Spirit"*.

lost on Paul's enemies, who accused him of *"defying Caesar's decrees, saying that there is another king, one called Jesus."*[8]

Paul begins his letter to the Romans by telling them that *the new King saves*, both objectively and in day-to-day experience (chapters 1–5 and 6–8). He then settles the conflict between Jewish and Gentile Christians by explaining to both groups that *the new King has a plan* (chapters 9–11). Next, in light of this, he gets specific about what it means for both groups to accept that *the new King is Lord* (12:1–15:13). Finally, he outlines his plans to preach the Gospel across the Western Mediterranean and warns his Roman readers that *the new King is advancing* (15:14–16:27).[9]

That's why we mustn't view Romans as a theological treatise that calls people to make a private response to an offer of personal salvation. Nero's ambassadors did not cross the Empire to encourage his subjects to experience the benefits of choosing him as their Lord. They simply announced that Nero was emperor, whether their hearers liked it or not, and that they needed to submit to his rule or face the deadly consequences. In the same way, Paul wrote this letter and sent it into Nero's backyard to proclaim that Jesus Christ was Lord, and they needed to surrender. Nero could execute Paul ten years later in Rome as one of the last desperate acts of his disintegrating reign,[10] but he couldn't resist his all-conquering message. Even today, when people read Romans, they discover that King Jesus really is Lord and that his plan to save all nations is nearing its grand finale.

So let's get ready to experience the message of Romans for ourselves. Whatever the world may have told us and

---

[8] Acts 17:6–7.

[9] Some people object to the idea that Jesus is the "new" King. Surely he has always been the Lord? Yes, but Acts 2:36 and Philippians 2:9–11 are clear that he also "became" Lord in a new way through the Gospel.

[10] See *Straight to the Heart of Acts* for how Luke's defence of the Gospel helped save Paul from being executed in Rome earlier in 62 AD.

whatever false gospels we may have believed, it is time for us to experience God's Gospel concerning his Son. It is time for us to wake up to what it means when Paul tells us that there is a new King in town.

Romans 1–8:

The New King Saves

It's Personal (1:1–7)

...the gospel of God...regarding his Son.

(Romans 1:1, 3)

Romans may be brilliant, but it isn't easy reading. It is the sixth of Paul's thirteen New Testament letters and the only one he wrote to a church he had neither planted nor visited,[1] which often makes it feel more like a lecture than a letter. Paul livens up his monologue by heckling himself with questions, and he tries to build bridges by naming lots of mutual friends in chapter 16, but none of this can stop Romans from feeling like a theological essay. It lacks the intimacy of 1 Thessalonians or the tailor-made teaching of 1 Corinthians. But don't let that fool you that this letter isn't personal.

Romans isn't primarily about sin or righteousness or justification or the role of Israel. It is about *"the gospel of God ...regarding his Son"*. In case we miss that Paul's message is primarily about a person, he also urges Timothy in another letter to *"Remember Jesus Christ, raised from the dead, descended from David. This is my gospel."*[2]

We need to note this as we start Romans, because so many people read the letter as a Gospel formula that *sin plus the cross plus repentance equals justification*. Unless we grasp that the Gospel is about a Jewish man, descended from King David, who was revealed as God's Son when he raised him from the dead,

---

[1] He had not visited the Colossian church either, but at least he had planted it through one of his converts.

[2] 2 Timothy 2:8.

then we will misunderstand Paul's teaching in 10:9.[3] We will treat it as a call to respond to the Gospel by following a formula, when in fact it is a call to respond to the Lord Jesus as a person.

Paul was not saying anything new to the Romans. This was, after all, how the Roman church began. Its earliest members had been there on the Day of Pentecost to hear the first Gospel sermon in Acts 2. After eight verses that responded to the crowd's immediate question, Peter launched into a message that began with *"Jesus of Nazareth..."* and which ended fifteen verses later with *"God has made this Jesus, whom you crucified, both Lord and Christ."*

Other church members had been there when Peter preached a Gospel sermon to a crowded room of Romans in Acts 10. Cornelius gave him carte blanche to preach anything he wanted – *"We are all here in the presence of God to listen to everything the Lord has commanded you to tell us"* – and Peter chose to give a ten-verse biography of Jesus, which recounted his baptism, his experience of the Holy Spirit, his healing ministry, his death and resurrection, and his post-resurrection appearances. He told them Jesus was Lord and that unless they received his forgiveness they would face his judgment.

So when Paul tells the Roman Christians that the Gospel is personal, he is not telling them anything particularly new. What is new is that he clarifies for them why conversion means more than assenting to certain Christian doctrines. When the Gospel is presented as a series of propositions by which listeners can escape God's judgment and go to heaven when they die, it creates stillborn, self-centred "converts" who are very different from the ones Paul describes in these first seven verses.

The Gospel we share affects how converts *see themselves*. The essence of sin is to act as if the world revolves around

---

[3] Paul stresses that Jesus is both man and God by two similar phrases in verses 3 and 4: *kata sarka* and *kata pneuma*, or *according to the flesh* and *according to the Spirit*.

us, so an impersonal gospel fails to deal with the root of the problem. It tells us that we are so precious that God sacrificed his Son because he couldn't bear to see people like us die. It pleads with us to accept God's salvation with a promise that he will improve our lives if we ask him to come into our lives. Those who respond to this "gospel" rise from their knees thinking that God just made a transaction with *them*, so they sit back and see whether he makes good on his promise to make their lives better. In contrast, those who respond to Paul's Gospel that Jesus is Lord rise from their knees understanding that they just made a transaction with God. They repent of acting as if the world revolves around themselves and accept nothing short of a Copernican Revolution in their thinking: they confess they are mere planets which must now revolve around God's Son.

To stress this, Paul begins his letter with a Greek phrase that was very offensive in Roman culture: *"Paul, a slave of Christ Jesus"*. When Tacitus, the great historian of Nero's reign, insults people he tells his readers they have *"the mind of a slave"*,[4] but Paul says that this is the essence of what it means to follow Christ. Praying a prayer cannot help us unless we accept that we now *"belong to Jesus Christ"* and authenticate our prayer with *"the obedience that comes from faith"*.[5] Responding to the Gospel means surrendering to King Jesus.

The Gospel we share also affects how converts *see their mission*. If they respond to a message that God wants to meet their needs, they become Christian consumers. They share testimonies that focus on what caused them to cry out to God and on what their decision has saved them *from*. They do not echo Paul's humility when he says three times in these seven

---

[4] He does this as much to noblemen (*Histories*, 5.9) as to former slaves (*Annals*, 15.54).
[5] Verses 5 and 6. Paul stresses the link between faith and obedience again in 15:18–19 and 16:26.

verses that it is God who calls us, or his excitement over what this means he has been set apart *for*.[6]

The Gospel we share also affects how converts *expect God to use them* to fulfil his purposes. If they are told that the Gospel is a message all about them, their involvement in mission will lead to either pride or despair because they will assume that success depends on their own hard work. They don't grasp that it is *"the gospel he promised beforehand through his prophets"* countless centuries before they were even born, or that Jesus makes us successful *"through him and for his name's sake"*. They cannot understand Paul's confidence in verse 13 that he will always be fruitful wherever he goes. They forget that when Paul finally made it to Rome he simply *"taught about the Lord Jesus Christ"*.[7] Luke also summarizes Paul's message in Rome as *"the kingdom of God"*. They think the Gospel is a set of propositions, but Paul insists it is a person.

John Piper puts it this way:

> *When we ask about God's design we are too prone to describe it with ourselves at the centre of God's affections. We may say, for example, his design is to redeem the world. Or to save sinners. Or to restore creation. Or the like. But God's saving designs are penultimate, not ultimate. Redemption, salvation, and restoration are not God's ultimate goal. These he performs for the sake of something greater.*[8]

He does it for his own glory through King Jesus, our Lord, as Paul tells us in this deeply personal letter about God's Gospel regarding his Son.

---

[6] The passive word *klētos*, or *called*, in verses 1, 6 and 7 sets Paul up for his teaching about God's initiative in chapters 9–11.

[7] Acts 28:31.

[8] John Piper, *Desiring God: Meditations of a Christian Hedonist* (1986).

You've Got Mail (1:8–15)

*I am bound both to Greeks and non-Greeks, both to
the wise and the foolish.*

(Romans 1:14)

Nero's surname was Ahenobarbus, meaning *Bronze-Beard*,
because his legendary ancestor had played postman to the
gods. The twin gods Castor and Pollux had made him their
evangelist in 496 BC when they ordered him to preach the
gospel that the Romans had defeated the Latins at Lake
Regillus. He hesitated because no word had yet arrived from
the battlefield, but when they touched his black beard and
turned it to bronze he evangelized Rome by faith and was
rewarded when its army returned in victory. He was invited
to lead their triumph and served as consul seven times. Now
Paul tells the Romans that this is nothing compared to what
King Jesus has in store for them.[1]

Paul has already described himself as Jesus' *slave* in verse
1, and now he also describes himself in verse 14 literally as his
debtor. The myth of Ahenobarbus was day-to-day reality for
Paul, since God had entrusted him with the Gospel of his Son.
He must come to the city where Nero used death threats to stay
in power and declare that one of Caesar's crucified victims had
broken death as a weapon through a miracle far greater than
turning a black beard to bronze. Paul was God's postman and
carried a message that Jesus was the new King in town.

Paul is not merely saying that he is a debtor to the Greek-
speaking wise men of Rome. Remember, Paul wrote Romans

---

[1] Suetonius records this dubious legend in his *Life of Nero* (1).

in Greek instead of Latin because this was the language of an empire that prided itself on its high-cultured wisdom. Paul tells them that he is also a debtor to *barbarians* and to the *foolish*, which means that they have a role to play in taking the Gospel to the rest of the world. He is preparing the Romans for his shock revelation in 15:28 that he actually plans to *"go to Spain and visit you on the way"*. They expected that they would be his final destination since everyone knew that all roads led to Rome, but Paul needed to teach them that they were as much in debt as he was, and that they needed to team with him in taking the Gospel to Spain and the rest of the Western Mediterranean.[2] They must not prove less obedient to the real God than the legendary Ahenobarbus had been to his idols.

There are two ways that we can fall into debt. We can borrow money for ourselves or be entrusted with delivering an item from one person to another. Either way, reneging on our debt is a serious matter. A few years ago, one of my local postmen started emptying his sack of letters in people's dustbins so he could go back to his depot with an empty sack after spending the morning relaxing at home. Someone saw him dumping letters in the dustbin to the rear of our church, and telephoned the police who identified the guilty postman from the postcodes on the letters. He was sentenced to jail for "interfering with Her Majesty's mail", but let's not be too shocked. We do it ourselves all the time.

Paul encourages us that a simple way to discharge our debt is to proclaim the Gospel by enjoying it ourselves. He tells the Romans in verse 8 that due to their wholehearted response to Jesus as Lord, *"your faith is being reported all over the world."* Another way is to pray for opportunities to share it, as Paul says he does *constantly* and *at all times* in verses 9 and 10. He tells the Romans that he prays to come to the mother-city Rome, of which he himself was a citizen by birth.[3] Prayer would pave the way for him to make an evangelistic visit.

---

[2] Luke uses this same word *barbaros* to describe the Maltese in Acts 28:2, 4.

[3] Acts 16:37–38; 21:39; 22:25–29; 23:27.

Paul also encourages us to discharge our debt by helping one another to understand the Gospel ever more deeply. He warns us not to treat the Gospel as an elementary message for non-Christians while we graduate to something meatier. He tells the Romans in verse 15 that *"I am so eager to preach the Gospel also to you"*, because he knows in verses 11 and 12 that it is only through discovering new depths to the Gospel that *"you and I may be mutually encouraged by each other's faith."* Lifestyle, prayer and sharing with one another form the prelude to discharging our larger debt of sharing the Gospel verbally with the millions of non-Christians to whom it is addressed.

Sometimes I wonder what kind of letters the postman must have thrown into our bin. Were cheques, tax rebates, job offers, love letters or other life-changing pieces of news left undelivered? Would it matter if most of the letters were only junk mail? The judge didn't think so when he sent the postman to jail because a price had been paid to deliver the letters and he had failed to discharge his obligation to the sender. God has not paid for his Gospel letter with a stamp but with blood, so we dare not defraud his addressees by considering them too wise or too foolish, too "Greek" or too "barbarian".

Paul knows that doubt is the reason why many of us fail to deliver the Gospel, since we lack his confidence in verse 13 that we will see fruit if we do. That's why he gives us some extra encouragement, which should keep us delivering the Gospel even when people close their ears and start singing "Return to Sender". He uses the Greek word *latreuō* to describe our calling to *serve* as God's postmen, which was the word used in the Old Testament for priests bringing offerings to God's altar, and which was used in the first century more generally to speak of believers worshipping the Lord. Paul is telling us that saying Jesus is Lord to non-Christians is just as powerful an act of worship as singing he is Lord in a gathering of Christians. As Mark Dever reminds us:

God is glorified in being known... We bring God glory as we speak the truth about him to his creation. This is not the only way that we can bring glory to God, but it is one of the chief ways that he has given us as Christians, as those who know him through his grace in Christ. It is not a way that we will bring him glory eternally in heaven; it is one of the special privileges of living now, in this fallen world... We do not fail in our evangelism if we faithfully tell the Gospel to someone who is not converted; we fail only if we don't faithfully tell the Gospel at all. Evangelism itself is not converting people; it's telling them that they need to be converted and telling them how they can be.[4]

That's why God wants us to understand the message of Romans, for our own sake and for the sake of others. He wants to teach us to worship him like Ahenobarbus by delivering his Gospel. If we do, then we will share in Jesus' royal triumph when he appears in glorious victory.

---

[4] Mark Dever, *The Gospel and Personal Evangelism* (2007).

Abraham, Martin and John (1:16–17)

For in the gospel a righteousness from God is revealed, a righteousness that is by faith from first to last, just as it is written: "The righteous will live by faith."

(Romans 1:17)

In 1968, a few months after the assassination of Martin Luther King, the singer Dion released a single entitled "Abraham, Martin and John".[1] It remembered three great martyrs of the black civil rights movement – Abraham Lincoln, Martin Luther King and John F. Kennedy. Now, as Paul moves from introductions into the main body of Romans, he summarizes its first eight chapters in verses 16 and 17 by singing his own version of "Abraham, Martin and John". Its lyrics summarize the message of the letter's first and longest section, setting out what Paul means when he says that the new King Jesus saves.

The first stanza looks back to the discovery of Abraham, the first Hebrew patriarch. Paul does not name him yet, but will mention him more often than anyone else but Jesus in the chapters which follow. Abraham was a former idolater, an instinctive liar, who even slept with the maid when he grew impatient with God's timing. Yet in spite of his sin we read in Genesis 15:6 that *"he believed the Lord, and he credited it to him*

---

[1] Laurie Records. Many artists have covered it since, including Marvin Gaye, Bob Dylan and Tori Amos.

as righteousness".[2] The word used by the Greek translators of that verse was *dikaiosunē*, which Paul uses together with its sister words a remarkable sixty-two times in Romans. It is a legal word which refers to a judge doing more than simply pardoning a guilty person from being punished. It means *justice* or *righteousness* or *vindication* because it carries the sense of declaring somebody not guilty and beyond the reach of punishment.

Paul uses the word at the end of verse 17 when he quotes God's Old Testament promise from Habakkuk 2:4 that *"The righteous will live by faith".*[3] He tells the Romans that God saves by giving us a righteousness we don't deserve when we lay hold of his Son. Abraham discovered *"a righteousness from God...that is by faith from first to last"*. Now Paul tells his readers to pick up the tune and sing along.

The second stanza of Paul's song illustrates what he means when he tells us in verse 16 that the Gospel *"is the power of God for the salvation of everyone who believes."* A German monk named Martin Luther started singing it when he got stuck on these two verses at the start of the sixteenth century:

> *I burned with desire to understand what Paul meant in his letter to the Romans... "The justice of God is revealed in the Gospel". I hated that phrase, "the justice of God", which I had been taught [meant]...the justice by which God is just when he punishes unrighteous sinners.*

---

[2] Paul quotes this verse again in 4:3, 22, as well as in Galatians 3:6. It joins with 1:2 and Psalm 130:8 to remind us that the Gospel is not a first-century innovation but the fulfilment of Old Testament Judaism.

[3] Since the Hebrew and Greek words *'emūnāh* and *pistis* both mean either *faith* or *faithfulness*, Habakkuk 2:4 in Hebrew reads *"the righteous man will live by his faith"*, and in Greek reads *"the righteous man will live by my faithfulness"*. Paul quotes the Greek translation but omits the word *"my"* in order to draw out both possible meanings. He did the same when he quoted this verse earlier in Galatians 3:11.

Despite the irreproachable character of my life as a monk, I felt I was a sinner before God and my conscience was extremely disturbed. I had no confidence that my satisfactions were sufficient to appease him. So I did not love this just and vengeful God. I hated him, and if I did not blaspheme his name in secret, I was certainly indignant and murmured violently against him. I said: "Is it not enough that he condemns us to eternal death because of the sin of our fathers, and that he makes us undergo all the severity of the Law? Must he increase our torment by the Gospel and even announce his justice and his wrath there?" I was beside myself, my conscience was so violently upset, and I ceaselessly puzzled over this passage from Paul in the keen desire to know what it meant.

When Martin Luther understood the broader meaning of the Greek word *dikaiosunē*, he learned to sing the same Gospel song as Abraham and triggered the Reformation which revived backslidden Europe.

Finally God took pity on me. While I was meditating, day and night, and examining the implications of the words "The justice of God is revealed in the Gospel, as it is written: 'the righteous shall live by faith,'" I perceived that the justice of God must be understood as the righteousness which God imparts and by which the righteous man lives if he has faith. So the meaning of the phrase is that the Gospel reveals to us the righteousness of God, and this is the passive righteousness by which God in his mercy justifies us by means of faith... Immediately I felt born again, and I seemed to have entered the open gates of Paradise itself. From then on I saw the whole of Scripture in a different light. I ran through the texts in my memory and noted other terms which had to be explained in similar fashion... Formerly I had detested this term "the righteousness of God", but now I loved and cherished so sweet a saying.[4]

John Wesley sang the third stanza of Paul's Gospel song two centuries later in 1738. He had returned to London after failing as a preacher in America and was increasingly convinced that he was not even saved at all. He lamented on his voyage home that *"I went to America to convert the Indians; but oh, who shall convert me?"* His prayer was answered when a Moravian missionary pointed out that he was relying on his own good works to save him, and dragged him to a meeting where he learned to sing the same song as Abraham and Martin:

In the evening I went very unwillingly to a society in Aldersgate Street, where one was reading Luther's preface to the Epistle to the Romans. About a quarter before nine, while he was describing the change which God works in the heart through faith in Christ, I felt my heart strangely warmed. I felt I did trust in Christ, Christ alone, for my salvation; and an assurance was given me that he had taken away my sins, even mine, and saved me from the law of sin and death.[5]

Abraham's first stanza had birthed the Hebrew nation, and Martin Luther's second stanza had saved millions across Europe. Now John Wesley's third stanza marked a turning point in Church history, as it catapulted the Gospel to every dark corner of Britain and to the unreached nations of the world.

Just before Dion recorded his single "Abraham, Martin and John", he heard the news that Senator Robert Kennedy, another supporter of black civil rights, had been killed. In tribute, he

---

[4] Luther recalls his conversion this way in the preface to his *Commentary on the Psalms*.

[5] Quoted from John Wesley's diary for that day.

ended his song by asking his listeners whether they had also seen his *"old friend Bobby"*. The song ends with him picturing Bobby Kennedy walking up over the hill with Abraham Martin and John, and that's how Paul wants to end his song too. He turns to us at the end of verses 16 and 17, and encourages us to climb the hill of these first eight chapters to sing the same Gospel song as Abraham, Martin and John.

Salvation Needed
(1:18–3:20)

*Jews and Gentiles alike are all under sin. As it is
written: "There is no one righteous, not even one."*

(Romans 3:9–10)

Like all the first churches, the one at Rome had begun as a
collection of converted Jews. A few Gentile converts to Judaism
also responded to the Messiah, but they didn't dilute the
church's very Jewish flavour.[1] The apostles took ten years to
start preaching the Gospel to ordinary Roman Gentiles in Acts
10, and almost another ten years to decide to do so wholesale
in Acts 15. Elsewhere in that same year of 49 AD, the Emperor
Claudius was making a church-changing decision of his own. He
decided to exile Rome's 40,000 Jews from the city.[2]

Almost overnight, the Roman church became completely
Gentile in its membership and leadership. It became the first
Gentile-majority church in the world, and its rump of Gentile
Christians grew to like their new-found power. When Claudius
died in 54 AD and Nero asked the Jews to return to their important
place in Rome's economy, it didn't take long for conflict to arise
between the returning Jewish Christians and the Gentiles they
had left behind.[3] Gentile Christians had been taught by Cicero

---

[1] See Acts 2:10–11. The scandal of Acts 10 was that they were God-fearing
Gentiles, not converts to Judaism.

[2] Acts 18:2 and Suetonius in his *Life of Claudius* (25). Suetonius blames it on
the Jews causing trouble *"at the instigation of Christ"*, but this seems to be
his anachronistic guess based on later events in the 60s AD.

[3] We do not know how big the Roman church was in 57 AD. Some argue it
was small since Paul avoids the word *church* in 1:7, but the same is true of

that Jewish culture *"was at variance with the glory of our empire, the dignity of our name and the customs of our ancestors."*[4] They had been brought up on the view of Nero's tutor Seneca that Romans should despise *"the customs of that most accursed nation."*[5] For their part, Jewish Christians came from a culture which labelled Gentiles unclean and made it a crime for *"a Jew to associate with a Gentile or visit him"*.[6] It is hard to make sense of Romans 1–3 or 9–11 without understanding something of this historical background.

But here's the interesting thing about Romans: Paul doesn't try to solve the conflict by offering the believers a course in race relations. He simply sticks to his message that Jesus is Lord and expects the Gospel to be the making of a loving, multicultural church in the city. Like an orator trying to unite Rome's divided senate before advancing barbarians, he spells out their problem. They have a far more dangerous enemy than one another. Both Jews and Gentiles have rebelled against the fact that Jesus is Lord, and this means that God himself has become their mortal enemy.

First Paul describes the utter wickedness of pagan culture in 1:18–32. The fact that the Roman Christians are still proud of their culture's catalogue of vice is simply proof they have been drinking from Rome's filthy fountain far too long. While the Jews are nodding at the former Pharisee's tirade, Paul surprises them by describing the wickedness of Jewish culture too. He is the apostle to the Gentiles[7] and points out to the Jews in 2:17–3:8 that their own sin is even more serious than that of the pagans. They have greater revelation of God's Word and

---

his letters to large churches at Ephesus, Philippi and Colosse.

[4] Marcus Tullius Cicero, *For Flaccus* (69).

[5] Augustine quotes Seneca's words in his *City of God* (6.11).

[6] Acts 10:28.

[7] 1:5 and 11:13, plus Galatians 2:8 and 1 Timothy 2:7.

therefore carry greater responsibility to obey it,[8] so their smug reliance on race and Law and circumcision was nothing short of blasphemy. Not only were they deluded that this had any power to save them, but their cultural arrogance was precisely the reason that so few Gentiles paid attention to the message of their God. Instead of squabbling like children, Jews and Gentiles needed to sit up and listen together to the verdict of 3:9–20 before it was too late. They were equally sinners before God, and must humble themselves in exactly the same way to receive God's righteousness as an undeserved gift through faith.

The Gentile Christians needed to humble themselves because their Jewish brothers and sisters had been entrusted with the Old Testament, which Paul describes in 3:2 as *"the very words of God"*. Their only hope was to believe the Gospel about a Jewish carpenter who was King of the Jews, which is why Paul insists in 1:16 that the Gospel is *"first for the Jew, then for the Gentile"*. To emphasize this, Paul packs Romans with more Old Testament quotations than any other book in the New Testament. He uses nine different quotes in chapter 3 alone.

The Jewish Christians needed to humble themselves because their Gentile brothers and sisters lay at the heart of their national calling in 1:5 *"to call people from among all the Gentiles to the obedience that comes from faith"*. Jesus had summarized the entire message of the Old Testament as *"The Christ will suffer and rise from the dead on the third day, and repentance and forgiveness of sins will be preached in his name to all nations, beginning at Jerusalem."*[9] The Jews had sinned by forgetting this commission and acting so lovelessly towards the pagans that Paul rebukes them, from Isaiah, in 2:24: *"God's name is blasphemed among the Gentiles because of you."*[10]

---

[8] The verses 2:1–16 form a no-man's-land which addresses both pagan and Jewish culture together.

[9] Luke 24:44–47.

[10] Paul's quotation from Isaiah 52:5 follows the Septuagint translation. It also links to Ezekiel 36:22.

The context of these two and a half chapters is therefore very specific, but it is also very relevant to our situations today. For a start, most Western cities are even more cosmopolitan than mid first-century Rome, so we need to learn from Paul's approach that we will never build multicultural churches by focusing on the symptoms of racism on their own. It is only by preaching the Gospel in all its glory that we will cause people from every nation to kneel together at Jesus' cross, finding that they no longer look down on one another – because Jesus is Lord and they are all his slaves upon their knees.

Furthermore, these two and a half chapters remind us that we can never receive the righteousness of God until we empty ourselves of our own attempts at righteousness. A friend of mine recently filled his car up with petrol, only to remember when he finished that his car ran on diesel. He could have shut his eyes and tried to drive away, but he wouldn't have got far before his engine stopped working and his car ground to a halt. He knew that he had to call for help and ask an expert to empty his fuel tank so that he could start all over again with the right kind of fuel.

That's why Paul begins these chapters about the new King's salvation by telling us that we had better admit we are in desperate need of saving. Whether our background is pagan or religious, immoral or moralizing, we need to confess that the fuel tanks of our righteousness are filled with the wrong stuff, and to ask the Lord to empty us as our first step towards receiving the gift of the righteousness of God.

What about People Who Have Never Heard the Gospel? (1:18–32)

For since the creation of the world God's invisible qualities – his eternal power and divine nature – have been clearly seen…so that men are without excuse.

(Romans 1:20)

When Paul preached the Gospel in Athens in 50 AD, he told the Greeks that *"in the past God overlooked such ignorance, but now he commands all people everywhere to repent."*[1] Some people use this statement as a promise that God will not punish anyone who, through no fault of their own, has never heard the Gospel. Paul wanted to clarify his meaning for the Gentile Christians in Rome because they were in danger of jumping to a similar conclusion.[2]

Few pagans in Rome knew very much about Jesus. They assumed that they would spend the afterlife in Hades, the Underworld where the demigod Minos judged souls very leniently. He rarely admitted a soul to the Elysian Fields to ride with the great heroes, but nor did he often consign one to eternal suffering in Tartarus.[3] Given this ignorant complacency, it seems from these verses that the Gentile Christians feared it might actually be cruel to tell their pagan neighbours about

---

[1] Acts 17:30.

[2] Paul is not trying to prove that God exists in 1:18–20. The Bible never feels the need to do that. Rather, he is proving that no one has any excuse before God's judgment.

[3] Peter uses the word *Tartarus* as a name for *hell* in 2 Peter 2:4.

Jesus. If ignorance meant immunity from God's judgment, then sharing the Gospel placed the pagan hearer's soul in jeopardy. The Gentile believers had decided it was kinder to the pagans if they kept their mouths shut altogether, so Paul warns them that the pagans are not ignorant at all.

He points out in 1:18–20 that the pagans are not ignorant *because of creation*. They can tell from the visible world that there is a powerful Creator God, and they can see so plainly what he is like that *"people are without excuse"*. Their problem is not ignorance but deliberate suppression of this truth in order to act like little gods themselves. Their root problem is *asebeia* (verse 18), which means a *refusal to fear God*, and their wickedness is simply the fruit of this decision. Similarly in verse 21, their root problem is a refusal to worship and thank the God they know is there. Their idolatry, sexual sin and depravity are simply natural outworkings of this primary act of rebellion.[4] Admittedly, creation speaks more about God's holiness and judgment than it does about the Saviour Jesus Christ – which is why we must finish the story by telling people the Gospel – but we will never share God's message with anyone who is not already guilty of deliberate sin against him and in desperate need of his salvation.

Paul adds in 2:14–15 that the pagans are not ignorant *because of their consciences*. Although God's judgment will take into account how much they were exposed to the Gospel,[5] Paul argues that their consciences are God-given legal teams, which *witness*, *accuse* and *defend* them in order to teach them God's requirements instinctively. They can drown out the voice of their legal team so determinedly that some of the sins listed in

[4] Together with Psalm 100:4, this verse teaches that thankfulness leads us more and more into God's presence, while ingratitude leads us further and further away from him.

[5] Romans 2:9–11; Matthew 11:20–24. Although God is just by judging everyone for their sin based on how much *revelation* they received, 2:12 makes it clear that the ignorant will *perish* nonetheless.

1:26–31 no longer strike them as serious, but this doesn't make them ignorant and it certainly doesn't make them innocent. It simply means they go against the standards that God has written on their hearts. They are judged because they gladly infect themselves with sin's disease, not because nobody told them that Jesus is its cure.

Paul also explains in 1:21–32 that pagans are not ignorant *because of the consequences* they can see of their rebellion. The same God who reveals his righteousness through the Gospel in verse 17 also reveals his wrath through his reaction to their sin in verse 18.[6] If his wrath were only visible in the past at Jesus' cross or in the future at Jesus' return, then a pagan might yet claim to be ignorant, but God *is revealing* his wrath against their sin every day so that they have no excuse when they fail to take his judgment seriously. He judges them by darkening their hearts so that they believe their own lie[7] and start worshipping puny little creatures instead of the Creator who alone can satisfy.[8] Then he judges them further by handing them over three times in verses 24, 26 and 28 to ever-increasing sexual immorality and depravity.[9] They feel the natural *"penalty for their perversion"* as a wake-up call that they are sinners who need to cry out for God to save them.

Paul's statement to the Athenians had in fact been intended to do the very opposite of promising that ignorance can spare anyone from God's judgment. He said it because the Greeks were struggling with the fact that "Jesus is Lord" meant by implication

[6] Paul uses the same verb *apokaluptō* in both verses, which is also the root of the Greek name for the book of Revelation.

[7] This repeats what Paul taught in 2 Thessalonians 2:10–11: *"They perish because they refused to love the truth and so be saved. For this reason God sends them a powerful delusion so that they will believe the lie."*

[8] Psalm 106:20 captures this contrast between worshipping the Creator and creation when it tells us that Israel *"exchanged their Glory for an image of a bull, which eats grass"*. Secular idols are just as deadly as statues.

[9] We also find this theme of God handing people over to their sin in Psalm 81:12; Ezekiel 20:25–26 and Acts 7:42.

that the heroes of Athenian history were all suffering in hell. They had understood that no pagan is innocent, because of creation and conscience and consequence. It was for that very reason that Paul urged them: *Leave such questions in the past where they belong, because you yourselves have heard the Gospel and must respond to it here and now!*

That's why Paul tells the Gentile Christians at Rome that they must face up to the fact that their countrymen are in desperate need of God's salvation. They must add to the voices of creation, conscience and consequence the Gospel of *Christ*, which alone has power to save. The pagans are already under God's judgment for deliberately suppressing the evidence that he pours into their lives. Their only hope is for a Christian to explain God's gift of righteousness as described in these first eight chapters of Romans. Paul exhorts us all in 10:12–15:

> *There is no difference between Jew and Gentile – the same Lord is Lord of all and richly blesses all who call on him, for "Everyone who calls on the name of the Lord will be saved." How, then, can they call on the one they have not believed in? And how can they believe in the one of whom they have not heard? And how can they hear without someone preaching to them? And how can they preach unless they are sent? As it is written, "How beautiful are the feet of those who bring Good News!"*

Gay Pride (1:26–27)

*Because of this, God gave them over to shameful
lusts. Even their women exchanged natural relations
for unnatural ones. In the same way the men also
abandoned natural relations with women and were
inflamed with lust for one another.*

(Romans 1:26–27)

Writing to Rome to say that homosexuality was sinful was like
writing to France to forbid the use of garlic in cooking. Gay
relationships were simply part-and-parcel of Roman life. They
had practically become a national institution.

When Paul wrote this letter in 57 AD, the city was as
entrenched in homosexuality as ancient Greece was before,
where the custom of pederasty made gay sex a rite of passage
for boys, and where the poetess Sappho wrote so many love
songs to the women of Lesbos that we still refer to her lifestyle
as lesbianism. Tacitus laments that under Nero, *"Promiscuity
and degradation throve. Roman morals had long become impure,
but never was there so favourable an environment for debauchery
as among this filthy crowd."* He even tells us that Nero *"went
through a formal wedding ceremony with one of the perverts
named Pythagoras. The emperor, in the presence of witnesses,
put on the bridal veil. Dowry, marriage bed, wedding torches, all
were there."*[1]

Suetonius gives a similar view of gay Rome: *"Having tried
to turn the boy Sporus into a girl by castration, Nero went through
a wedding ceremony with him – dowry, bridal veil and all – took*

---

[1] Tacitus, *Annals* (14.15 and 15.37).

him to his palace with a great crowd in attendance, and treated him as a wife." He adds a third story that Nero "was dispatched – shall we say? – by his freedman Doryphorus. Doryphorus now married him – just as he himself had married Sporus – and on the wedding night he imitated the screams and moans of a girl being deflowered."[2]

In light of this, Paul's comments here about homosexuality were both controversial and dangerous. Why does he tackle this issue in particular, and what can it teach us in our own cities which are similarly affected by gay pride?

Paul makes this his focus because *gay sex is sinful*. That's about as unpopular a sentence as any you could read in our culture, but it was just as unpopular in first-century Rome. Paul writes in these two verses that homosexuality is *shameful*, *unnatural*, *indecent*, and *a perversion*. He is so clear about this that the only way we can miss it is by having already made up our minds to disregard the things he says. Yet note that Paul does not insult gay people themselves. Instead, he states something even more controversial: he says that their actions are simply the outworking of a culture which has rejected God.

Paul makes this his focus because *gay attraction is a symptom of a race that has rejected God*. Note his argument: People know from creation what God is like, but they deliberately resolve to suppress the truth about him. He responds by "darkening their hearts" so that they begin to worship creatures, and by handing them over to reap what they have sown. Since they reject God the Father, Son and Spirit – different yet one – their blind eyes no longer recognize that *"in the image of God... male and female he created them"*.[3] They forget in verse 21 that sex is a way to glorify God and be thankful, because *"refusing to know God, they soon didn't know how to be human either"*.[4] Although Paul wasn't part of the modern debate over whether

---

[2] Suetonius, *Life of Nero* (28–29).

[3] Genesis 1:27.

[4] This is a paraphrase of verse 26 in *The Message*.

gay attraction is a matter of nature or nurture, he answers the question by telling us it is neither. It is the natural expression of a culture that rejects God. Being gay actually feels right to homosexuals because they live in a culture that has suppressed God's truth and been given over *"to a depraved mind, to do what ought not to be done"*. Conservatives may feel an instinctive repulsion to this behaviour, but since they cannot articulate why they feel it, they quickly lose the cultural battle. Very soon they wake up in the world of verse 32, where people *"not only continue to do these very things but also approve of those who practise them"*.

Enough of Paul confronting Gentile homosexuality in Rome. Are you ready now for something even more surprising? Paul also makes this his focus because *homophobia is sinful too*. If you find yourself nodding at Paul's teaching and revelling in his attack on homosexuality, then he also chose to highlight this as an issue because of you. He is laying a trap which he springs in 2:1 on the moralists who are guilty of first-century homophobia: *"You, therefore, have no excuse, you who pass judgment on someone else, for at whatever point you judge the other, you are condemning yourself!"* He knew that Jewish Christians quoted Leviticus 18:22 and 20:13 to push gay people away as *"detestable"*. Therefore he lists it alongside envy and lying and hatred and gossip to demonstrate that it is simply one of many expressions of human rebellion. Was Nero worse in his homosexuality than when he raped a Vestal Virgin, committed incest with his mother, took a freedwoman as his mistress or kicked his pregnant wife to death during an argument?[5] Of course not. Paul focuses on homosexuality because it roots out moralizers, so that he can deal with them at the beginning of chapter 2.

But beyond all these things, Paul makes this his focus because *King Jesus saves both homosexuals and homophobes*. If

---

[5] Suetonius, *The Life of Nero* (28 and 35) and Tacitus, *Annals* (13.12 and 16.6).

we pretend that gay pride isn't sinful then we won't ask him to deliver gay people, but if we rail against the gay community we will lead them to believe that church is the last place for them to find any deliverance. If we try to help them when they come by addressing their homosexuality as if it were the root issue, then we won't manage to help them either. Yet if we treat it – like Paul in chapter 1 – as one of the fruits of rejecting God, while avoiding the judgmentalism he tackles in chapter 2, then we will truly build churches where gay people can be saved. We will be able to say along with Paul in 1 Corinthians 6:9–11:

> *Do not be deceived: Neither the sexually immoral nor idolaters nor adulterers nor male prostitutes nor homosexual offenders nor thieves nor the greedy nor drunkards nor slanderers nor swindlers will inherit the kingdom of God. And **that is what some of you were**. But you were washed, you were sanctified, you were justified in the name of the Lord Jesus Christ and by the Spirit of our God.*[6]

That's why Paul got so excited when he wrote to gay Rome and told them the Gospel that the new King Jesus saves.

---

[6] Paul uses two specific words here in Greek. One refers to the submissive partner in homosexual sex, and the other refers to the dominant partner. Both are sinful and both can be saved.

Dr Jekyll and Mr Hyde (2:1–16)

You therefore have no excuse, you who pass judgment on someone else, for at whatever point you judge the other, you are condemning yourself, because you who pass judgment do the same things.

(Romans 2:1)

Robert Louis Stevenson understood something of Paul's argument in the first half of Romans 2. He tried to illustrate it in 1886 in his novel *The Strange Case of Dr Jekyll and Mr Hyde*. He found a powerful way of conveying Paul's warning not to make the mistake of trying to counter ungodliness with moral self-improvement.

Henry Jekyll is a London doctor who is acutely aware of the problem of sin. He sees himself as a good person, but he believes he is prevented from unleashing his full potential by an internal battle with his sinful nature at work in his body.[1] He produces a potion that is able to separate the good Dr Jekyll and the evil Mr Hyde, and he hopes to drive his sinful nature underground. He hopes this will make him a picture-perfect figure of Victorian respectability.

But Dr Jekyll is in for a shock. He has forgotten what Paul tells the Romans in verse 13. People are not saved by hearing God's standards or even by agreeing with them. What matters is whether they actually do them! Jekyll is shocked to find that the

---

[1] Stevenson's book therefore also illustrates Romans 7:18–25, since Dr Jekyll tries to reform himself through self-improvement instead of crying out for Jesus to rescue him.

villain hiding away inside him (Mr *Hyde* is a deliberate play on words) is far more repulsive than he ever imagined. Stevenson doesn't mention all of the sins that Paul lists in chapter 1, but tells us that a turning point comes when Hyde commits murder and shocks Jekyll into action. He suddenly understands why Paul repeats the same word *anapologētos*, or *without excuse*, in verse 1 which he used to describe the immoral pagans back in 1:20. It didn't matter that Henry Jekyll was a respectable man who looked down on the sins of his ungodly neighbours. Inside him was lurking an ugly alter ego which was every bit as guilty as the people he despised. That's why Paul warns moralists in verse 16 that *"God will judge men's secrets"* and not just their outward veneer.

Dr Jekyll decides to stop taking the potion, and embarks on a path of religious self-improvement. *"I began to spy a danger that, if this were much prolonged, the balance of my nature might be permanently overthrown...and the character of Edward Hyde become irrevocably mine... I resolved in my future conduct to redeem the past; and I can say with honesty that my resolve was fruitful of some good."*

Soon, however, he begins to discover why Paul warns the Romans that moralism is so deadly. It quickly turns into judgmentalism, a form of spiritual pride, which is every bit as sinful as out-and-out wickedness. Whereas the immoral Mr Hyde suppresses the truth about God in order to run after his perversions, the moral Dr Jekyll suppresses the truth about God in order to pat himself on the back for not needing God's salvation. Conservative moralists look down on sinful people and liberal moralists look down on narrow-minded people, but either way they fail to look up and see the truth about God's standards and how far their man-made morality falls short of them.

"It fell out with me, as it falls with so vast a majority of my fellows, that I chose the better part and was found wanting in the

strength to keep to it... Not that I dreamed of resuscitating Hyde; the bare idea of that would startle me to frenzy: no, it was in my own person that I was once more tempted." Dr Jekyll goes for a walk in Regent's Park and sits down on a bench to congratulate himself on the successes of his past few months as a respectable Victorian: *"I smiled, comparing myself with other men, comparing my active goodwill with the lazy cruelty of their neglect. And at the very moment of that vainglorious thought, a qualm came over me, a horrid nausea and the most deadly shuddering... I looked down; my clothes hung formlessly on my shrunken limbs; the hand that lay on my knee was corded and hairy. I was once more Edward Hyde."*

It doesn't matter that we are not first-century Romans or nineteenth-century Englishmen. Paul tells us that the first half of chapter 2 is meant for us. He addresses 1:18–32 very clearly to Gentiles and 2:17–3:8 very clearly to Jews, but he deliberately makes these sixteen verses a no-man's-land in between which addresses the reader as "whoever you are".[2] All of us are in danger of falling into moralism when we think that sin means committing bad deeds and forget it also means trusting in good deeds to make us righteous. Paul warns in verse 5 that self-reliant religion not only fails to save us from God's judgment, but it also stores up for us far more of his judgment because it is as much a form of proud rebellion as immorality. Dr Jekyll finds that he has no need of a potion to turn his virtuous self into a monster. The immoral Mr Hyde and the moral Dr Jekyll are simply two different ways of suppressing the truth about God and our need to receive his salvation.

Thomas Schreiner summarizes the lesson Dr Jekyll learned, when he contrasts legalism – the attempt to save ourselves through morality by following God's Law – with God's gift of

---

[2] He does this by addressing his reader as *ō anthrōpe*, meaning *O man!* in verses 1 and 3. He only addresses his reader as a Jew when he gets to his Jewish-specific teaching in verse 17.

righteousness through Jesus as described in these first eight chapters of Romans:

> *Legalism has its origin in self-worship. If people are justified through their obedience to the law, then they merit praise, honour and glory. Legalism, in other words, means the glory goes to people rather than God. The desire to obey the law, though it appears commendable, is actually an insidious attempt to gain recognition before God.*[3]

At the end of Robert Louis Stevenson's novel, Dr Jekyll understands that he must destroy himself as well as Mr Hyde. In the same way, Paul tells us to let our moralism die in this no-man's-land before we step any further through his letter. Take time to confess to God that spiritual pride in your obedience is as much a suppression of his truth as your outright disobedience. Only then, when you have let that truth empty you of all self-righteousness, are you ready to be filled with the undeserved righteousness of God.

[3] Thomas Schreiner, *The Law and Its Fulfilment: A Pauline Theology of the Law* (1993).

Surely a Loving God Wouldn't Judge Me? (2:4)

Do you show contempt for the riches of his kindness, tolerance and patience, not realizing that God's kindness leads you towards repentance?

(Romans 2:4)

Paul isn't embarrassed about God's judgment. He actually thinks that it's very good news. He uses the Greek word for *judging* ten times and the words for *wrath* and *anger* four times in 2:1–16, then tells us that this is his Gospel. He tells us that anger and judgment play a vital role in what *"my gospel declares"*, so we had better make sure that they also do in ours.

Most people don't like the idea of God judging. Correction: they don't like the idea of God judging *them*. Every movie producer knows that people love stories in which evil people end up getting what they deserve. Every news editor knows that people are incensed by stories about corrupt dictators, powerful drug barons and fat-cat directors getting away with their crimes scot-free. We all nod our heads when Proverbs 17:15 tells us that *"Acquitting the guilty and condemning the innocent – the Lord detests them both."* What we struggle to accept is what Paul tells us in this passage: that we ourselves are the guilty ones and that justice demands God punish us as we deserve. We plead, with Alexander Pope, that *"to err is human, to forgive divine"*.[1] We point out that there is very little evidence of God's judgment in our lives so far. We even suggest that our comfortable lives are actually a sign he has decided to go easy on our sin. That's the

---

[1] This comes from Alexander Pope's poem *An Essay on Criticism* (1711).

attitude which Paul wants to nail by giving us five statements about God's judgment.

First, he tells us that God's judgment *is sometimes silent*. When we think of judgment, we tend to think of lightning bolts and hurricanes and earthquakes and great balls of fire, not the gentle whisper that took the prophet Elijah unawares. We feel like Jim Carrey's character in the film *Bruce Almighty* when he shouts at God, *"C'mon, lemme see a little wrath! Smite me, O mighty smiter! You're the one who should be fired! The only one around here not doing his job is you!"*[2] Paul tells us that God's judgment is more subtle than Jim Carrey. He told us three times in 1:24, 26 and 28 that God's scariest form of judgment is not pestilence or plague, but a decision to stay silent and hand us over to our sin. The English Puritan Thomas Watson warned that *"The greatest judgment God lays upon a man in this life is to let him sin without control. When the Lord's displeasure is most severely kindled against a person, he does not say, I will bring the sword and the plague on this man, but, I will let him sin on."*[3]

Second, Paul tells us that God's judgment *is sometimes unrecognized*. When he told us in 1:27 that many pagans have "received in themselves the due penalty for their perversion", was he meaning that they notice God's hand of judgment on their lives? Almost certainly not. Proverbs 19:3 observes that *"A man's own folly ruins his life, yet his heart rages against the Lord."* When promiscuous people contract infections, when greedy people are dissatisfied, when liars lose their jobs and when gossips lose their friends, they very rarely come to the conclusion that God is judging them. They either explain his judgment away by attributing it to natural causes, or they use it as a reason to blame God for unfairly ruining their lives.

When Adolf Hitler's evil empire collapsed and he prepared himself for inevitable death, he insisted to the end that *"God*

---

[2] *Bruce Almighty* (Universal Pictures, 2003).

[3] Thomas Watson, *The Doctrine of Repentance* (1668).

*the Almighty has made our nation. By defending its existence
we are defending his work. The fact that this defence is fraught
with incalculable misery, suffering and hardships makes us even
more attached to this nation."*[4] Paul told us in 1:18 that God's
judgment is already being revealed; the question is whether we
are wise enough to listen.

Third, he tells us that God's judgment *is always just*, which
means that nobody can avoid it for too long. He stresses this
through an unusual word in 2:5, which occurs nowhere else in
the Bible and means literally *righteous judgment*, and by quoting
in the following verse from Psalms and Proverbs to remind
us that God *"will give to each person according to what he has
done"*.[5] Can we really believe that the Lord will waive justice
for the self-seeking, truth-denying evildoers Paul describes in
2:8? Since justice demands that he punish them, and we are all
like either Dr Jekyll or Mr Hyde, we must not misinterpret God's
slowness to judge as a lack of resolve.

Fourth, Paul tells us that God's judgment *is always both now
and not-yet*. Note his choice of words in 2:5 when he talks about
*"storing up wrath...for the day of God's wrath, when his righteous
judgment will be revealed"*. Whether or not we receive a gracious
foretaste through God's discipline today, he has appointed a Day
of Judgment in the future and is storing up each evil deed for
that final moment of reckoning. *"The sins of some people are
obvious, going before them into judgment,"* he explains, *"but for
others, they show up later."*[6] Whether or not they are obvious
now, they will be on that Final Day.

Fifth, Paul tells us that God's judgment *is always kind,
tolerant and patient*. God's tolerance does not mean that he turns
a blind eye to right and wrong, but that he patiently endures our

---

[4] Adolf Hitler in a radio speech on 30th January 1945.

[5] This quote is word-for-word Psalm 62:12 and Proverbs 24:12 in the
Septuagint. Paul clarifies in 2:9–11 that God will take into account the amount
of revelation each person received when he looks at their deeds.

[6] 1 Timothy 5:24 (New English Translation).

sin because his true desire is to save us before that Final Day comes.[7] Our judge in 2:16 is Jesus, the very one who died to save us, so this slowness to punish is not caused by indecision. *"Do you show contempt for the riches of his kindness, tolerance and patience, not realizing that God's kindness leads you towards repentance?"* Paul asks us in amazement.

No. We cannot use God's patience as false reassurance that his judgment isn't coming, and nor can we fight Paul when he tells us that everyone will deserve it when it comes. We must face up to the fact that the only thing standing between us and judgment is the mercy of the God we have offended. We must turn from the wickedness and moralism described in chapters 1 and 2, because we need to make room for the Gospel of the righteousness of God in Jesus Christ.

Another English Puritan, this time Stephen Charnock, writes:

> *Presume not upon God's patience. The exercise of it is not eternal... You know not how soon His anger may turn His patience aside, and step before it. It may be His sword is drawn out of the scabbard, His arrows may be settled in His bow, and perhaps there is but a little time before you may feel the edge of the one or the point of the other, and then there will be no more time for patience in God to us, or petition from us to Him.[8]*

---

[7] 2 Peter 3:9.

[8] Stephen Charnock, *Discourses upon the Existence and Attributes of God* (1682).

Coffee Stains (2:17–3:8)

As it is written: "God's name is blasphemed among the Gentiles because of you."

(Romans 2:24)

When Jan Carlzon became president of SAS Airlines in 1981, the company was losing thirty million dollars a year and teetering on the brink of failure. In only twelve months, he turned the airline around and surprised business analysts by posting a profit. When asked the secret of his success, he said the pivotal moment had been telling his cleaning staff to wipe the coffee stains off all the flip-down trays after every flight. The analysts laughed and assumed he was joking.

But Jan Carlzon was being deadly serious. His success with SAS Airlines was based on what he described as "moments of truth" with each of their passengers. Since travellers could not see inside the cockpit or the engines, they formed impressions of an airline's safety from the little details they could see. If there were coffee stains on the flip-down trays, they assumed similar negligence over engine safety. If the trays were wiped clean, they felt reassured that the pilot must be giving his flight controls equally close attention. Carlzon explained that

> *Last year each of our ten million customers came in contact with approximately five SAS employees, and this contact lasted an average of 15 seconds each time. The SAS is "created" 50 million times a year, 15 seconds at a time. These 50 million "moments of truth" are the*

moments that ultimately determine whether SAS will succeed or fail as a company.[1]

It was time for Paul to tell the Jewish Christians at Rome that their confidence in Jewishness was covered in coffee stains. Having dealt with pagan immorality in 1:18–32 and with moralism in 2:1–16, he now turns to the Jews and tells them they are as in need of God's gift of righteousness as anyone else. Their Jewishness, their familiarity with the Law of Moses, their circumcision, their history and their calling to be a light to the Gentiles – none of this had any power to save them since they had fallen woefully short of their calling as God's People. God wanted to be seen through the Jewish nation, but there were dirty coffee stains all over the flip-down trays of their lives.

Don't switch off at this point if you are not Jewish. Paul is actually making a more general point here too. God has given the same calling to the Church as he gave to Israel,[2] and he still wants to make himself visible through us. We can be every bit as guilty of misplaced confidence and spiritual arrogance – it's just that our temptation is to rely on the faith of our parents, on the fact we have been baptized or on our role in a local church. Paul says exactly the same two words to us as he did to the Jewish Christians in Rome: coffee stains.

He insists in 2:17–24 that being entrusted with the Bible is no guarantee that we will be saved.[3] What matters is whether or not we actually obey it, and Paul has already convinced us that none of us lives as righteously as it demands. He adds in 2:25–29 that being circumcised is no guarantee either that we are truly part of God's saved People. Paul shocks the Jewish Christians by reminding them of the teaching of Deuteronomy

---

[1] Jan Carlzon, *Moments of Truth* (1987).

[2] Compare, for example, Exodus 19:5–6 with 1 Peter 2:9–10.

[3] Although Paul uses the word *Law* technically in 3:19–20 to refer to the Pentateuch, we can see from John 10:34; 12:34 and 15:25 that the word *Law* also referred more generally to the Old Testament as a whole.

10:16 and Jeremiah 4:4 that circumcision only matters as an outward sign of an inward commitment to obedience, and that therefore many uncircumcised Gentile Christians are in fact more "circumcised" than they are![4] The Christian Gentiles they despised were actually more "Jewish" than the die-hards in the synagogue, since outward ritual can never make a person part of God's saved People.[5]

Paul demonstrates just how coffee-stained their ethnic boasting is by referring to the promise of Isaiah 42:6–7 that God would make the Jews into *"a light for the Gentiles, to open eyes that are blind...those who sit in darkness"*. They were to be like flip-down trays which represented God's invisible character to the nations, but Paul quotes the verdict of Isaiah 52:5 that *"God's name is blasphemed among the Gentiles because of you"*.[6] Their sin-stained lives, breaking the Law while at the same time judging the pagans they were meant to be saving, were so covered in dirt that the pagans assumed that their God was as bad as they were. Instead of looking down on pagans, they should be apologizing to them for deceiving them at Jan Carlzon's spiritual "moment of truth". They should stop bragging about their privileged status as Jews and start facing up to the fact they were the worst offenders of them all!

God had said a similar thing to David in 2 Samuel 12:14 after his adultery with Bathsheba and his murder of Uriah. When God's prophet warned him that *"By doing this you have made the enemies of the Lord show utter contempt"*, David repented and found himself restored to his former place in God's missionary

---

[4] 2:27 echoes Jesus' warning in Matthew 12:41–42 that many Gentiles will condemn Jews on Judgment Day.

[5] Paul uses a pun in 2:29 because the word *Jewish* comes from the name *Judah*, which means *Praise*. C.K. Barrett tries to convey this pun by translating it *"He is a **Jew** whose **due** comes not from men but from God"*.

[6] Paul takes the Septuagint reading of this verse, which is also similar to Ezekiel 36:22. In its original context, the Lord was not so much telling Israel that their sin made him look wicked, as that their sin stopped him from blessing them and therefore made him look weak.

plan. That's why Paul quotes from David's great psalm of repentance in 3:1–4 and tells the Jewish Christians that God remains faithful to this promise. Despite their unfaithfulness, he has a plan to clean away their coffee stains and use their lives to win the nations to himself as originally planned. Paul expects them to remember that Israel's disobedience after Isaiah 42 led to the Messiah coming in 49:6 and being told that *"I will also make you a light for the Gentiles, that you may bring my salvation to the ends of the earth."* He expects them to link this to 51:4–5 when the Messiah promises that *"My justice will become a light to the nations. My righteousness draws near speedily, my salvation is on the way, and my arm will bring justice to the nations."*[7] God has not finished with ethnic Israel, but their calling is completely tied to the coming of the new King Jesus.

Like the pagans and moralizers, the Jews were faced with a choice. They could whine and make the excuses in 3:5–8, or they could confess "Jesus is Lord" and let him start cleaning their coffee stains. God still wants to be seen through his People, but only *his* righteousness, *his* salvation and *his* Messiah can make us equal to the plan.

We need to repent of relying on Jewishness or on Christian externals, and to confess that our only hope is receiving the righteousness of God. Our Bible studies, liturgies and Christian rituals can simply never be enough. Like everyone else, we need the Gospel message that the new King Jesus saves.

---

[7] Jesus says that he fulfils these promises in John 8:12 and 9:5, and he commissions us to share this ministry with him through the Gospel in Matthew 5:14–16.

Parachute Drill (3:9–20)

Therefore no one will be declared righteous in his sight by observing the law; rather, through the law we become conscious of sin.

(Romans 3:20)

Paul has already given us two chapters which argue that everyone is a sinner and subject to God's judgment. Now he gives us half a chapter more. Since the Greek word *euangelion*, or *gospel*, literally means *good news*, this can come as a bit of a surprise. Paul's negative focus in the first three chapters of Romans can even leave us wondering why the Gospel concerning Jesus is called good news at all.

That's why it helps to remind ourselves that the word *euangelion* had a technical meaning in the first-century Roman Empire. We have already noted that it was used to describe the news that a future emperor had been born, or that a major battlefield victory had been won. This meant that when an angel told the shepherds (in words which echoed the Priene calendar inscription about Augustus which we quoted earlier) that *"I bring you the euangelion of great joy that...a Saviour has been born to you; he is Christ the Lord"*, it was good news to the shepherds but such bad news for King Herod that he slaughtered Bethlehem's babies in his anger.[1]

Similarly, when evangelists were despatched to Rome from Britain in 61 AD to announce the gospel that General Suetonius Paulinus had defeated Boudicca's rebellion, it was good news

---

[1] Luke 2:10–11. If you are in any doubt how dangerous it was to announce in the Roman Empire that there was a new King in town, then read Matthew 2:1–18.

for the Romans but terrible news for the Britons. Paul's purpose in these first three chapters is to convince us that all people are enemies of God who need urgently to change sides. If the Gospel about Jesus sounds like bad news so far, it is only because Paul starts out by warning us that the whole human race is fighting on the losing team. The message that "Jesus is Lord" always starts that way.

So before Paul launches into five and a half more positive chapters about how we can change sides, he needs to make sure that we have understood our problem. We are guiltier than any rebel against his earthly ruler, for we have deliberately suppressed the truth about God. Our pride doesn't need flattering but flattening so that we can be saved. Otherwise we treat the Gospel as an offer we don't need from a God who promises to improve our lives. That's a false gospel which produces false converts who fail to last the distance in the marathon race of following Jesus. Only hearing that we are rebels makes us ready to be made righteous.

Imagine that you and I are on a long-haul flight together. As the plane reaches cruising height, one of the stewardesses hands us parachutes and asks us to put them on. *"This will make you feel like paratroopers,"* she encourages us. *"If you enjoyed 'Band of Brothers' then you will love wearing these."* She is so charming and convincing that we do as she says, but pretty soon we find the parachutes aren't as much fun as she made out. They make it hard for us to sit comfortably in our seats, and an hour into the flight they begin to feel very heavy. *"What were we thinking of, listening to that stewardess?"*, we ask each other. We stop believing her flattery and take the parachutes off our backs.

Now imagine that same situation, but with a different stewardess who follows Paul's example. As we reach cruising height, she hands us parachutes with a warning that *"The cockpit is on fire and the plane is going down!"* This time it doesn't bother us that the parachutes feel uncomfortable and heavy. We know that they are the only things which can save us from certain destruction, so we keep them on and ready ourselves to jump out of the plane.

It's this difference which makes Paul step up his warnings in these last twelve verses of his teaching on "salvation needed". He lists seven back-to-back quotations from the Old Testament to convince us that the message we are God's enemies runs right the way through the Jewish Scriptures. It is in the Pentateuch in verses 19 and 20, and in the Psalms, Solomon's wisdom and the prophets in verses 10–18.[2] Paul emphasizes that sin is *very widespread* by asserting nine times in verses 9–12 that it affects *everyone*, and that sin runs *all over* by choosing quotes that mention *throats*, *tongues*, *lips*, *mouths*, *feet* and *eyes*. Gentiles refuse to seek God as Lord in 1:18–32, moralists refuse to seek him as Saviour in 2:1–16, and Jews refuse to seek him as either in 2:17–3:8, since *"There is no one righteous, not even one; there is no one who understands, no one who seeks God."* We are all on a plane which is engulfed in flames, and we had better all get ready to put on Paul's Gospel parachute.

This, Paul tells us, was actually the primary purpose of Moses' Law all along. It was never meant to be a self-help guide for humans to construct their own path to righteousness. It was always a wake-up call which listed God's holy standards in order to shut us up long enough to listen to the Gospel! When we read Leviticus or Deuteronomy, we find the books defy neat structure, bouncing back and forth between legislation that shows how guilty we are and blood sacrifices that show what we must do about it. They are designed to silence us long enough to hear the stewardess's warning that we are guilty, under God's judgment,

---

[2] Although a few Greek Old Testament manuscripts place all the words quoted in 3:10–18 in Psalm 14:1–3, they were added by later copyists who were influenced by Paul. In fact these seven or eight quotations come from Psalm 5:9; 10:7; 14:2–3; 36:1; 53:2–3 and 140:3 and from Ecclesiastes 7:20 and Isaiah 59:7–8.

and in need of God's Gospel parachute as the only way we can be saved.

Martyn Lloyd-Jones writes:

> *You are not a Christian unless you have been made speechless! How do you know whether you are a Christian or not? It is that you "stop talking". The trouble with the non-Christian is that he goes on talking... They are forever talking about God, and criticising God, and pontificating about what God should or should not do... You do not begin to be a Christian until your mouth is shut, is stopped, and you are speechless and have nothing to say.*[3]

We need to shut our mouths and listen at the end of Paul's teaching on "salvation needed". We need to let these chapters search our hearts and silence our false sense of safety and self-righteousness. We need to open our mouths to speak differently to God, to lay hold of his righteousness before he marches out in judgment. We need to agree with Paul's conclusion as summarized by the nineteenth-century evangelist D. L. Moody:

> *The Law was given not to save men, but to measure them... It was never meant for men to save themselves by... I can always tell a man who has got near the kingdom of God: his mouth is stopped.*[4]

---

[3] Martyn Lloyd-Jones, *The Righteous Judgment of God* (1989).

[4] D.L. Moody, *Twelve Select Sermons* (1881).

Salvation Given (3:21–5:21)

But now a righteousness from God, apart from law, has been made known, to which the Law and the Prophets testify.

(Romans 3:21)

A few weeks ago, I took my young children to the gates of Buckingham Palace to try and catch a glimpse of the Queen. It was a sunny day and we had a lot of fun, but it wasn't a gospel moment. Even as fans of Queen Elizabeth, her arrival made very little difference to our lives which we could hail as good news.

Contrast that, however, with the end of a good Robin Hood movie. King Richard the Lionheart is away on the Crusades and his evil brother John is turning England into an island hell. He is stealing the lands of loyal knights like Robin of Locksley, forcing himself on beautiful women like Maid Marian and taxing the peasants into the ground. Robin and his merry men do all they can to rob from the rich to save the lives of the poor, but everything changes when King Richard reappears. *"Hold, I speak!"* he commands as he appears, and every Englishman falls to his knees.[1] There's no more place for Prince John or cruel taxes or the need to live in Sherwood Forest now that King Richard is home. There's no doubt about it, his appearance is pure gospel.

So think "King Richard" instead of "Buckingham Palace" when you read Paul's teaching in 3:21–5:21 about "salvation given". He deliberately links back to where he broke off in 1:17

---

[1] Sean Connery says this as King Richard at the end of *Robin Hood: Prince of Thieves* (Warner Brothers, 1991). This is my favourite Robin Hood gospel moment.

by using the same key phrase *dikaiosunē theou*, the *righteousness of God*. It's as if he is telling us that his teaching on "salvation needed" was simply a necessary prelude to unpacking what that actually means. I had to tell you about your spiritual Prince John, he explains. I had to tell you that you are outlaws with a price on your head. I had to show you the nightmarish kingdom of Satan so that you can now see the value of the Gospel as the Saviour King Jesus rides into view.

The next two and a half chapters are possibly the richest in the Bible. Paul has so much to say and so little space to say it that he crams each verse with condensed truth, yet it still makes Romans the longest surviving letter in the ancient world! He uses 3:21–22 as an overall summary of these first eight chapters which announce that the new King Jesus saves: *"But now a righteousness from God, apart from law, has been made known, to which the Law and the Prophets testify. This righteousness from God comes through faith in Jesus Christ to all who believe."* These two verses are a headline for the verses which follow, and because they are so dense and so important, let's draw out the big picture of where Paul wants to take us before we dive into the detail.

Paul is going to give us *five pictures of the Gospel*, in order for us to view it from five different angles. He will spend the rest of this chapter painting the first three pictures, which are (excuse my love of old classic movies) "The Accused", "Cry Freedom" and "Trading Places". He will then call an interval before painting the last two pictures in chapter 5, which are "The Bodyguard" and "Tomb Raider". The Gospel concerning Jesus means such a show-stopping turnaround that unless we see it from all five angles we will miss out on all it means.

Paul is also going to give us *two characters from the Old Testament*. The five pictures explain what he means by *"the righteousness of God"*, but his reflections on the lives of Abraham and David explain what he means by that righteousness *"coming through faith in Jesus Christ to all who believe"*. He will tell us in chapter 4 about "Abraham's Credit Card" and "David's Accountant", as a God-given guide from the pages of the Old Testament for what it means to confess by faith that the new King Jesus is Lord.

As Paul does this, he is going to answer *four more key questions* along the way. He will heckle himself to keep his monologue interactive, guessing our four biggest questions and answering them each in turn. "What about other religions?" he will ask at the end of chapter 3. "What about the Promised Land?" he will ask in chapter 4, mindful that this was a point of conflict between the Jewish and Gentile Christians, as indeed it still often is today. He will finish off in chapter 5 by asking "Now I'm a Christian, what next?" and "How many people will be saved?" He tries to predict our questions because the Gospel is too important for us not to investigate its every little corner.

So let's get ready to engage with these five pictures, two characters and four questions that unpack the Good News of "salvation given". Martin Luther called these chapters *"the most importance piece in the New Testament and the very purest Gospel"*, and urged every reader to pore over them as much as he did. God used them in his life to revive a nation, a continent and eventually the whole world:

> *It is well worth a Christian's while not only to memorise it word for word, but also to occupy himself with it daily, as though it were the daily bread of the soul. It is impossible to read or to meditate on this letter too much or too well. The more one deals with it, the more precious it becomes and the better it tastes... It is in itself a bright light, almost bright enough to illumine the entire Scripture... Without doubt, whoever takes this letter to heart possesses the light and power of the Old*

Testament. Therefore each and every Christian should make this letter the habitual and constant object of his study. God grant us his grace to do so. Amen.[2]

---

[2] Martin Luther in his *Preface to Romans* (1522).

First Picture: the Accused (3:24)

*For all have sinned and fall short of the glory of God,
and are justified freely by his grace.*

(Romans 3:23–24)

On 30th July 1998, the London Court of Appeal overturned Derek Bentley's conviction for murder. Nothing too unusual about that, you might think – after all, the Court of Appeal quashes convictions all the time – but what made this case different was that Derek Bentley had already been hanged for the murder almost half a century earlier in 1953. That belated ruling from the Court of Appeal reminds us why Paul's first Gospel picture in 3:24 is so important.

Iris Bentley began her campaign to have her brother acquitted shortly after his execution. She was granted a concession in 1966 which permitted her to disinter his body from the prison graveyard and give it a respectable burial in a churchyard, but a slightly better burial plot simply wasn't enough. In the 1970s, 1980s and 1990s a series of TV documentaries and a feature-length movie highlighted the case and swung public opinion in Derek Bentley's favour, but this didn't change the fact that he was still officially guilty of murder, so his sister's legal battle carried on. Even when he received a posthumous royal pardon in 1993, along with an embarrassed confession that he never should have hanged, his sister still refused to be satisfied. Pardon was not the same thing as exoneration, so she carried on fighting to overturn his conviction. A year after his sister died, the Court of Appeal finally ruled that he was innocent of murder. Derek Bentley had been justified and vindicated under English law, just as Paul says in his first Gospel picture that Jesus justifies convicted sinners like ourselves.

To understand Romans, we need to know what the word *justified* means. It is one of the most important words in the letter. It is a legal term which Paul took from the courtroom and does not mean the same thing as being *pardoned* or *forgiven*. Pardoning is the opposite of sentencing, whereas justifying is the opposite of condemning. Pardoning Derek Bentley meant saying that, even though he was guilty, he shouldn't have been executed. Justifying Derek Bentley meant saying that he wasn't actually guilty of murder at all; not only should he not have been executed, but there were no proper grounds on which to punish him at all. Can you see the important distinction between *forgiveness* and *justification*? Then let's enjoy Paul's first Gospel picture of what it means to say that the new King Jesus saves.

The picture begins with Jesus sitting in the courtroom as judge and jury, and with us standing in the dock to await his decision. Paul has no time for the sloppy idea that the Father plays the role of judge on his own and the Son only enters the scene to play the role of Saviour. No, Paul told us in 2:16 that Jesus is the judge and jury, and he passes a clear verdict: we are guilty as charged of rebellion against God, and the fixed penalty for that crime is death. The final Judgment Day has yet to arrive, but Jesus anticipates that Day by revealing his verdict and sentence ahead of time.

Suddenly, Jesus changes his position in the picture. Now he is standing next to us and arguing our case. 1 John 2:1 can be literally translated *"If anyone sins, we have a defence lawyer arguing our case to the Father – Jesus Christ, the Righteous One."* Paul now paints the Father as judge, and Jesus as the attorney who points out an unconsidered factor which will reverse the initial verdict. New evidence came to light in 30 AD when Jesus was himself put on trial and declared innocent of any crime. A life of perfect Law-keeping as a working-class Galilean had made him righteous. Now he brings that "righteousness from God" into the courtroom and tells the judge that it is ours because we trusted in his Gospel. The accused is guilty through his own deeds but deemed entirely innocent through the deeds of another!

Suddenly the galleries erupt with clamouring spectators who oppose the defence lawyer's proposal. The accused is guilty as charged of rebellion and sin, so the judge cannot simply pretend those actions never happened. Faith is all very well, but whatever happened to the Old Testament promise Paul quoted in 2:6 that God *"will give to each person according to what he has done"*? Jesus replies by telling the judge that his argument rests on the fact that through the Gospel he and the accused possess one legal identity. *"You are **in Christ Jesus**, who has become for us...our righteousness,"* Paul explains in 1 Corinthians 1:30. We stand in the dock, united with Jesus, and hear God pass two verdicts in verse 26, *"so as to be just and the one who justifies those who have faith in Jesus."*

Paul's picture therefore ends with Jesus being convicted and condemned to crucifixion because of our guilt, and with our being justified and exonerated because of his innocence. We find ourselves outside the courtroom listening to the sound of nails being driven into Jesus' hands and feet, when suddenly we feel the hand of a court official on our shoulder and spin around. But it's not a team of appeal lawyers demanding a retrial because *"there is now no condemnation for those who are in Christ Jesus"*.[1] The official simply wants to reassure us that this not-guilty verdict is a once-for-all decision. We have been vindicated of every charge – past, present and future – so that

---

[1] Romans 8:1. The word *katakrima*, or *condemnation*, means literally *a guilty verdict*.

no one can lodge a fresh accusation against us. That's what it means to be united with Jesus by faith in the Gospel concerning God's Son.[2]

It wasn't easy for Paul to write to the Roman mother-city, with all its pomp and imperial splendour, to announce that the new King in town was a convicted felon who had been executed after a trial before one of Caesar's top provincial judges. He confessed to his readers that he was tempted to be ashamed of such a message, but this picture of God's courtroom spurred him on to preach it in all its counter-cultural glory:

> *I am not ashamed of the gospel, because it is the power of God for the salvation of everyone who believes: first for the Jew, then for the Gentile. For in the gospel a righteousness from God is revealed, a righteousness that is by faith from first to last, just as it is written: "The righteous will live by faith."*[3]

---

[2] In fact Paul uses a present tense in 3:23 to talk about us *going on falling short* of the glory of God. This once-for-all verdict deals with our present and future sins as much as with our past.

[3] Romans 1:16–17. Paul is not just saying in a roundabout way that he is proud of the gospel. He is saying that he needed to remind himself of pictures like this one to fight off his temptation to be ashamed of it.

Second Picture:
Cry Freedom (3:24)

*…justified freely by his grace through the redemption
that came by Christ Jesus.*

(Romans 3:24)

There's no better place to see God's unflinching commitment to justice than in Paul's second Gospel picture in 3:24. Paul paints the picture with a single word that was almost as offensive to a Gentile Roman as when he called himself *"a slave of Christ"*. Paul's second picture is all about *redemption*, a dirty word that spoke of helpless slaves, defeated prisoners of war and convicted criminals.

The Roman Jews viewed this unpleasant word very differently. This was the word the Lord had used to describe the way he rescued their nation from slavery in Egypt and brought them to the freedom of Mount Sinai. They remembered God's promise to their ancestors in Exodus 6:6 that *"I am the Lord, and I will bring you out from under the yoke of the Egyptians. I will free you from being slaves to them, and I will redeem you with an outstretched arm and with mighty acts of judgment."* When they looked at Paul's second Gospel picture, it looked familiar. God had repainted the Exodus story in new and better colours.

God began the Exodus by demonstrating that he was stronger than all of Egypt's idols put together. He took them on through ten devastating plagues on the Egyptians, and when he blew the final whistle he had beaten them ten–nil. There was nothing to stop him from freeing the Hebrews from their slave-masters by force. The only thing which held him back was his fierce commitment to justice.

God demanded their freedom by telling Pharaoh that his slaves were actually first and foremost God's family. *"Israel is my firstborn son...so I will kill your firstborn son"* he warned through Moses in Exodus 4:22–23. Nevertheless, he recognized that the Egyptians possessed legal ownership of those slaves under the ancient rules of civil war and hostage-taking. The Hebrews had been the allies of the fallen Middle Kingdom, and they had natural links with the Canaanite Hyksos who invaded Egypt during the Second Intermediate Period. When the new Pharaoh's dynasty established the New Kingdom, they had a legal right in their culture to treat the Hebrews as prisoners of war. God therefore refused to free the Hebrews by might at the expense of honouring what was right. He paid a ransom price to legitimize their freedom.

On the night of the tenth plague, which killed the Egyptian firstborns, the Lord redeemed the Hebrews by telling them to kill a Passover lamb and smear its blood onto their doorframes. The New Testament explains this was a picture of God's firstborn Son Jesus[1] dying later on a wooden cross to buy freedom for God's People.[2] Once he had led them through the Red Sea as a kind of "baptism" which united them with Jesus' future death and resurrection, they looked at the drowned corpses of their former slave-masters and praised the Lord that he had *ransomed*, *redeemed* and *purchased* them through the death of his own firstborn. The Jewish Christians could look at Paul's second Gospel picture and grasp what Jesus meant in Matthew 20:28 when he told his followers that he had come *"to give his life as a ransom for many"*.

---

[1] *Firstborn* in Romans 8:29, Colossians 1:15, 18 and Hebrews 1:6 and 12:23 refers to Jesus' status as God's beloved Son, not to him having been born first. Ephraim is called the firstborn in Jeremiah 31:9 despite being the second son of the eleventh son of the second son of a second son!

[2] See 1 Corinthians 5:7, or compare Exodus 12:46 with John 19:31–36.

This second picture is important because the Gospel is not just about forgiveness, but also about freedom. Most Western Gospel sermons address sinners as the accused and deal more with the issue of guilt and condemnation than they do with how we can break free from sin's power. They give rise to testimonies that rejoice in our being counted righteous despite our past, but hold little expectation for a changed life in the present. Yet Jesus promised, *"If the Son sets you free, you will be free indeed."* Paul adds that

> The grace of God that brings salvation has appeared to all men. It teaches us to say "No" to ungodliness and worldly passions, and to live self-controlled, upright and godly lives in this present age, while we wait for…Jesus Christ, who gave himself for us to redeem us from all wickedness and to purify for himself a people that are his very own, eager to do what is good.[3]

This second picture informs us that Jesus has shattered Satan's rule, and has freed us to live under the rule of the new King in town.

Stephen Biko, the South African campaigner whose life is celebrated in the movie *Cry Freedom*, is famous for his refusal to act like a slave to apartheid. *"It is better to die for an idea that will live, than to live for an idea that will die"*, he proclaimed as part of his message of freedom and redemption.[4] Paul paints this second Gospel picture as a prelude to unpacking how we can experience our salvation in chapters 6–8. He reminds us that God paid justice (not Pharaoh, who died!) when he redeemed the Hebrew slaves from Egypt, and he tells us God has done the same for us through Jesus, the better Passover Lamb. *"The God of peace will soon crush Satan under your feet,"* because the Gospel

---

[3] John 8:36 and Titus 2:11–14.

[4] Stephen Biko, quoted in Dickson A. Mungazi, *The Mind of Black Africa* (1996).

has freed you by right as well as by might.[5] It gives us freedom from the Devil's legitimate hold on our lives, so we can say with Jesus in John 14:30: *"The prince of this world is coming...he has no hold on me."*

So feast your eyes on this second Gospel picture. Justice and mercy have come together at the cross. Let's look at our old slave-master Satan and tell him: *"I don't work for you any more!"*

---

[5] Romans 16:20.

Third Picture: Trading Places (3:25)

*God presented him as a sacrifice of atonement,
through faith in his blood. He did this to demonstrate
his justice, because in his forbearance he had left the
sins committed beforehand unpunished.*

(Romans 3:25)

Imagine that you are Charles Darnay in the Dickens novel *A Tale of Two Cities*. You are a hated French nobleman in the midst of the Revolution, and you have been arrested and sentenced to die by the guillotine. As the minutes tick away in your dark and lonely prison cell, you accept that this is the day you will die. Dickens tells us that Charles Darnay *"sustained himself with no flattering delusion... He had fully comprehended that no personal influence could possibly save him."*

Suddenly you hear footsteps in the corridor, and a key turns in the lock. It is Sydney Carton, a London barrister who once promised your wife that he would die to protect your family. You both look so much alike that he once had you acquitted in an English courtroom by pretending to be you and fooling the jury. Now he tells you that he has come to Paris to perform the same trick again, fulfilling his vow to your wife by going to the guillotine as if he were you. How would you respond?

Charles Darnay refuses. His saviour is forced to overpower him with chloroform and go to the guillotine in his place by force. While a drugged Charles Darnay is smuggled to freedom in England, Sydney Carton goes silently to the guillotine in his place. *"I see the lives for which I lay down my life, peaceful, useful, prosperous and happy,"* he encourages himself in the novel's closing lines. *"It is a far, far better thing that I do, than I have ever done."* He goes down as one of literature's greatest tragic heroes.

Paul picks up a different paintbrush in verse 25 and begins to paint his third Gospel picture. He tells you that Jesus has traded places with you in a drama more breathtaking than any Dickens novel. *"The wages of sin is death,"* he explains later in 6:23 as a reminder that all of us were once waiting on death row, *"but the gift of God is eternal life in Christ Jesus our Lord."*

John Stott puts it this way:

> *The concept of substitution may be said, then, to lie at the heart of both sin and salvation. For the essence of sin is man's substituting himself for God, while the essence of salvation is God substituting himself for man. Man asserts himself against God and puts himself where only God deserves to be; God sacrifices himself for man and puts himself where only man deserves to be. Man claims prerogatives which belong to God alone; God accepts penalties which belong to man alone.*[1]

Jesus has done something far greater than Sydney Carton.

The Lord tried to teach this to the patriarchs by telling them to sacrifice sheep on their altars. He taught it through the Law when he told the Hebrews to do the same. He told their priests to enter the Most Holy Place in the Tabernacle on the Day of Atonement and sprinkle sacrificial blood on the *hilastērion*, the lid of the Ark of the Covenant, which is translated the *atonement cover* or *mercy seat*.[2] The wages of sin is always death, so someone had to pick up the paycheque for their sin. Paul tells us in verses 25 and 26, *"He did this to demonstrate his*

---

[1] John Stott, *The Cross of Christ* (1986).
[2] Leviticus 16:15. The Greek word *hilastērion* comes from the Septuagint translation which Paul used.

justice, because in his forbearance he had left the sins committed beforehand unpunished – he did it to demonstrate his justice at the present time."

Take a closer look at Paul's brushstrokes in his third Gospel picture, and you will find this same Greek word *hilastērion*: *"God presented him as a **sacrifice of atonement**, through faith in his blood"*. Paul therefore points us back to the Day of Atonement and tells us that those blood sacrifices were ancient sketches of the Gospel, only bringing forgiveness to the Hebrews because of what Jesus was going to do. He is the great Sydney Carton who has burst into our death-row prison cell and taken our place so that we can live again. Like Charles Darnay, we have a chance to accept or resist him, but Jesus will not force himself on any prisoner who is too proud to let him take their place and die.

This picture is important because Paul doesn't want us to stop at the first half of 6:23 – *"the wages of sin is death"* – but to carry on reading that *"the gift of God is eternal life in Christ Jesus"*. The Gospel isn't just a message that Jesus is Sydney Carton and died the death we should have died. It is also the message that we wake up like Charles Darnay and discover ourselves in the London where Sydney Carton once walked free. Salvation is more than failure to get what we deserve; it is a positive invitation to step into all that Jesus has deserved. The Day of Atonement was also the day on which the trumpet was sounded to announce the Year of Jubilee, when slaves were freed, the poor made rich and beggars extended the favour of God.[3]

My house is near the Tower of London, the castle where the English kings kept their prisoners on death row. Although visitors can sit in the cells where they awaited execution, that's not the real reason why so many tourists crowd to the Tower. At the heart of the castle is a display of the Crown Jewels, a collection of over 23,500 royal gems. Tourists swarm to the castle to see

[3] Leviticus 25:8–55. The Hebrew word for *Jubilee* comes from the word for the horn of a dead sheep.

these royal treasures, not to look at the darkness of a cell which isn't theirs. In the same way, Paul's third Gospel picture reminds us to preach the Gospel as the promise of blessing, and not just as the avoidance of death. Let's not try to attract non-Christians by preaching a message which does nothing more than threaten death unless they receive God's sacrifice. Let's remind them of the kingly riches which can be theirs through Jesus' sacrifice as well. Let's study this third Gospel picture for ourselves, and praise God for what it means that Jesus took our place and gave us his.

Dickens describes Charles Darnay's fight against Sydney Carton and his chloroform: *"For a few seconds he faintly struggled with the man who had come to lay down his life for him; but, within a minute or so, he was stretched insensible on the ground."* Paul does not come at you with chloroform; he comes at you with faith. He asks you to surrender gladly to the Saviour, to accept him freely as your sacrifice, and to enjoy the riches of the royal life which King Jesus traded for your own.

What About Other Religions? (3:27–31)

A man is justified by faith... There is only one God, who will justify the circumcised by faith and the uncircumcised through that same faith.

(Romans 3:28, 30)

Ancient Rome had as many gods as taverns. Its citizens prided themselves on their religious diversity. Each was free to tailor-make his own particular version of paganism at the family shrine in the corner of his home. If he preferred, he could even choose Judaism or one of the Eastern mystery religions instead. So when Paul wrote to the city and said that there was only one God and only one way to be saved, it wasn't the message which most Romans wanted to hear. It just sounded so – well – *arrogant.*

Not much has changed in the past 2,000 years. In Western societies any religion still goes. It doesn't matter how beautiful we find Paul's three Gospel pictures personally, it can still feel embarrassing to display them on our wall. It's one thing to tell people that Jesus is *a* way or even the *best* way for them to be saved, but is he really the *only* way? Paul sees this question coming and breaks off halfway through his five pictures to sketch out a reply.

He begins by confessing that God's People ought to share this message with humility. He was a former Pharisee, so he had seen at first hand the Jewish tendency to treat God's Word an as excuse to behave like spiritual know-it-alls. Stop boasting, he tells his fellow Jewish Christians in verses 27–31, because God wants to save the pagans too, and to use their tough questioning to hone our understanding of the Gospel. He would say the same thing to Philemon later when he told him to *"be active in sharing your faith, so that you will have a full understanding of every good thing we have in Christ."*[1] The fact is, we don't know it all, and God can even use the enemies of Christ to point out our religious blind spots.

As for the Law which had led to their boasting, Paul reminds them that all it meant was that *"in his forbearance he had left the sins committed beforehand unpunished."* It stopped them from being punished as they deserved, but it didn't atone for their sins as they were going to be. The Lord had always warned them not to let the *"things revealed"* in the Law make them forget that *"the secret things belong to the Lord our God."*[2] Christians need to put these three Gospel pictures on display, but they must frame them with humility and grace.

That said, there was nothing arrogant about the Gospel message itself. It was actually pluralist paganism which was breathtakingly arrogant under a cloak of false humility. The Roman government was constantly drawing a line between religions that were acceptable and religions that were not. Julius Caesar had officially legalized Judaism in 63 BC, and Claudius had ignored this ruling in 49 AD.[3] Even in 57 AD, the very year that Paul wrote this letter to the Romans, their city was gripped by the trial of the wife of the general who conquered Britain for Claudius, and who was *"charged with foreign superstition"* for her conversion to Christianity.[4] Our pluralist culture draws its

---

[1] Philemon 6. The implication is that unless we discuss the Gospel humbly with people who don't believe it, we won't fully understand its riches ourselves.

[2] Deuteronomy 29:29.

[3] Josephus tells us in *Antiquities of the Jews* (14.10.17–26) that Caesar passed this landmark ruling after the conquest of Judea in 63 BC. Luke tries to prove in Acts that it should extend to cover Christianity.

[4] Tacitus, *Annals* (13.32). Although Tacitus does not actually name her crime as Christianity, many historians view this as the first account of Roman

own lines like the Romans to outlaw the views of hate-preaching clerics or abusive cult leaders. What Paul does with his Gospel pictures is take the paintbrush out of our own hands so that God can mark where the line ought to go. Pluralism is the arrogant creed of human paintbrush snatchers. The Gospel is humble because it lets God do the painting.

Paul points out in verse 28 that God has not painted a line between paganism and Judaism, or even between paganism and Christianity. The issue is not that one religion is right and the others are all wrong, but that every religion is cripplingly flawed. Paganism, Judaism and even misunderstood Christianity are all differently packaged ways of trying to impress God through human effort. These pictures drew the same line Paul had painted in Athens when he preached that *"God is not served by human hands, as if he needed anything"*.[5] There are no religious deeds we can perform to acquit the accused, free the slave or rescue the prisoner on death row. Our only hope is to cry out to Jesus who has stepped in to do what we couldn't do ourselves.

Of course the Romans could disagree with Paul and argue that human effort is able to save, but note what they had to do to hold that opinion. They had to live in a world where every heartbeat and every harvest time shouts that human life depends on God, and yet insist that eternal life depends upon ourselves. They had to drown out the warning siren of conscience with ever-louder shouts of self-congratulating piety. They had to believe that even though the great Achilles confessed in the Underworld that *"I would rather be a paid servant in a poor man's house above ground than be king of kings here among the dead"*, they had a better hope than the hero of Troy.[6] That kind of self-confidence was more arrogant than anything Paul had painted.

It also meant that God was less worthy of their worship,

---

persecution against a Christian.

[5] Acts 17:25.

[6] Homer, *Odyssey* (11.488–491).

since he had sent his Son to die an unnecessary death and had short-changed him when he pleaded in the Garden of Gethsemane, *"My Father, if it is possible, may this cup be taken from me."*[7] It meant disbelieving verse 26, that Jesus' death and resurrection were God's acts which *"demonstrate his justice at the present time, so as to be just and the one who justifies those who have faith in Jesus."* At the very least, it meant that Christianity was a lie, and that all religions therefore do not lead to God. It meant breathtaking arrogance and rejection of the Gospel.

No. Paul paints these Gospel pictures precisely because their message is so radical. He wants to show us where God has painted his line, and to call us to turn from human effort to faith in Christ. Jesus has made a way to the Father which religion can never copy. No number of religious deeds can replicate what he did when he died as our Saviour, Redeemer and Substitute with the religion-busting cry that *"It is finished!"*[8]

---

[7] Matthew 26:39.
[8] John 19:30.

Abraham's Credit Card
(4:1–25)

*To the man who does not work but trusts God
who justifies the wicked, his faith is credited as
righteousness.*

(Romans 4:5)

Sometimes it helps to know the story behind great paintings. Paul certainly thought so. Instead of rushing to complete his five Gospel pictures, he slows down to illustrate the meaning of the first three with a story. He takes the life of Abraham, the founder of the Jewish nation and familiar even to the newest Gentile convert, and explains what the patriarch discovered about these three Gospel pictures in Genesis.

Abraham was spiritually broke, flat broke. He knew only too well that all religions do not lead to God. He grew up in Ur of the Chaldees as a worshipper of the Mesopotamian moon-god Nanna, until God appeared to him and told him to leave behind his country and its gods to start offering blood sacrifices and calling on the name of the Lord.[1] Abraham didn't try to argue that he had any credit before God through his devotion to Nanna. He repented of his old religious views and started following the only true God.

But Abraham's spiritual bank balance wasn't getting any better. God told him to leave his household behind, but he decided to take his troublesome nephew along for the ride. God told him to go to the land he would show him, but he settled in the

---

[1] Genesis 12:1–8 and Joshua 24:2. He must have gone with his father to the temple of Nanna, chief god of Ur.

city of Haran halfway there instead. God told him to leave Haran and live in the land of Canaan, but when famine threatened he absconded to Egypt without stopping to ask permission from the Lord.

It got worse. Abraham had run to Egypt for protection, but he soon got scared that Pharaoh would murder him for his pretty wife, so he forced her to lie that she was merely his sister. Sure enough, Pharaoh sent for her and added her to his harem, all because Abraham had failed to do the work God had given him. His spiritual bank balance was seriously in the red.

But here's the thing Paul wants us to notice in the story: God continued blessing Abraham all the same. He not only rescued Abraham's wife from Pharaoh's clutches, but brought them back to Canaan from Egypt *"very wealthy in livestock and silver and gold"*. Once home, he not only delivered Abraham from Lot's selfish scheming, but promised to give him the length and breadth of the land of Canaan. He made him the richest man in Canaan when he defeated and plundered the foreign invaders who attacked Lot. Abraham's own actions had made him spiritually bankrupt, but he seemed to have a credit card that never reached its limit.

Finally, in Genesis 15:6 we reach the verse which Paul quotes here in verses 3 and 22. He reminds us that *"Abraham believed the Lord, and he credited it to him as righteousness."*

Things didn't immediately get much better. For all God's promises, Abraham's wife had failed to provide him with an heir, so he fell back on the practices of the city he had left behind. Mesopotamian tradition permitted the husband of an infertile wife to take her maidservant as a concubine in order to have an heir.[2] Abraham sinfully did so then drove her away to die, but instead of judging him God promised to grant an heir through his infertile wife after all. Even when Abraham lied to the king

---

[2] We can see how this issue was handled in ancient Mesopotamia from the Law Code of Hammurabi (c.1800 BC) and the Nuzi Tablets (c.1500 BC).

of Gerar that his wife was just his sister, in order to save his own neck yet again, and the king took his newly fertile wife into his harem and might have slept with her and cast doubt on the paternity of Abraham's heir, the Lord stepped in to save him. He brought Abraham back home with his wife plus a compensation payment of 1,000 shekels of silver – a vast sum for a spiritual bankrupt who had disobeyed the Lord at almost every turn along the way.[3] How could Abraham keep receiving God's blessing? Because the credit card of faith paid off his crippling bills every time.

One day the credit card bill had to arrive, and it did in Genesis 22. The Lord told Abraham to take his beloved son Isaac, representing all the spiritual credit he had been given, and commanded him to sacrifice his son on Mount Moriah, which had a craggy outcrop known later as Calvary. Abraham tied up his son and laid him on the altar, then raised the sacrificial dagger to pay the credit card bill in full. He had promised Isaac in faith that *"God himself will provide the lamb for the burnt offering, my son,"* and suddenly his faith in God transformed the way in which his credit card bill was paid. The Lord stopped Abraham from killing Isaac and showed him a ram with its head entangled in a thorn bush, as a picture of the one who would be sacrificed at Calvary with a crown of thorns on his head. As Abraham wept over the glory of the Gospel, he prophesied that *"On the mountain of the Lord it **will be** provided."* The Lord had credited his faith as righteousness because his own beloved Son would die to pay the credit card bill of his spiritually bankrupt People.

It is time for Paul to apply this to the Roman Christians, and to link this story to his first three Gospel pictures. Abraham was found guilty of compromise, lying and sexually abusing his wife's maidservant, yet he was *justified* because Jesus died to

---

[3] The Lord talks graciously about Abraham's obedience in Genesis 26:5, but only because of John 6:28–29.

become his righteousness. Abraham was trapped in Egypt and later in Gerar, yet he was *redeemed* because Jesus died to set him justly free.[4] Abraham's sin demanded swift retribution, yet Jesus put on the clothes of a death-row prisoner so that Abraham could wear the robes of a king.

Paul turns to the Jewish Christians and reminds them that Genesis 15:6 mentions Abraham's credit card before circumcision and long before Moses' Law. Abraham needed neither of those things to work off his debt because *"when a man works, his wages are not credited to him as a gift, but…to the man who does not work but trusts God who justifies the wicked, his faith is credited as righteousness."*[5]

Paul turns to the Gentile Christians and reminds them that Genesis 17:5 describes Abraham as *"the father of many nations"*. The story that illustrates Paul's first three pictures belongs as much to the Gentiles as it does to the Jews. The PIN code for God's credit card isn't race or works or circumcision or the Law. It is faith in the one who justifies, frees and sacrifices himself for spiritual paupers who believe the Gospel concerning God's Son.

Paul ends this picture by encouraging us that *"The words 'it was credited to him' were not written for him alone, but also for us, to whom God will credit righteousness – for us who believe in him who raised Jesus our Lord from the dead."* Let's learn to live out these Gospel pictures like the patriarchs. Let's receive them by faith, which was Abraham's credit card.

---

[4] Silver shekels speak of redemption money in Genesis 20:16, Exodus 21:32 and 30:11–16, and Matthew 27:3–4.

[5] 4:4–5. When Paul addresses the Jewish Christians in verse 1, he calls Abraham *"our forefather"*. When he addresses both Jewish and Gentile Christians in verse 16, he calls him *"the father of us all"*.

David's Accountant (4:6–8)

David says the same thing when he speaks of the blessedness of the man to whom God credits righteousness apart from works.

(Romans 4:6)

Sometimes one story just isn't enough. Paul has told us about the pauper; now he tells us about the king.

David was very different from Abraham. He had everything going for him spiritually. As a teenager, he spent his spare time writing psalms and working so diligently as a shepherd that God singled him out to become the future ruler of his People.[1] As a teenager, he even shamed King Saul and his army by daring to fight and kill Goliath in the Lord's name. David's spiritual bank balance was as good as Abraham's was bad.

After he became king, he carried on in the same fashion. He defeated Israel's enemies, conquered Jerusalem and became the first Hebrew ruler to take full possession of the Promised Land. He built a tabernacle for the Lord on Mount Zion and brought the Ark of the Covenant into the city with great rejoicing. Of particular relevance to the Jewish Christians in Rome was the fact that he coupled this with deep love for Moses' Law. *"The law of the Lord is perfect,"* he wrote in Psalm 19 in praise of its commands. *"They are more precious than gold, than much pure gold; they are sweeter than honey, than honey from the comb."*[2] David was everything that Abraham was not. He lived a life of

---

[1] His friend Asaph links this choice to David's obedience as a shepherd in Psalm 78:70–72.

[2] Psalm 19:7, 10. David probably also wrote the anonymous Psalm 119, which is a love song about the Law.

such impeccable virtue that his story illustrates the other side of Paul's first three Gospel pictures.

You see, David sinned, badly. He had a month of spiritual madness later on in life that undid all the years of obedience that went before. He lusted, committed adultery and then murdered his lover's husband. He discovered that no number of good deeds in the past can offset a brief moment of sin in the present. The wages of sin is death, and death is so powerful that it drains even the healthiest bank balance into the red. David was forced to confess that he was no better than Abraham, and to cry out to God not to count his sin against him. David wrote Psalm 32 as a *maskil*, which is Hebrew for a *teaching psalm*, in order to share what God taught him in reply. Paul quotes its opening stanza here in verses 7 and 8: *"Blessed are they whose transgressions are forgiven, whose sins are covered. Blessed is the man whose sin the Lord will never count against him."*

The Greek word at the end of Paul's quotation is *logizomai*, a word borrowed from the business world. It was not a term from the law court, but from the accountant and his ledger. It meant *counting* a payment against a particular column, just as modern-day accountants do in their spreadsheets. *Logizomai* occurs forty-two times in the New Testament, thirty-five of which are Paul, nineteen of which are Romans and eleven of which are here in chapter 4. Paul used it in verse 3 when he quoted from Genesis to tell us that disobedient Abraham's faith was *reckoned* to him as righteousness, and he uses it twice in verses 6 and 8 to tell us David's sin was not *reckoned* against him and God's righteousness was. Paul therefore uses the story of Law-loving David in order to illustrate that we all need these Gospel pictures.

David loved and studied the Law, which is why he understood it so much better than the Jewish Christians in Rome. Even in his virtuous youth, he never fooled himself that he could ever earn his way to righteousness. He knew the Torah began with Adam and Eve finding their years of unbroken obedience in Eden undone by one solitary sin. God taught them that no amount of man-made coverings from fig leaves could place their sin in a different column. Instead, he painted the first Gospel picture by shedding innocent blood so as to clothe them in the skin of an animal sacrifice.[3] Similarly, David knew from the Torah that Moses' years of complete obedience could not offset one single act of folly in Numbers 20 which barred him from entering the Promised Land. David knew that sin carries such a heavy penalty that it cannot be offset by filling the same column with good behaviour.

Yesterday I turned right at a no-right turn. I was driving in an unfamiliar part of town and hadn't seen the signs which told me that a right turn was prohibited. Unfortunately, the policeman who saw me was very clear that my ignorance did not make me innocent. What could I do? Tell him that I had been driving for years without ever once turning right at a no-right turn before? Tell him that I had fifteen years of spotless driving record to my credit? No. My years of past obedience could not offset one present sin. I had broken the law, regardless of my yesterdays, and my only hope was to follow David's lesson in Psalm 32. I got out of the car, confessed my transgression and pleaded with the officer not to hold my sin against me. Thankfully, he decided to reckon my sin against a car full of noisy and distracting children. As I drove away, I whispered to myself the words of Romans 4: *"Blessed is the man whose sin is not counted against him."*

Paul wants the Jewish Christians to admit that they neither love nor obey the Law as consistently as David. He wants them to recognize that no amount of Law-keeping can offset a single sin. He wants all of us to feel sin's guilt, enslavement and penalty as tenderly as David, and to believe the same Gospel that David found in Psalm 32. When David was confronted with his sin,

---

[3] Adam felt guilty despite his fig leaves in Genesis 3:7–11. He needed to be clothed in Christ in 3:21.

he exclaimed, *"As surely as the Lord lives, the man who did this deserves to die!"*[4] God wants to save us from the executioner, just as he did David, as we believe that through Jesus our sin is not counted against us.

Above all, Paul wants to convince us that these Gospel pictures were all painted for us. We may be compromised like Abraham or virtuous like David, but either way our only hope of salvation is for God to act as our accountant. We need our sins to be reckoned in the column headed "Jesus", and to have his righteousness reckoned in the column which bears our name.

David prayed to God for you and for me as he wrote Psalm 32: *"Let everyone who is godly pray to you while you may be found."* Paul pleads with us as we finish these verses to be the answer to David's prayer, and to take his story as the reason to make Paul's Gospel pictures our own.

---

[4] The Lord's prophet Nathan traps David into passing this judgment on himself in 2 Samuel 12:5.

What About the Promised Land? (4:13-17)

It was not through law that Abraham and his offspring received the promise that he would be heir of the world, but through the righteousness that comes by faith.

(Romans 4:13)

If being a Jewish Christian in Rome felt difficult in 57 AD, then it was about to get a whole lot harder. Perhaps that's why God inspired Paul to make his throwaway comment in verse 13. In our own day, as Jews and Arabs continue to battle it out over who should possess the Promised Land, we certainly mustn't let Paul's comment slip by unnoticed. Terrible things were about to happen in the Roman province of Judea, so Paul prepares the Roman Christians to react wisely when they did.

Five years after Paul wrote this letter, Governor Porcius Festus died unexpectedly. The high priest had recently been thwarted by the Romans in his plan to assassinate Paul, so he seized this as a golden opportunity to arrest and execute James, the leader of the church in Jerusalem, instead. Nero's new governor responded to the high priest's defiance of Roman law by deposing him so heavy-handedly that it provoked the Great Jewish Revolt of 66 AD.

When Jewish rebels ambushed and slaughtered an entire Roman legion, Nero sent a general to teach the Empire what happened to any race that resisted Caesar's rule. General Titus captured Jerusalem in 70 AD and slaughtered over a million

Jews when he razed both the city and its Temple to the ground.[1] Titus felt so sickened by the one-sided massacre that the Greek historian Philostratus tells us he refused a victory wreath because he saw *"no merit in vanquishing people forsaken by their own God."*[2] The province of Judea ceased to exist, and the Emperor Hadrian added insult to injury in 132 AD by building a temple to Jupiter on the site of the old Jewish Temple.

All of this was still to come for the Jewish Christians at Rome, but Paul gives them God's perspective to see them through the days ahead. If they understood his Gospel pictures, it would stop the Jewish and Gentile Christians from turning on one another when their countrymen did in Judea.

The Jewish Christians argued from Genesis 13:15 and 17:8 that the Lord had promised them the land of Canaan forever. The Hebrew word *'ōlām* in those verses meant *everlasting*, so they claimed Pompey had been wrong to annex the land for Rome in 63 BC. Christian Zionists still quote those verses today, along with the sister promise in Psalm 105:8–11 that God gave the land to the Jews as *"an everlasting covenant...for a thousand generations"*. They use them to argue that the Jews have a divine right to the land which used to constitute Judea, and that Palestinian Arabs are therefore illegal squatters. Paul made his throwaway comment almost 2,000 years ago, but the passage of time hasn't made it any less relevant today. Paul tells the Jewish and Gentile Christians in verse 13 that God promised Abraham *"he would be **heir of the world**"*.

Nobody loved the Jewish nation more than Paul. He tells the Romans in chapter 9 that he would gladly be damned to hell personally in order to save more of his Jewish countrymen to heaven. He had been brought up as a Pharisee to hate Roman rule and to see the Promised Land as the pinnacle of God's covenant

---

[1] Josephus was an eyewitness and reports this in his *War of the Jews* (6.9.3). He adds in 7.1.1 that Titus destroyed Jerusalem so thoroughly that *"nothing was left there to make visitors believe it had ever been inhabited."*

[2] Philostratus II, *The Life of Apollonius of Tyana* (6.29).

with his People. But he has been painting Gospel pictures for too long to settle for such a black and white sketch any more.

Sure, Genesis referred to the land of Canaan as an *everlasting* inheritance, but it also called circumcision an *everlasting* sign of God's covenant in 17:13. That sign had been upgraded through Jesus into something far greater than the shadow pictured in Moses' Law. The same might therefore also be true of the Land.[3]

Yes, the Psalms had promised God's People would inherit the land, but Jesus had explained what those verses meant in Matthew 5:5 by upgrading Psalm 37:11 to read, *"Blessed are the meek, for they will inherit **the earth"**. Jesus used the Greek word *gē*, which was ambiguous and could mean either *land* or *earth*, but Paul chooses the unambiguous word *kosmos* in Romans 4:13 to upgrade God's promise to Abraham so it encompasses the *world*. To underline this, he quotes from Genesis 17:5 and points out that *"Abraham...is the father of us all. As it is written: 'I have made you a father of many nations.'"* The Jewish and Gentile Christians at Rome must not waste their energy on chasing sketches that belonged to a pre-Christian era. The coming of Jesus had repainted those pictures in the far brighter colours of New Covenant salvation.

It was this truth which made the Christians in Jerusalem sell their precious tracts of land in the days after Pentecost to build Christ's Kingdom until it filled the earth.[4] It was what caused the writers of the New Testament to place such little importance on the Land when they wrote letters after the Temple and city of Jerusalem had been destroyed.[5] It was

---

[3] God always made it clear in the Law in Deuteronomy 28:63–68 that if the Hebrews rejected their Messiah then they would lose the Promised Land. See also Jeremiah 7:5–7.

[4] Acts 4:32–37. Contrast this with godly Naboth's attitude towards the Land in 1 Kings 21.

[5] John is most conspicuous in his failure to mention the recent destruction of Jerusalem in 70 AD when he writes Revelation and his letters. He refused to distract anyone from God's better Gospel pictures.

what made angry Jewish mobs attack Paul as *"the man who teaches all men everywhere against our people and our law and this place".*[6] Ultimately, it was this refusal to flatter with Old Covenant sketches which eventually won tens of thousands of Jews over to Jesus as Messiah. Only when they saw that their black and white sketches had been upgraded did they finally surrender to Jesus as the new King in town.

I hope you love the Jewish nation. I hope you support their right to live in the land which is legally theirs under UN Resolution. I hope you never forget that the Gospel is *"first for the Jew, then for the Gentile"*. But I also hope that you love them enough not to humour their obsession with 8,000 square miles of sun-scorched land. I hope you love them enough to tell them that a new King reigns on David's throne, just as God promised, and that if they will not receive him as King then the Gentiles will. I hope you play your part in God's plan as Paul describes it in chapters 9–11, to make the Jews so jealous at the sight of him blessing the Gentiles that they turn en masse to Jesus as their King.

I hope you refuse to indulge your Jewish friends in their hope in the sketchy promises of yesteryear. *"Ask of me, and I will make the nations your inheritance, the ends of the earth your possession,"* God the Father urged the Son.[7] That's what Paul means when he tells us that God promised Abraham a descendant through the Gospel who would be heir to the whole world.

---

[6] Acts 21:28.

[7] Psalm 2:8. Jesus tells us in Revelation 2:26–27 that this promise is for his People as well as for him.

Now I'm a Christian, What Next? (5:1–5)

Therefore, since we have been justified through faith, we have...

(Romans 5:1)

David Dickson liked his dirty old painting of Salome with the head of John the Baptist, but it was so old and covered in grime that he decided to take it to Christie's auction house in London. Their expert identified it as the work of a student of the Venetian artist Titian, and told him not to waste thousands of pounds on trying to restore it. He sold it through Christie's in December 1994 for £8,000. At the time, he was happy to have some extra Christmas spending money.

Ten years later, that all changed. David Dickson was visiting an exhibition of Titian's work at the National Galleries in Edinburgh, when he suddenly came face to face with his painting. The new owner had decided to clean away the grime and had discovered that the painting was an original Titian, once owned by King Charles I of England and still bearing his royal monogram on the back. When the rival auction house Sotheby's put the same painting under the hammer for almost £4,000,000 in 2010, a disconsolate David Dickson sued Christie's for damages. What he won was a fraction of the millions he had lost.[1]

That's why Paul refuses to rush into painting his last two Gospel pictures. He has said enough to convince us that the

---

[1] This story was reported by the British newspaper *The Independent* on 25th February 2010.

Gospel is very precious, but he is still concerned we haven't grasped its true value. We might treat it purely as something that saves us *from* evil, instead of remembering that it also saves us *for* great glory. We might receive it simply as the promise of a better life to come, instead of embracing it as the promise of a better life right now – the kind of life John has in mind when he tells us that *"I write these things to you who believe in the name of the Son of God so that you may know that **you have eternal life**"* (not *"will have"*).[2] We might treat the Gospel as a ticket to heaven when we die instead of as an invitation to experience heaven today. So before Paul paints his last two Gospel pictures, he gets out his tools and begins to clean away the grime to reveal the true value of his paintings.

Therefore. That's a powerful word. Paul uses it to uncover five things which are ours from the very moment we surrender our lives to Christ. The first two serve as a prelude to his fourth Gospel picture, and the other three serve as a prelude to his fifth. Together they answer the question, *"Now I'm a Christian, what next?"* We mustn't be spiritual David Dicksons and miss what Paul's therefore is there for.

First, Paul reminds us in verse 1 that being justified through faith in Jesus does not just mean our sins are forgiven. It means God exonerates us of any crime and removes whatever grounds he had to feel hostile towards us as sinners. We have *peace with God*, complete reconciliation, which is why the Christian life is so exciting. When a toddler says *"Daddy"* for the first time, her relationship with her father is not complete. She has just started out on a lifetime of getting to know him.

Second and linked to this, Paul goes further in verse 2 and tells us that we have *access to God's presence* as recipients of his grace. We deserved to be dragged away like the death-row prisoners that we are, but instead he looks on us as he looked on Jesus when he said, *"This is my Son, whom I love; with him I am*

---

[2] 1 John 5:13.

well pleased."[3] Hebrews 10:19–22 encourages us, *"Since we have confidence to enter the Most Holy Place by the blood of Jesus...let us draw near to God with a sincere heart in full assurance of faith,"* but Paul goes one step further. He uses a Greek perfect tense to tell us literally that grace is now the place where *we have taken our stand*. Paul is not telling us to screw up our eyes and get intense about intimacy with God. He is telling us it is already ours if we open our eyes to see the true value of the Gospel.

Third, Paul tells us in verses 2–4 that the Gospel means *a share in the glory of God*. It reveals God's glory through brushstrokes of grace and mercy and forgiveness and salvation, then promises that God will reveal that glory through us! He makes himself more visible through his People today than he did through Moses when he came down from Mount Sinai with such a beaming face that he had to wear a veil. He promises to make his glory ever more visible through us until we share his glory fully on the Day Christ comes again. This should make us rejoice even when we go through difficult trials, since suffering can actually develop our character to steward more of his glory.[4] The "hope" of the Gospel is not just longing for the future. It's what gives us strength to follow Jesus in the present.

Fourth, Paul tells us in verse 5 that we have received *the gift of the Holy Spirit*. John the Baptist, whose execution was the subject of David Dickson's much undervalued picture, preached that Jesus would be known as the Baptizer-in-the-Holy-Spirit. This message has been buried under the grime in many churches. Paul is not telling us that being filled with the Spirit happens automatically at conversion (which would contradict Acts 8:15–17 and 19:1–7), but that being filled with the Spirit is God's gift to every Christian. He will explain in 8:9–17 how we can be filled with the Holy Spirit, and he urges us to treat that

---

[3] Matthew 3:17; 17:5.

[4] Paul explains what he means by rejoicing in the hope of the glory in 8:17–18 and 2 Corinthians 3:18 and 4:17.

gift as a down payment today on the glory which is to come.[5] We do not merely have access to dwell with God in heaven. He also invites us to give him access to dwell with us on earth.

Fifth, Paul tells us in verse 5 that when we receive the Holy Spirit we know *God's love as a heartfelt experience.* We feel the objective truth of his love and find it strengthening us to follow him, bearing fruit in Christian character which convinces us that the glory we hope for is sure to come. Paul will spend three chapters unpacking this in chapters 6–8, but for now he begins to scrape away the grime and to warn us not to underestimate the value of his Gospel pictures. They haven't merely saved us *from* a terrible fate in the future; they have saved us *for* a priceless Christian life today.

Paul is reassured that we have seen beneath the grime which can obscure the riches of the Gospel, so he finally picks up his paint brush once again. It is time for him to paint his last two Gospel pictures – paintings greater than anything sold by Christie's or Sotheby's.

[5] See also 2 Corinthians 1:22; 5:5; Ephesians 1:13–14; 4:30. Paul cannot even imagine in 1 Corinthians 12:12–13 that anyone might respond to the Gospel but not want the gift of the Holy Spirit.

Fourth Picture: the Bodyguard (5:6–11)

Since we have now been justified through his blood,
how much more shall we be saved from God's wrath
through him!

(Romans 5:9)

Paul's fourth Gospel picture is horrible and beautiful, both at the same time. It is a battle scene in which you stand in the foreground in a soldier's uniform, looking like you're fighting for your life. Your face betrays your certain knowledge that the battle will go against you, because the enemy marching to attack is God himself.

Some Christians don't like this Gospel picture. They hate Paul's statement in verse 10 that Jesus died to save us at a time *"when we were God's enemies"*. They dislike Paul's insistence from the Old Testament Scriptures that God hates sinners as well as loving them, and that he is angry as well as patient towards their sin.[1] Paul tells us that *"God's wrath"* burns against all people until they surrender to the Gospel. These verses prompted Jonathan Edwards to tell his eighteenth-century hearers that:

> *However unconvinced you may now be of the truth of*
> *what you hear, by and by you will be fully convinced of*
> *it... The God that holds you over the pit of hell, much as*
> *one holds a spider or some loathsome insect over the*

---

[1] God calls sinners his *foes* and his *enemies* in Isaiah 1:24. He adds in Hosea 9:15 that he *hates* sinners as well as their sin. We must balance this against verses such as Romans 5:8, but not ignore it altogether.

fire, abhors you and is dreadfully provoked; his wrath
towards you burns like fire; he looks upon you as worthy
of nothing else but to be cast into the fire; he is of purer
eyes than to bear to have you in his sight; you are ten
thousand times so abominable in his eyes as the most
hateful venomous serpent is in ours. You have offended
him infinitely more than ever a stubborn rebel did his
prince: and yet 'tis nothing but his hand that holds you
from falling into the fire every moment... You hang by a
slender thread with the flames of divine wrath flashing
about it, and ready every moment to singe it and burn it
asunder; and you have no interest in any mediator and
nothing to lay hold of to save yourself, nothing to keep off
the flames of wrath, nothing of your own, nothing that
you ever have done, nothing that you can do, to induce
God to spare you one moment.[2]

Paul tells us that unless we understand this fourth Gospel picture like Jonathan Edwards, we can never grasp the full extent of God's love towards us. He begins verse 6 with the little Greek word *gar*, meaning *for*, in order to link verses 6–8 back to his reference to God's love in verse 5. Unless we grasp that Jesus died to save us when we were powerless, ungodly and out-and-out sinners,[3] we will never know the certainty of God's love towards us every day. If we think we weren't all that bad or fool ourselves we caught God's attention through our piety, we will constantly worry that our slip-ups and failures might forfeit his love. When we grasp that we never deserved his love in the first place, we stop worrying that our ups and downs might ever

---

[2] Jonathan Edwards preached this sermon entitled "Sinners in the Hands of an Angry God" on 8th July 1741 at Enfield, Connecticut. It is widely viewed as the greatest and most effective sermon of the Great Awakening.

[3] The Greek word *asebēs*, which is translated *ungodly*, means literally *devoid of reverential awe towards God*. We did not sin and become sinners. We were sinners and therefore sinned.

undeserve it. We only find security in God's love towards us when we realize how much he once had reason to hate us.[4]

On 4th December 2006, a nineteen-year-old American soldier named Ross McGinnis was manning the turret of an armoured vehicle on patrol in east Baghdad. Suddenly, a hand grenade fell into the vehicle, thrown from the rooftop by an insurgent Iraqi. From his vantage point in the turret, Ross McGinnis could see that his crew were all about to die, because there was no time for them to exit the vehicle before the blast. He could have jumped clear but instead he jumped down and threw his body on the grenade to smother the explosion. He died instantly, but the rest of the crew all survived. His selfless act to save his friends earned him the posthumous Medal of Honor.

Unlike the Iraqi grenade, God's wrath towards us was completely justified. In fact, God would have been unjust not to burn with anger against us. What is more, unlike the crew of Ross McGinnis's Humvee, we were all Jesus' enemies instead of his friends. Paul tells us literally in verse 8 that God *commends* his love for us through the fact that his Son became our bodyguard when we were fighting on the wrong side.[5] Picture Ross McGinnis throwing himself on a hand grenade to save a bunker filled with Iraqi insurgents, and you are closer to grasping what it meant for Jesus to shield us from the wrath of God with his mangled body. That is Paul's horrible and beautiful fourth Gospel picture. It is baffling and humbling, and it rules out all boasting.[6]

It is also deeply offensive to human pride. Some Christians object that this sounds like *"a form of cosmic child abuse – a*

---

[4] John Calvin explores this in his *Institutes of the Christian Religion* (2.17), concluding that *"in a manner which cannot be expressed, God, at the very time when he loved us, was hostile to us until reconciled in Christ."*

[5] The word *sunistēmi* is the same word which Paul uses repeatedly in 2 Corinthians for apostles *commending* themselves to churches. God showcases and advertises his love through this fourth Gospel picture.

[6] This is Paul's ironic point in verse 11 when he tells us literally that we can only *boast* in God through Jesus.

vengeful Father, punishing his Son for an offence he has not even committed... Such a concept stands in total contradiction to the statement 'God is love'. If the cross is a personal act of violence perpetrated by God towards humankind but borne by his Son, then it makes a mockery of Jesus' own teaching to love your enemies and to refuse to repay evil with evil."[7] What this objection misses is that God did not inflict punishment on somebody else. Jesus *is* God, and Paul reminds us in 2:16 that he is God the Judge at that. The Triune God is able to play three out of four roles in this picture: the Judge, the Saviour and the Comforter who uses the picture to fill our hearts with a deep understanding of his love. He leaves the fourth role to us, his enemies-turned-friends, through the death and resurrection of Jesus the Bodyguard.[8]

Don't fight Paul's fourth Gospel picture and its message that God hates sinners and attacks them in his wrath. If you do, you will miss the bright caption painted on the dark background: *"God demonstrates his own love for us in this: While we were still sinners, Christ died for us."*

---

[7] Steve Chalke and Alan Mann, *The Lost Message of Jesus* (2003).

[8] This theme is also explored in Isaiah 53:1–12 and Colossians 1:19–23.

Fifth Picture: Tomb Raider (5:12–21)

If, by the trespass of the one man, death reigned through that one man, how much more will those who receive God's abundant provision of grace and of the gift of righteousness reign in life through the one man, Jesus Christ.

(Romans 5:17)

General George Patton was not a happy man. He had led his troops to victory in North Africa and Sicily, but the US high command had ruled that he would not take part in D-Day. Instead, they had posted him to south-east England with a decoy army in order to convince the Germans that the Allied landings would take place in the Pas-de-Calais region. He didn't even hear until the evening of D-Day that the Normandy landings had been successful and Hitler's Fortress Europe had been breached. When news came, he was convinced that the Nazis were defeated and that the Allies had effectively won the War without him.

This realization didn't make him passive, however. General Patton was the man who told his officers that *"When we land against the enemy, don't forget to hit him and hit him hard. When we meet the enemy we will kill him. We will show him no mercy... Stick him between the third and fourth ribs. You will tell your men that. They must have the killer instinct."*[1] Now he practised what he preached and pleaded with his superiors to send him and his army to France without delay. His new belief that the

---

[1] Patton said this to his troops before the invasion of Sicily. He gave a longer, expletive-filled speech to the US Third Army on the evening of D-Day.

War was definitely won made him more eager than ever to be placed at the very thick of the action. Fresh certainty of victory had made him thirsty for a fight.

Paul expects certainty of victory to have the same effect on us, which is why he has saved this fifth Gospel picture till last. He reminds us in verses 12–14 that long ago the human race fell under the power of an enemy even fouler than Hitler. When Satan launched his surprise attack on an unsuspecting Adam in the Garden of Eden, he outflanked his defences as easily as the French Maginot Line. He tempted Eve within earshot of Adam to eat the fruit about which the Lord had warned, *"When you eat of it you will surely die"*.[2] Paul uses the Greek word *basileuō* three times in these verses, which means *to reign as king*, in order to tell us that when Adam sinned Satan became king over the world. Adam and his children lost their God-given dominion, and were as powerless as Frenchmen before D-Day to throw off the authority of Satan.[3]

But the Lord promised his People that invasion day was coming. He gave the prophet Daniel a dream in 553 BC in which he saw the future Roman Empire and the coming of a better King than Caesar: *"He was given authority, glory and sovereign power; all peoples, nations and men of every language worshipped him. His dominion is an everlasting dominion that will not pass away, and his kingdom is one that will never be destroyed."*[4]

This vision of the Messiah forms the background to Paul's fifth Gospel picture, which he paints in verses 15–17. He tells

---

[2] Genesis 2:17 fulfilled in 3:22 and 5:5. Genesis 3:6 tells us that Adam *"was with her"* but failed in his duty to protect her, which is why Scripture tells us that Adam, not Eve, was responsible for the Fall.

[3] Some people struggle with the principle of "federal headship" here and in Hebrews 7:9–10. How could Adam's sin bring the whole human race under Satan's authority? Again, D-Day provides a useful parallel. French babies were all born under Nazi rule because the failure of a parent affects the fortunes of a child.

[4] Daniel 7:14. The Roman Empire is described in verses 8–9, and the *horn* may well refer to Caesar himself.

us that God has performed his own D-Day landing by invading earth as the man Jesus, the true and better Adam,[5] in order to deliver Satan's kingdom a mortal blow. Satan's General Death appeared to have repulsed God's invasion when Jesus was crucified, died and was buried in a tomb. He discovered too late that this was part of God's strategy to shatter Satan's rule on the earth once and for all. Jesus had come to be the ultimate Tomb Raider, despatching General Sin through his crucifixion and General Death through his resurrection.[6] Paul uses the word *basileuō* twice more in these verses to proclaim that now there is a new King in town. The reign of Satan, Sin and Death is officially over. The reign of Jesus and Grace has officially begun.

Do you see why Paul saves this Gospel picture till last, and why these two and a half chapters on "salvation given" build up to a grand finale? He doesn't want us to treat the Gospel as an excuse for spiritual passivity, but as the war cry that rallies us into the thick of the spiritual battle. He urges us to treat the message that Jesus is the new King in town with the same vigour as General Patton on the evening of D-Day. As Jesus put it to the disciples after his resurrection, referring back to Daniel's dream: *"All authority in heaven and on earth has been given to me. Therefore go and make disciples of all nations."*[7] His invasion had been successful; he had defeated all comers to be the new King in town; now it was time for them to go and get the spoils. Paul tells us in verse 17 that we reign with Jesus through the Gospel, and we must rise up to press home our Saviour's certain victory.

Think how important this message must have been to the

---

[5] Paul calls Adam a *pattern* of Jesus in verse 16, and Jesus *"the Last Adam"* in 1 Corinthians 15:45. We were born sinners in Adam and therefore sinned, but we are reborn in Christ and therefore justified.

[6] Paul sings a victory song over Generals Sin and Death in 1 Corinthians 15:54–57.

[7] Matthew 28:18–19. Note that the Gospel is not about completing Jesus' victory, but about recognizing it.

Roman Christians. Emperor Nero was a murderer who used death as his greatest weapon, and within a few short years he would be using it on the Church. The Christians would be tempted to tone down the challenge of their Gospel and to hang these pictures in a private gallery for fearful fellowship and withdrawn worship. They would be tempted to retreat and leave the world to Satan and his defeated generals. This fifth Gospel picture gave them courage to withstand Nero's persecution and to go on the counter-offensive by preaching across the Roman Empire that Jesus is the new King in town.

General Patton instructed his troops that

> *In landing operations, retreat is impossible. To surrender is as ignoble as it is foolish... Above all else remember that we as the attackers have the initiative. We know exactly what we are going to do, while the enemy is ignorant of our intentions and can only parry our blows. We must retain this tremendous advantage by always attacking: rapidly, ruthlessly, viciously and without rest... However tired and hungry you may be, the enemy will be more tired and more hungry – keep punching. No man is beaten until he thinks he is.*[8]

This begs the natural question: Are we acting like men and women who think that they are beaten? Do we live as men and women who understand that Satan's kingdom is reeling from Jesus' killer blow, and that we have only to press forward to win new families, new cities and new nations for Christ? Do we live in the light of Paul's fifth Gospel picture and preach Jesus as the great Tomb Raider, who has won back what Adam lost and much, much more?

---

[8] Part of Patton's order to the Seventh Army on 27th June 1943 before the Sicily landings.

How Many People Will Be Saved? (5:18–19)

For just as through the disobedience of the one man the many were made sinners, so also through the obedience of the one man the many will be made righteous.

(Romans 5:19)

Being an art critic isn't as easy as it looks. Just ask Rolf Anderberg of the Swedish newspaper *Posten*. He raved in his column about a brilliant new French artist called Pierre Brassau, whose paintings he had discovered in a gallery in Gothenburg: *"Brassau paints with powerful strokes, but also with clear determination. His brushstrokes twist with furious fastidiousness. Pierre is an artist who performs with the delicacy of a ballet dancer."* He refused to see the funny side when a rival journalist revealed that he had tricked him by planting four paintings by a chimpanzee in the gallery under a false name. He continued to insist that one of the chimp's works was *"still the best painting in the exhibition"*.[1]

Paul doesn't want us to blunder like Rolf Anderberg over his fifth Gospel picture, so he stops for a moment to clarify. He wants to spare us the blushes of those who misinterpret what he means when he tells us to lay hold of Jesus' victory. The last of the four questions with which he heckles himself over these pictures is *"How many people can we expect to be saved?"*

Some readers go the way of Rolf Anderberg and assume that Paul is preaching *universalism*, the belief that everyone will

---

[1] Included by Richard Saunders in his book *The World's Greatest Hoaxes* (1980).

be saved. They home in on verse 18 where Paul tells us that *"just as the result of one trespass was condemnation for all men, so also the result of one act of righteousness was justification that brings life for all men."* All means all, they insist, so everyone will be saved regardless of how they responded to Jesus. Adam's sin meant condemnation for all, so Jesus' death and resurrection must mean forgiveness for all. They also point to Paul's statement in 11:32 that *"God has bound all men over to disobedience so that he may have mercy on them all"*, but they haven't studied Paul's brushwork carefully enough.

For a start, they overlook the fact that Paul uses the words *all* and *many* very loosely in verse 19, just as Luke does in Acts 2 and 19 when he tells us that the apostles preached to *every* nation and to *all* those who lived in the province of Asia. Paul was clear in chapters 1–3 that everyone stands condemned, but he is equally clear here in verse 17 that Jesus' rescue plan only saves *"those who receive God's abundant provision of grace and of the gift of righteousness."*[2]

Other readers are like Rolf Anderberg in the way they assume that Paul is advocating *pessimism*, the belief that only a small remnant will be saved. They home in on verse 15 where Paul tells us that *"the gift is not like the trespass"*, and the fact he uses what debaters call an "a fortiori" argument. *How much more* refers to the *quality* of assurance we receive, not to the *quantity* of people who receive it. Since the gift is not like the trespass, Jesus' action undoes Adam's, but not the other way around.

It sounds very plausible, but think a little harder. Imagine your friend goes into a casino with £20,000 and emerges hours later with only £2,000. He is excited about his winnings and crows about his skill at the card table. You would think of calling him lots of things, but none of them would be "winner". In the

---

[2] Paul offends Gentiles in 5:13–14 by saying that ignorance does not make pagans innocent. He offends Jews in 5:20 by saying that their precious Law actually *increases* sin and makes them need Jesus even more!

same way, if Jesus' victory only saves a tiny remnant then no amount of bluster about quality can convince us he has won. That's why Paul *never* applies the "remnant" prophecies of the Old Testament to the Church. He quotes one in 9:27 and applies it to ethnic Israel, but talks here in verse 20 about grace *overflowing* to the Church. Jesus is not a failed gambler, deluding himself as Satan drags a majority down to hell. Our expectation should be for God to save many, not few, through the power of the Gospel.

John Calvin understood these verses to mean that *"Christ is much more powerful to save than Adam was to destroy... As the sin of Adam has destroyed many, Paul concludes that the righteousness of Christ will be no less efficacious to save many."*[3] Charles Hodge went one step further to argue that *"The number of the saved shall doubtless greatly exceed the number of the lost... We have reason to believe that the lost shall bear to the saved no greater proportion than the inmates of a prison do to the mass of the community."*[4] John Stott sees this as a reason to expect a great end-time revival, since it means that *"Christ will raise to life many more than Adam will drag to death... 'The many' does not mean 'all'...[but] it certainly means 'a very great multitude', in other words, a majority."*[5] Paul will explain in chapters 9–11 how we can reconcile this expectation with the Church often looking weak and small, but for now he simply tells us to expect Jesus' victory over the Devil to be reflected in the final tally.

In the meantime, Paul warns us not to act like Rolf Anderberg by embracing a naïve *triumphalism* which assumes the Gospel will be instantly popular and universally accepted. He tells us to expect the Gospel to flourish in 1:13 and 15:29, but that it will do so in 8:35–36 against a backdrop of *"trouble or hardship or persecution or famine or nakedness or danger or sword. As it is written: 'For your sake we face death all day long;*

---

[3] John Calvin, *Commentary on Romans* (1540).

[4] Charles Hodge, *Commentary on Romans* (1835).

[5] John Stott in *"The Message of Romans"* (1994).

we are considered as sheep to be slaughtered.'" Universalism and pessimism both hold us back from pressing forward, but triumphalism saps our fighting spirit with empty hope that the Devil and his generals have already surrendered and left the field.

But if we study this fifth Gospel picture and avoid these three mistakes, Paul tells us it will stir us to great exploits for Christ's Kingdom. As we receive these five Gospel pictures from Paul's chapters on "salvation given", we are able to march forward with the victory cry that there is a new King in town!

Salvation Experienced
(6:1–8:39)

We died to sin; how can we live in it any longer?...
Christ was raised from the dead through the glory of
the Father, [so] we too may live a new life.

(Romans 6:2, 4)

It was the mid-nineteenth century and the penniless dockhand was weary of loading cargo onto the cruise liners to America. He heard tales that in the New World it was possible for a man like him to become rich and famous through his talent, not his birth. He started putting aside part of his meagre income against the day when he could afford to buy a ticket of his own.

Finally the day arrived. He had scraped together enough money to pay for his fare but had nothing left over to pay for food at the ship's restaurant. He filled a bag with as much bread as his leftover change could buy and began the ten-day voyage from London to the land of his dreams.

He rationed himself to eat his bread slowly but by the end of the third day his bag was empty. He went to bed early and tried to sleep away the hunger, but the darkness made the emptiness in his stomach hurt all the more. He was woken by the smell of cooked breakfast from the restaurant, and spent the day dreaming of America and tasty mealtimes to come. After a fifth, sixth and seventh day, the smell of food was so tormenting that he knocked on the kitchen door of the restaurant to beg for scraps of leftover food. The surprised chef asked for his ticket and told him to read the small print. The price of the ticket included three meals a day in the ship's restaurant. He had been starving in his cabin when he could have been dining up above.

Paul is concerned we might be like that London dockhand. That's why the first section of Romans is split into three parts, not just two. It's not enough for him to tell his readers about "salvation needed" and "salvation given". He also gives us chapters 6–8 as a reminder that the Gospel is also about "salvation experienced". The Gospel isn't just the promise of a mystic destination which we will reach at the end of the hungry voyage we call life. Paul will tell us that there are groans and hunger pangs in chapter 8, but his main message in these three chapters is that the Gospel transforms our lives straight away. Eternal life is not just something to look forward to when we die or when Jesus returns as King. It is something which God's People get to eat and drink today.[1]

Paul starts by heckling himself with a question: If we are counted righteous through Jesus in spite of our sin, can we simply go on sinning because we know God will forgive us? That's a good question to ask because it shows we have understood the extent of God's mercy in Paul's five Gospel pictures. If our message doesn't raise this question, it may not be the Gospel at all. Paul answers with an emphatic no, because receiving Jesus as the new King in town means total turnaround today.

First, Paul reminds us in 6:1–7 that the Gospel means we have been raised to new life with Jesus, so we cannot go on sinning as we did in our old lives. Second, he illustrates this in three different ways by telling us in 6:8–7:6 that the Gospel gives us a new nationality, a new employer and a new husband. Paul spends most of chapter 7 describing the difference that this makes to our lives. He wants to make sure we are not starving in our cabins, unaware of the experience which the Gospel brings in the here-and-now.

In chapter 8, Paul describes the contents of the restaurant

---

[1] The apostle John also stresses this in John 17:3 and 1 John 5:13.

upstairs. He talks in 8:1–17 about our being adopted as children of God, being filled with the Holy Spirit and changed from the inside out to look more like our new Father. He enlarges on this in 8:18–27 by promising that this is a foretaste of what will happen to the universe when Jesus returns, which means that our enjoyment of our salvation advertises the Gospel to the world. This leads into the promise of two intercessors in 8:26–27 and 8:34, who help us to lay hold of our salvation and gain assurance that it is ours forever. We need to read these chapters slowly to spare us from the London dockhand's folly.

The Devil hates these three chapters. He will do anything to stop you from understanding them and taking them seriously. Even if we believe Paul's five Gospel pictures, he still hopes he can stop us from displaying them to the world. If he can make us treat the Gospel as good news about the future, then he still hopes to cling on to his kingdom in the present. He hopes to make us so miserable that we don't share our faith, or so miserable that no one pays attention when we do. What he mustn't allow is for people like us to experience the same life-transforming power as Paul.

I spent my first three years as a Christian largely oblivious to Paul's teaching in these chapters about "salvation experienced". Mine was the driven faith of a new believer who was determined to endure hunger for the sake of a better life to come. I shared the Gospel with those around me, but grew discouraged that no one seemed interested in my invitation to come and starve with me in my cabin. Then I read a book that explained the message of these three chapters and turned my "salvation given" into "salvation experienced".[2] I discovered the joy, the assurance, the freedom and the power which Paul describes in Romans 6–8.

What happened next was staggering. The same unbelievers

---

[2] Terry Virgo has subsequently reprinted the book under the title *God's Lavish Grace* (2004).

who used to change the subject whenever I shared the Gospel started to notice my new-found joy and peace, and began to question me themselves. Christians began asking me to help them discover this Gospel experience too. The same people who had turned down my call to share my hungry cabin on a long-haul trip to Paradise started wanting to know how to join me in the ship's restaurant to *"taste the heavenly gift...and the powers of the coming age."*[3]

So come and feast on these three chapters, not just for your own sake but for the sake of others. Feast on them because the Gospel is the message that heaven has been unleashed on earth today. Feast on them as a testimony to the world that God's salvation can be experienced because there is a new King in town.

---

[3] This is how Hebrews 6:4–5 describes the Gospel.

East Side Story (6:1–7)

*Don't you know that all of us who were baptized into
Christ Jesus were baptized into his death? We were
therefore buried with him through baptism into death
in order that, just as Christ was raised from the dead
through the glory of the Father, we too may live a
new life.*

(Romans 6:3–4)

Passover night was when the Israelites were saved from slavery,
but that didn't mean they experienced their salvation straight
away. Pharaoh had changed his mind many times before, so they
"went up out of Egypt armed for battle" and looked back fearfully
over their shoulders.[1] When they reached the western shore of
the Red Sea their worst fears came true. Pharaoh was pursuing
them at the head of his army of crack charioteers. Unless the
Lord translated their salvation into immediate experience, they
were all about to be re-enslaved or slaughtered.

Paul explains at the beginning of 1 Corinthians 10 that God
led the Israelites to the Red Sea in order to "baptize" them as a
nation: *"I do not want you to be ignorant of the fact, brothers, that
our forefathers...were all baptized...in the sea."* Moses told them
it was time to experience what God had purchased for them
at the Passover: *"Stand firm, and see the salvation of the Lord,
which he will work for you today. For the Egyptians whom you
see today, you shall never see again."*[2] As the Israelites watched,

---

[1] Exodus 13:18.

[2] Exodus 14:13 (English Standard Version).

God carved a tomb out of the Red Sea and led them through to the opposite shore in time to turn around and see him drown their old king Pharaoh and his army of slave-masters. They looked back at the tomb where their old life had been buried, and sang the opening song of their East Side Story. It was a song about "salvation experienced": *"The Lord is my strength and my song; he has become my salvation."*[3]

Hold that thought and re-read the question with which Paul heckles himself at the beginning of Romans 6: *"Shall we go on sinning so that grace may increase?"* He knows that some of his readers will object that his five Gospel pictures make salvation sound so easy that people will use it as an excuse for further sin. He doesn't answer by back-pedalling and insisting that he has been misunderstood, but by fleshing out his Gospel in even more detail. The truth is that God is even more generous in his grace than his critics can possibly imagine.

After dealing with his question very strongly in verse 2,[4] Paul gives a long succession of "aorist verbs", which are a Greek way of referring to completed one-off actions. Like the Israelites at the Red Sea, *"we were baptized"* as an expression of the fact that we are united with Jesus through the Gospel. *"Our old self was crucified with him so that the body of sin might be done away with"*,[5] and *"we were buried with him through baptism into death in order that, just as Christ was raised from the dead through the glory of the Father, we too may live a new life."*[6]

---

[3] Exodus 15:2.

[4] The Greek *mē genoito* is a strong way of saying *"by no means!"* or *"no way!"* Paul tells the Romans that if anyone does not live out God's salvation, it is actually a sign they have not truly received it.

[5] The last of these five aorist verbs is the same word used in Matthew 27:44, Mark 15:32 and John 19:32 to refer to the two robbers who were *crucified with* Jesus at Calvary. We need no more doubt that our old self has been crucified with Jesus than that the robbers were. Paul also uses this same verb in Galatians 2:20.

[6] *The Glory of the Father* is probably a Jewish way of referring to the Holy Spirit. See 8:11.

Were the Israelites free on the western shore of the Red Sea? Of course, because of their faith in the Passover lamb. There was no need for any further price to be paid, but they still had to learn how to experience their salvation. They needed to look at the corpses of their former slave-masters on the shore in Exodus 14:30, and to start eating and drinking the reality of their salvation.[7]

Think about it. On the western shore of the Red Sea the Israelites still lived in fear of being recaptured and dragged back to a life of slavery, but on the eastern shore they lived a very different story. Nobody fears being re-enslaved by a corpse, much less volunteers to still serve as a slave to one. So if anyone thinks that responding to the Gospel means we are free to keep on sinning, then they haven't really understood Paul's five pictures. To demonstrate this, he deliberately uses the word *dikaioō* in verse 7, which normally means *to justify* but here means *to set free*. Anyone who has truly been saved from their sin will want to live differently as a result.

More than that, they will also be empowered to follow through on their desire to live differently. Of course we can choose to continue in our sin, but we do so out of choice and not because sin is still our master.[8] Paul uses the word *sumphutos* at the start of verse 5 to insist that we have been *planted together* with Jesus in resurrection soil and are naturally set up to bear godly fruit through the Holy Spirit inside us. He adds in verse 6 that our old self has had its sinful power *deactivated* through the Gospel so that now *"the grace of God that brings salvation… teaches us to say 'No' to ungodliness and worldly passions, and to live self-controlled, upright and godly lives in this present age."*[9]

---

[7] Quite literally, in fact. God gave the Israelites manna from heaven and water from a rock in Exodus 16–17.

[8] Paul clarifies in 12:1; 12:9 and 13:14 that the fact we *need not* sin does not mean we *cannot* sin.

[9] Titus 2:11–12. The verb *katargeō* in Romans 6:6 means *to deactivate* rather than *to destroy*, since the old self still tries to reassert his lost authority. Paul

Grace not only forgives us for our sins, but also delivers us from sinning. It sanctifies as well as justifies, because "salvation experienced" is still our East Side Story.

If you have never been baptized in water (and, at face value at least, Paul's logic only works if we understand baptism to mean something that happens when believers go under water), this should challenge you to take Jesus seriously when he tells his disciples to *"Go and make disciples of all nations, baptizing them"*.[10] If you have been baptized, then it should challenge you to view the waters of your baptism as dramatically as the Israelites on the eastern shore of the Red Sea. It should help you grasp that what happened was a picture of your crucifixion, burial and resurrection with Christ. It spoke of "salvation experienced" by cutting off Satan's authority over you forever. It means you cannot keep on sinning on the opposite shore, as you sing the songs which make up your own East Side Story.

It means salvation isn't just a pious hope for the future. It is the daily bread and butter of God's People in the here-and-now.

tells us in Ephesians 4:22 that it still tries to deceive us.

[10] Matthew 28:19. Hebrew babies were "baptized" in the Red Sea, but we are part of God's People through faith, not through family. Acts 16:31–34 stresses that only households which all believed were all baptized.

The Diplomat (6:8–14)

Do not let sin reign in your mortal body so that you obey its evil desires.

(Romans 6:12)

Necdet Kent was a Turkish diplomat sent to represent his government to the Nazi regime in occupied France. Although Turkey was officially on friendly terms with the Germans, he was determined to do all he could to thwart their plans to exterminate France's large Jewish population. He issued Jewish visitors to his office with Turkish papers, which protected them from deportation to one of Hitler's extermination camps. Then one day in 1943 a junior official came running to his office with news that eighty of his Turkish Jews had been loaded into cattle cars at the railway station.

Necdet Kent had to move fast. He rushed to the station and demanded that the Gestapo officer release the eighty Turkish citizens at once. *"These are not Turks or anything of the sort, but just plain Jews,"* he was told by the officer, who motioned for the train to leave. Faced with no alternative, Kent made his decision in a moment. He pushed past the officer and boarded one of the cattle cars as the train began to pull away from the station.

At the next stop, a team of Gestapo officers were waiting on the platform to meet him. They apologized for letting the train leave Marseilles station with him on board, and pointed to a luxury Mercedes which would take him straight back to his office. *"I explained that more than eighty Turkish citizens had been loaded on to these animal wagons because they were Jews, and that I was a representative of a government that rejected such treatment,"* he later recalled. The Gestapo officers were dumbfounded by his audacity. Nobody had ever dared to stand up to them this way. After much heated discussion, they finally allowed Necdet Kent and his eighty Jews out of the cattle cars. They were freed, and he was able to send them to safety in Istanbul until the end of the War. *"I would never forget those embraces,"* he told a reporter many decades later, *"the expressions of gratitude in the eyes of the people we rescued."*[1]

That is the kind of picture Paul wants us to have in mind as he illustrates what it means for us to experience our salvation. It doesn't matter how bitterly a state hates one of its subjects, so long as that subject has been granted citizenship by another ruler who cannot be defied. The Israeli government awarded Necdet Kent a medal which declared that *"Saving one life is like saving all the world"*, but Paul tells us that Jesus really did save the world when he stood up to Satan and stepped into our cattle car. He has made us citizens of a Kingdom that Satan cannot defy, and we get to experience that deliverance every day.

Paul uses three key words in this passage, the first of which is in verse 9 where he tells us that death no longer has mastery over Jesus. The word for having mastery is *kurieuō*, which comes from *kurios*, or *Lord*, one of the Emperor Nero's favourite titles.[2] While Jesus lay for three days in the tomb, General Death *lorded it over* him on behalf of his master Satan, but on the third day his authority was broken forever when Jesus rose back to life as the new King in town. Unsurprisingly, therefore, the second key word in verse 12 is *basileuō*, as Paul exhorts us not to let sin *reign as king* over our bodies any more. General Sin reigned on behalf of the Devil over Jesus as he hung on the cross, but his rule was broken once and for all when Jesus died

---

[1] Quotes taken from Necdet Kent's obituary in the British *Daily Telegraph* on 1st October 2002.

[2] Acts 25:26. Remember, the Romans tended to reserve the word "king" for puppet rulers, so Paul uses the word *kurios* over forty times in Romans to stress that Jesus is the new King in town.

and rose again to declare sinful people righteous. Sin and Death are as powerless to harm us today as the group of dumbstruck Gestapo officers who released Necdet Kent's Turkish Jews. We are citizens of a country which they know they can't defy. We are subjects of Jesus Christ, the new King in town.

Paul begins to apply this to our lives when he reuses the word *kurieuō* in verse 14 to tell us that *"Sin shall not be your master, because you are not under law, but under grace."* Satan loves to dupe us into trying to make progress in our Christian lives through gritted teeth and human effort, as if we were still living on the western shore of the Red Sea. He tries to rubbish our citizenship papers and convince us he is still our lord, supported by his evil henchmen: Law, Sin and Death. That's why Paul's third key word in verse 11 is *logizomai*, the same word which he used in chapter 4 to describe God *counting*, *reckoning* or *crediting* Abraham's faith to him as if it were righteousness. He tells us it is time for us to recognize that Jesus is our new Lord through his gentle servant Grace. It is time for us to do some reckoning of our own: *"Count yourself dead to sin but alive to God in Christ Jesus."* We were granted salvation as a free gift through faith, and we get to experience it daily through that selfsame faith as well.

Earlier we defined what Christians mean by the technical word *justification*. It describes the way that God exonerates the guilty of every charge because another has been condemned in their place. To understand Romans 6–8, we need to grasp the difference between justification and *sanctification*. Justification means being declared righteous, but sanctification means being *made* righteous in day-to-day experience. Justification is immediate and complete at our conversion, but sanctification is a lifelong process.[3] Paul therefore tells us to recognize that Jesus' death and resurrection is as much the basis of our sanctification

---

[3] *Sanctified* literally means *set apart as holy*. Therefore, strictly speaking, God sets us apart at conversion and then calls us to learn to live out our new set-apart identity. See 1 Corinthians 1:2.

as it was our justification. Paul told King Agrippa in Acts 26:18 that Jesus promises to save people through the Gospel *"from the power of Satan to God, so that they may receive forgiveness of sins and a place among those who are sanctified by faith in me."*

Jesus is your Necdet Kent, but you are not to wait passively inside the cattle car. Every day you get to jostle with the Enemy on the station platform, your citizenship papers in your hand. You get to defy his agents when they bark orders to obey, and to assert your new nationality with all the stubborn resilience of a Turkish diplomat to France. As the great preacher A.W. Tozer puts it:

> *The devil's business [is] to keep the Christian's spirit imprisoned... But when the devil starts tampering with you, dare to resist him! I stand for believing in God and defying the devil – and our God loves that kind of courage among His people... It is time for you to dare to rise and in sweet faith in the risen Jesus Christ declare: 'I will not take this any longer.'"*[4]

---

[4] A.W. Tozer, *I Talk Back to the Devil* (1990).

Write Your Resignation
Letter (6:15–23)

*Just as you used to offer the parts of your body
in slavery to impurity and to ever-increasing
wickedness, so now offer them in slavery to
righteousness, leading to holiness.*

(Romans 6:19)

When I worked in business, I used to receive calls from head-hunters offering me a better job if I switched to a different company. They would offer me a better position, better prospects and a better pay packet if I would come to an interview and start drafting my resignation letter. Paul does something similar when he moves on from describing us as *subjects* transferred from one kingdom to another in verses 8–14, and illustrates the same point by describing us as *slaves* transferred from one master to another.

Paul's original Roman readers didn't like the idea of being anyone's slave at all. Church members who were free citizens had been taught to take great pride in their freedom, while those who were slaves had been drawn to the Gospel because it spoke of redemption and of a Son of God who set people free. Yet Paul doesn't tell his readers that they must choose to become slaves of righteousness. He tells them that if they have been saved then this transfer has taken place already, and that if they haven't been saved then they are in a far worse situation. God has made human beings to work for a master, and we are all born into Adam's family under the cruel slave-master Sin. Our only hope of freedom lies in choosing a better master. Paul began his letter by telling us that he is *"a slave of Christ Jesus"*, and now he urges us to accept our own new status as slaves of righteousness so that we can begin to enjoy the fruit of our salvation.[1]

In verses 15–18, Paul tells us that our new master has given us a *far better position*. He repeats the same basic question as he posed in verse 1, asking if his five Gospel pictures give us licence to keep on sinning. Once more he is emphatic that those who have genuine faith in Jesus as Lord will simply not ask that question from their new position. Sanctification does not mean resigning from Sin's workforce in order to become something which we are not. When we *"wholeheartedly obeyed the form of teaching to which you were entrusted"* – Paul's rich way of describing our conversion to Christ[2] – we were instantly set free from our old slave-master Sin and became slaves to the righteousness which was given us by God. The paradox of salvation is that only as slaves can we experience God's total freedom.

In verses 19–22, Paul tells us that our new master offers us *far better prospects*. As impure unbelievers, we had nothing to look forward to except for *"ever-increasing wickedness"*, which ultimately ends in death. In contrast, our new slave-master promises ever-increasing holiness, which in turn results in an active experience of the eternal life that has been given us through Christ. We would be mad to carry on serving Sin for a moment longer. Paul urges us to place our resignation letter on our old master's desk where it belongs.

In verse 23, Paul makes the contrast even stronger as he reveals the *far better pay packet* that is offered by our new master. He mixes his metaphors by using a word that normally referred to the meagre *soldier's salary* paid to Nero's Roman legions.[3]

---

[1] This theme even appears in the Exodus story. Moses deliberately and repeatedly uses the same Hebrew word to describe the Israelites leaving Egypt to *serve* the Lord as he does for them serving as slaves in Egypt.

[2] Paul also links conversion and obedience in 1:5 and 15:18.

[3] Paul also refers literally to *weapons* rather than *instruments* twice in verse 13. He wants us to understand that these two employers are at war with one another.

Although this verse is often used to persuade unbelievers to come to Jesus to be saved and justified, Paul actually writes it as a call for believers to come to Jesus to experience their salvation and be sanctified. Sin's pay packet contains death, and consequently swift judgment and hell, but God grants a lavish gift instead of a pay packet to anyone who willingly serves his righteousness. He is the one who *imputed* righteousness in 4:5 by justifying *"the man who does not work but trusts God who justifies the wicked."* Now he promises likewise to impart righteousness as a gift by sanctifying anyone who will let him do so. God grants us *"eternal life in Christ Jesus our Lord"*, so that we can experience its power changing us today.[4]

As with his first metaphor of us being transferred as subjects from one kingdom to another, Paul wants to make us grateful that our conversion has also transferred us from one master to another. He is, however, after much more than mere gratitude. He turns up the contrast so that we will put our gratitude into action by writing Sin a resignation letter and by giving ourselves wholeheartedly to God's work to sanctify us.

We cannot sanctify ourselves any more than we can justify ourselves, but Paul will not let this make us passive in our daily battle against sin. He uses "present imperatives" in verses 11–13 as a Greek way of telling us to *"Keep on counting yourselves dead to sin... Do not let sin keep on reigning... Do not keep on offering the parts of your body to sin."* Then he changes his tense and uses an "aorist imperative" when he tells us to *"Offer yourselves to God [as a decisive action]... Offer the parts of your body [as a decisive action] in slavery to righteousness leading to holiness."* We need to break the habit of a sinful lifetime by resigning from Sin as a decisive pledge to follow righteousness instead. A God-pleasing lifestyle is not brought about by cheerful optimism, but by carefully considering the facts of our salvation and then

---

[4] John 17:3 and 1 John 5:13 emphasize that eternal life begins at conversion, not death.

putting a resignation letter down on Sin's desk and walking away from his payroll for good.

I always said no to the head-hunters who called my office until I found myself working for the worst boss of my career. His undermining style of leadership and his regular habit of stealing credit for my work made it a pleasure to walk into his office and hand him my resignation letter. A few weeks after I left the company, I received a phone call from his office saying that he needed my help to prepare an important presentation. Similarly, we can expect our old slave-master Sin to keep on calling us long after we have terminated our employment with him. Paul encourages us to give Sin the same reply which I was able to give to my old boss down the phone: *"I'm sorry, but I don't work for you any more."*

Paul tells us that it's time for us to stop obeying Sin. It's time to get to know our new employer and to start enjoying our salvation.

The Happy Widow (7:1–6)

You also died to the law through the body of Christ, that you might belong to another, to him who was raised from the dead, in order that we might bear fruit to God.

(Romans 7:4)

When she met him, she thought she had found her Mr Right, but they were still on their honeymoon when the marriage turned sour. He became very demanding and refused to lift a finger to help, and when she failed in his commands he began to beat her black and blue. She was stuck in a marriage to the most miserable of husbands, and the pain grew even stronger when each of their pregnancies together ended in miscarriage or stillbirth.

Then one day her husband died. She was finally free to marry the kind and gentle suitor who had been waiting many years for the proper time to make his move. Her excited friends arranged great celebrations on her second wedding day, but it didn't take long for them to notice that something was very wrong. She still kept a photo of her old husband on her side of the bed, and she would gaze longingly at his angry-looking face while her tender new husband lay beside her. She would bury her face in her old husband's clothes in the wardrobe to catch his scent and reminisce about the fear she used to feel when she heard his rasping voice. Sometimes she missed his wife-beating company so much that she would cry.

Does that strike you as a very odd story? Good. That

means you are ready for one more metaphor from Paul. He has likened our experience of salvation to waking up as *subjects* of a far better kingdom and as *slaves* of a far better master, and now his third illustration is of us being *wives* to a bad husband who are freed through his death to marry the man of our dreams.[1] Paying taxes to our old king would be mutiny, serving our old master would be stupidity, and looking back fondly on our first husband would be spiritual adultery.

We might have hoped for Paul to be clearer in stating exactly who our first husband was. Was it the *Law of Moses*, which the New Testament tells us elsewhere is prone to nag us, accuse us, condemn us, curse us and beat us when we fail?[2] Was it *Sin*, which Paul cast as Satan's viceroy and slave-master in 6:8–14 and 6:15–23? Was it our *Old Self*, which Paul refers to in 7:5 as *"the sinful nature"* and which he told us in 6:6 was put to death through our conversion? Ultimately, it doesn't really matter since the end result of the death of the Law or of Sin or of our Old Self is that we are free to "marry" Jesus instead, a better husband and a fruitful union to replace our first husband's abortive beatings and death. Regardless of which husband Paul had in mind, hanging on to any of those three things makes us spiritual adulterers. At our moment of conversion and baptism, we died and rose again with Jesus and became part of the Bride of Christ.[3]

The temptation for the Jewish Christians in Rome was to look back lovingly at Moses' Law and try to live a God-pleasing lifestyle through commitment to their late husband. That's why Paul continues the shock tactics of 3:20 and 5:20 by telling them that, far from being an ally in their struggle

---

[1] Paul is primarily teaching about sanctification rather than marriage, but verse 3 ties in with Matthew 19:9 when it says that remarriage after divorce is adultery. It warns us to hold marriage vows in high regard.

[2] John 5:45; Romans 3:20; 2 Corinthians 3:9; Galatians 3:10.

[3] See Revelation 19:7; 21:9 or 2 Corinthians 11:2–3; Ephesians 5:22–33.

against sin, the Law actually fought on the opposite team! Far from dealing with their sinful passions, it actually gave them suggestions about how they could act even more wickedly than before.[4] Paul repeats what he wrote in 1 Corinthians 15:56 and 2 Corinthians 3:6–7, telling the Jewish Christians that the Law is a powerless written code which delivers bondage and death instead of liberty and life.

The contrasting temptation for the Gentile Christians in Rome was to look back lovingly at sin and use God's grace as a licence not to turn completely from their pre-conversion pagan lifestyle. That's why Paul warns them that "salvation given" will always result in "salvation experienced" – otherwise they are not actually saved at all. He uses an aorist tense again in verse 4 to remind them that *"You died [once and for all] to the Law through the body of Christ, that you might belong to another, to him who was raised from the dead, in order that we might bear fruit to God."*[5] If they were not bearing the fruit of holiness which he promised them in 6:22, then it might be due to committing adultery with Sin, like the Jews who committed adultery with the Law. J.C. Ryle observes that:

> *I fear it is sometimes forgotten that God has married together justification and sanctification. They are distinct and different things, beyond question, but one is never found without the other. All justified people are sanctified, and all sanctified are justified. What God has joined together let no man dare to put asunder. Tell me not of your justification, unless you have also some*

---

[4] Paul will clarify in verse 7 that the Law itself was good. It was simply never designed to be used as a man-made route to holiness, and if we abuse it as such then Sin easily recruits it to its side.

[5] Paul's word for *bearing fruit* in 7:4 is deliberately linked to the word for *fruit* in 6:22 (sometimes translated *benefit*). Those truly saved bear holiness as a fruit of experiencing God's gift of eternal life.

*marks of sanctification. Boast not of Christ's work **for you**, unless you can show us the Spirit's work **in you**.*[6]

Paul is about to turn from these three metaphors to get very practical on how to win this daily battle against sin, but first he wants to make sure that we have understood this basic principle. He wants us to acknowledge that our position changed completely at the moment of our conversion. We are no longer bound as subjects, slaves and wives to Satan, sin, death or the Law. We are free to start enjoying the eternal life we have been given through our new ruler, master and husband, the Lord Jesus, who is the new King in town.

A.W. Pink felt the same passion for holiness as Paul, and mourned:

> *The nature of Christ's salvation is woefully misrepresented by the present-day "evangelist". He announces a Saviour from hell rather than a Saviour from sin. And that is why so many are fatally deceived, for there are multitudes who wish to escape the lake of fire who have no desire to be delivered from their carnality and worldliness. The very first thing said of Him in the New Testament is, "Thou shalt call His name Jesus, for He shall save His people", not "from the wrath to come", but "from their sins" (Matthew 1:21). Christ is a Saviour for those realising something of the exceeding sinfulness of sin, who feel the awful burden of it on their conscience, who loathe themselves for it, who long to be freed from its terrible dominion; and a Saviour for no others... No one can receive Christ as his Saviour while he rejects him as Lord.*[7]

---

[6] Bishop J.C. Ryle, *Holiness: Its Nature, Hindrances, Difficulties and Roots* (1879).

[7] Arthur W. Pink, *Studies on Saving Faith* (1937).

Paul hopes he has convinced us that God wants us to experience the salvation we have received. The moment has now come for him to explain exactly how we can do so.

Our Man on the Inside
(7:7–25)

*What a wretched man I am! Who will rescue me from
this body of death? Thanks be to God – through
Jesus Christ our Lord!*

(Romans 7:24–25)

If scaling the peaks of Paul's theology in Romans can sometimes
feel a bit like the Alps, then chapter 7 is the north face of the
Eiger. Some mountain guides try to help us by explaining that
Paul is describing his pre-conversion battle against sin (but
this doesn't fit with his having an inner desire to follow Jesus),
while others try to help by arguing he is talking about his post-
conversion battle (which doesn't fit either since he tells us in
chapter 8 that the normal Christian life is much more positive).
Many readers simply give up in confusion and take a detour
around this passage altogether. But this is a peak which is most
definitely worth scaling because it sets the scene for chapter
8's teaching on how we can experience our salvation every day.
Let's therefore stop and read these nineteen verses slowly. They
tell us how God sanctifies his People.

Paul has just told us in verse 5 that Sin makes an ally of the
Law to infect our Christian lives with death instead of proper
Gospel freedom. He is therefore not describing his pre- or post-
conversion state at all, but rather the experience of any believer
who tries to rely on Moses' Law to sanctify. He told us in 3:21–
5:21 that no one can be justified by human effort through the
Law, and now he tells us that neither can anyone be sanctified
by human effort through the Law. Unless we understand this, we

will miss the importance of chapter 8, so let's read these verses in their proper context and analyse what Paul has to say:

In verses 7–13, he tells us that Moses' Law is intrinsically good, but that Satan's evil henchman Sin is an expert in using it as a powerful ally against us.[1] He uses the army word *aphormē* in verses 8 and 11 to tell us that Sin uses the Law as its *base for military sorties*. It takes simple commandments such as *"Do not covet"* and uses them to incite us into fresh acts of coveting which had never even crossed our minds.[2] As I write this, my children's Christmas present is hidden under a blanket in the spare bedroom next door, but I know better than to tell them not to go in the room because it's there. A command like that would guarantee them sneaking into the bedroom as soon as my back is turned! Paul tells us that trying to sanctify ourselves by willpower through the Law is equally foolish and equally certain to fail.

In verses 14–20, he tells us that Sin has a second willing ally in the form of our Old Self. Although Paul told us in 6:6 that our Old Self was crucified with Jesus, he now tells us it keeps on trying to climb out of the grave like the villain in a low-budget horror movie. If Sin manages to recruit the Law as his ally, even though it is *pneumatikos*, or *set-in-place-by-the-Holy-Spirit*, then we are utter fools if we think he will have any trouble recruiting our Old Self since it is *sarkikos*, or *governed-by-the-flesh*. Paul uses the words *"I"* and *"me"* twenty-four times in these seven verses, sometimes to mean our crucified Old Self and sometimes to mean the New Self we have been raised to be. These two selves can no more work together than the generals of two

---

[1] Paul delights in the Law in verse 22 like the writers of Psalm 19 and 119. It reveals God's character to us and exposes our need of a Saviour. It simply has no power to sanctify us.

[2] Exodus 20:17; Deuteronomy 5:21. It is interesting that Paul chooses to single out the secret sin of *coveting*. Perhaps he is echoing Matthew 23:25–28 by pointing out that even if the Law enforces outward conformity, it still leaves a person's inside like a dirty cup or filthy tomb.

opposing armies on the battlefield. Our Old Self tries to help Sin re-establish itself as our ruler, slave-master and husband. We must view the Law and our Old Self as enemy agents who cannot sanctify, and rely as much on God's grace to experience our salvation as we did to receive it in the first place.

This then leads into verses 21–23, where Paul describes the way the battle always goes when a Christian tries to break free from sin through willpower alone. He uses the Greek word for *law* five times in these three verses as a play on words to illustrate that the Law is a very unstable ally. However much our New Self may want to break free, the Law helps our Old Self to capture it as a prisoner of war. This doesn't detract from Paul's teaching in 6:1–7:6 that we have a new King, a new Master and a new Husband, but it does warn us that we need to lay hold of the Gospel to enjoy our salvation in day-to-day experience. Thankfully, Jesus' name is not simply *The-Lord-Who-Justifies* in Jeremiah 23:6. It is also *The-Lord-Who-Sanctifies* in Exodus 31:13.

C.S. Lewis tried to explain the message of Romans 7 through one of his Narnia stories in *The Voyage of the Dawn Treader*. The unpleasant Eustace Scrubb is punished for his greed by being turned into a grotesque dragon, a symbol of our sin-scarred Old Self. When he repents of his greed, he tries to tear away his dragon skin in order to bring out the human flesh he knows is on the inside. When he finds that no amount of effort or willpower can strip away his scales, the Christlike lion Aslan tells him how he can be changed:

> *Then the lion said… "You will have to let me undress you." I was afraid of his claws, I can tell you, but I was pretty nearly desperate now. So I just lay flat down on my back to let him do it. The very first tear he made was so deep that I thought it had gone right into my heart. And when he began pulling the skin off, it hurt worse than*

anything I've ever felt. The only thing that made me able to bear it was just the pleasure of feeling the stuff peel off... After a bit the lion took me out and dressed me...in new clothes.[3]

Paul therefore ends chapter 7 with a promise of help from Jesus, the new King in town. Because Sin makes an ally out of Moses' Law to resist our new identity in 6:1–7:6; because he makes a second ally out of our Old Self and enlists it as Satan's man on the inside; because together these two allies can capture our New Self as their powerless prisoner of war; because we need the Gospel to sanctify us every bit as much as we needed it to justify us; because we cannot win the battle against sin on our own – the new King Jesus comes and dwells within us through his Holy Spirit. He is God's own man on the inside and he turns the tide of battle in our favour.

We have now scaled the north face of the Eiger together. We are ready to gaze out from its summit on the splendour of chapter 8 and to revel in the view.

[3] C.S. Lewis, *The Voyage of the Dawn Treader* (1952).

What It Means to Experience the Gospel (8:1–17)

If the Spirit of him who raised Jesus from the dead is living in you, he who raised Christ from the dead will also give life to your mortal bodies through his Spirit, who lives in you.

(Romans 8:11)

My wife and I met some fascinating people when we visited rural China. One of them was a man in his thirties with an unusual obsession with anything English. He worked as an English teacher, was an expert in English history and spent his leisure time reading English books and watching English movies. In short, he talked about England for hours, but we discovered in conversation that he had never actually been to England or even visited an English-speaking country. Denied a passport by his government, he had never been able to turn his obsession with England into practical experience. Paul is concerned that many Christians are the same, which is why he gives us four clear indicators in 8:1–17 to help us know if we are experiencing the Gospel or just learning more about it.

The first sign is *knowing that we are justified,* since verse 1 reminds us that *"there is now no condemnation for those who are in Christ Jesus."* Charles Hodge explains that *"To condemn is not merely to punish, but to declare the accused guilty or worthy of punishment; and justification is not merely to remit that punishment, but to declare that punishment cannot be justly inflicted...that no ground for the infliction of punishment still exists."*[1] Mature Christianity does not involve wallowing in shame out of consciousness that we are sinners, but rejoicing with complete confidence that God has declared us not guilty and that Satan and our Old Self have no power to gainsay him.

If this emphasis on justification seems out of place at the heart of three chapters on sanctification, then remember that failure in our daily battle against sin is so often why we succumb to condemning voices and start doubting that the Lord truly accepts us. We appease ourselves with promises that we will make it up to him by trying harder next time, but Sinclair Ferguson insists that Paul is telling us that those who have learned to experience the Gospel never put themselves on such probation before God:

> *The glory of the gospel is that God has declared Christians to be rightly related to him in spite of their sin. But our greatest temptation and mistake is to try and smuggle character into his work of grace. How easily we fall into the trap of assuming that we remain justified only so long as there are grounds in our character for justification. Paul's teaching is that nothing we do ever contributes to our justification.*[2]

Experiencing salvation means being so aware of Paul's five Gospel pictures that they remove all condemnation.

Paul's second sign is *seeing the fruit of God's sanctification* in our lives. He continues the reasoning he began in chapter 7 and tells us that with Jesus as our ally we can overpower the combined forces of Sin and the Law and our Old Self put together. The Gospel is not simply that message that God declares us righteous because the Law has been completely fulfilled for us in Christ. It is also the promise of verse 4 that by grace God has

---

[1] Charles Hodge, *Commentary on Romans* (1835).

[2] Sinclair Ferguson, *Know Your Christian Life* (1981).

condemned Sin *"in order that the righteous requirements of the law might be fully met **in us**"*! Paul tells us that our transformed lives are irrefutable proof that Jesus has come to our aid to give us victory over sin. John Piper responds to Paul's teaching in chapters 7 and 8 by warning us that *"Assurance of salvation is a precious thing, so precious and so necessary that we dare not dilute it with feelings of safety apart from transformed lives."*[3]

Paul's third sign in this passage that we are experiencing the Gospel is us *knowing that we have been filled with the Holy Spirit.* He uses the Greek word for *Spirit* seventeen times in these seventeen verses and insists in verse 9 that *"if anyone does not have the Spirit of Christ, he does not belong to Christ."*[4] Since Peter promised on the Day of Pentecost that anyone who repents and is baptized will be forgiven and filled with the Holy Spirit, our experience of the Spirit is convincing proof that we have been forgiven and possess everything else which is promised through the Gospel.

Very few people try to deny that Romans 8 is a chapter about the Holy Spirit. Even fewer dare to tell the Lord that they do not want to be filled. Yet countless Christians sidestep Paul's promise by saying that they have already received the Holy Spirit as a fact and therefore do not need to experience him as a feeling. Martyn Lloyd-Jones responds sharply to this delusion:

> *[Do you say]* *"It happened when I was born again, at my conversion; there is nothing for me to seek, I have got it all". Got it all? Well, if you have "got it all", I simply ask in the Name of God, why are you as you are? If you have "got it all"...why are you so unlike the New Testament Christians?... You cannot be baptised or filled with the Holy Spirit without knowing it. It is the greatest experience one can ever know. The teaching that assures*

---

[3] John Piper, *A Godward Life* (1997).

[4] Paul also says this in 1 Corinthians 6:19; 12:13; 2 Corinthians 1:22; Ephesians 1:13–14; Galatians 3:2–3.

us that we may feel nothing at all runs entirely contrary not only to the teaching of the Scripture but to the recorded experiences of countless Christians throughout the centuries.[5]

Paul's fourth sign that we are experiencing the Gospel is therefore *seeing that the Holy Spirit controls our minds and our bodies*. If Paul's argument in chapter 7 felt like climbing the Eiger, these seventeen verses take us down the opposite side. He calls the Holy Spirit *"the Spirit of Christ"* in verse 9 to explain that this is how Jesus comes to us as God's man on the inside and frees us from our sin.[6] When we believe that our Old Self died with Jesus on the cross, and when we trust that through Jesus' resurrection we are subject to a new King, slave to a new Master and wife to a new Husband, it paves the way for Jesus to sanctify us as a gift of grace through our faith in the Gospel. Suddenly the battle against Sin tips irreversibly in our favour. Our regenerate mind which was taken captive as a prisoner of war in 7:23 now bursts its chains through the same Holy Spirit who raised Jesus' body from the dead, and it takes control of our bodies so that Sin and the Law and our Old Self must run away.

These are the four signs that Paul highlights to us as proof we are experiencing the Gospel. He therefore uses the same word in verse 12 as he did in 1:14 in order to tell us we are just as obliged to live in the good of the Gospel as we are to pass it on to others. Let's not be like the Chinese man who studied England from afar yet never got on a plane to experience it first-hand. This is what it means to live a normal Christian life. Let's not settle for experiencing anything less.

---

[5] Martyn Lloyd-Jones in *The Christian Warfare* (1976) and *The Sons of God* (1974).

[6] Like Jesus in John 14:16–18, Paul adds in verse 10 that when the Holy Spirit fills us, *"Christ is in you"*. Jesus is therefore the fulfilment of Ezekiel 36:26–27 through the Holy Spirit.

Your Gospel is Too Small
(8:14–25)

We ourselves, who have the first-fruits of the Spirit, groan inwardly as we wait eagerly for our adoption as sons, the redemption of our bodies. For in this hope we were saved.

(Romans 8:23–24)

Paul hasn't finished listing all we can experience as a result of our salvation. He now widens his focus beyond justification and sanctification to expand on what it means to live in daily enjoyment of our salvation. Most Christians need to be reminded not to neglect at least one of the three areas that Paul addresses in verses 14–25. Whichever one of the three you are most regularly tempted to forget, Paul wants to make sure that your Gospel is not too small.

As twenty-first century readers of Romans, we can fail to grasp what Paul means in verses 14–17 when he tells us that we have been *adopted as sons of God*. Adoption is relatively uncommon in our culture – fewer than 1 per cent and 3 per cent of British and American births respectively – but in Roman culture it was much more common. Augustus had become emperor because he was the adopted son of Julius Caesar, and he in turn adopted his successor Tiberius. Caligula became emperor because Tiberius adopted his father, and Nero himself was the current emperor by virtue of his adoption by Claudius. Not one of the Romans emperors by the time Paul wrote this letter had actually been the natural son of the emperor who had reigned before him. So when Paul tells us in verse 15 that the

Holy Spirit is *the Spirit of adoption* who turns us into children of God, there was nothing unusual or second-rate about the promise. On the contrary, he is reminding us that God has made us part of his royal family through the Gospel.

Being a child of God – Paul only refers here to sons but clarifies in 2 Corinthians 6:18 that he also means *daughters* – means that we get to experience unprecedented intimacy with God. The Old Testament refers fourteen times in total to God being Father to the nation of Israel, but the New Testament exceeds this total by only its fifth page. What is more, by telling his followers to address God as *Abba*, the Aramaic word for *Daddy*, Jesus told us to expect this father–son relationship to be full of tender warmth through the Holy Spirit.[1] The Jewish leaders were so offended by this idea, when even the great Moses had only known God *"as a man speaks to his friend"*, that they tried to murder Jesus for teaching it in John 5:18.[2] Paul therefore uses the same word *Abba*, both here and in Galatians 4:6, as a warning not to settle for a Gospel which is far too small.

Being adopted in Roman culture also meant becoming someone's heir. Julius Caesar had only adopted Augustus posthumously in the terms of his will because adoption and inheritance went together in the Roman mind. Paul therefore tells us in verse 17 that having God as our Daddy also means we have become *"heirs of God and co-heirs with Christ"*. God already has a Son and Heir, but he unites us with that Son through the Gospel and adopts us as fellow heirs alongside him. Since Jesus is the new King in town, we get to rule over sin, death and sickness with him, as co-rulers on his throne.[3] Since he is Heir to the riches of God's glorious Kingdom, we get to hear God tell us in

---

[1] Matthew 6:9 and Mark 14:36. *Abba* was a cross between the English words *Daddy* and *Dad*, since it continued to be used by grown-up Jewish men to address their fathers.

[2] Exodus 33:11. 1 John 3:9–10 emphasizes that adoption means starting to look more our like Dad.

[3] See Revelation 5:10 and 22:5, as well as Daniel 7:18, 27.

Luke 15:31 that *"everything I have is yours"*. Our experience of salvation must not be shrunk to something less.

The Jewish Christians at Rome also needed Paul to remind them in verses 18–22 that *the inheritance God gives us is far bigger than a patch of land in the Middle East*. Even Jesus' disciples still clung in Acts 1:6 to the traditional Jewish hope that the Messiah would fight the Romans and *"restore the kingdom to Israel"* along its historic borders. Jesus had to lift their eyes beyond Jerusalem and Judea to encompass God's plans for *"the ends of the earth"*. Paul started to do the same for the Jewish Christians in Rome when he told them in 4:13 that God promised Abraham *"he would be **heir to the world"***. Now he expands still further on that theme.

Adam sinned outside Israel's borders, and the consequences of the Fall affected all of creation. Since Adam's sin brought the whole universe under *"bondage to decay"*, Paul warns them not to shrink down the scope of Christ's redemption to Judea! *"The whole of creation has been groaning as in the pains of childbirth right up to the present time,"* Paul insists. The Gospel is not just the promise of personal salvation, or even the promise of national victory for Israel. It is the promise that both Jew and Gentile are made part of the same heavenly family,[4] as a foretaste of the whole universe experiencing *"the glorious freedom of the children of God."*[5] This was what Jesus meant when he promised in Matthew 19:28 that his Second Coming would inaugurate the rebirth of the universe as God always intended it to be.[6] To treat the Gospel as a promise about Jews getting

---

[4] Perhaps this is why 8:15, Galatians 4:6 and Mark 14:36 all refer to God as *Abba ho Patēr*, using both the Aramaic and Greek names for God as one unit to stress that God's adopted family comes from every nation.

[5] Not only does Paul tell us that the Fall of the universe was part of God's plan, but he also tells us that the whole universe waits in *anxious and persistent expectation* for the plan to be fulfilled through the saving of many lives. Paul will return to the theme of God's great plan in chapters 9–11.

[6] The Greek word *palingenesia* in Matthew 19:28 is also used for us being *born again* through the Holy Spirit in Titus 3:5. See also Acts 3:21; 2 Peter

back to the Land or Christians getting up to heaven is to make the Gospel far too small. It is a promise that heaven is coming down to earth, and that people in every part of the world must surrender to the new King while they still can.

Finally, the Gentile Christians at Rome were in danger of forgetting Paul's teaching in verses 23–25 that God will resurrect our bodies. Their culture had taught them that a trip to the Underworld was always one-way, and that the very idea of bodily resurrection was laughable[7]. Once converted, the Gentile Christians found it easier to believe in a disembodied afterlife in heaven than in Jesus' promise that the dead will be raised and inhabit his new heavens and earth in resurrected glory.[8] Paul was fighting a battle in Corinth as he wrote this letter with a group of Gentile false teachers who claimed that the resurrection was just a metaphor. No, he insists, the Gospel is about *"the redemption of our bodies"*. Our spiritual resurrection through the Holy Spirit is simply *"the first-fruits"* of an even greater harvest yet to come, when Jesus comes in power and renews the world so we can live in it with resurrection bodies.

Tom Wright warns Christians not to downsize the Gospel to merely the promise of an airlift to heaven:

> *"The gospel" in the New Testament is the good news that… God is God, that Jesus is Lord, that the powers of evil have been defeated, that God's new world has begun. This announcement, stated as a fact about the way the world is rather than as an appeal about the way you might like your life, your emotions or your bank balance to be, is the foundation of everything else.*[9]

THE NEW KING SAVES

3:13 and Revelation 21–22.

[7] Acts 17:32 and 26:8

[8] John 5:28–29. See also 1 Thessalonians 4:13–18 and 1 Corinthians 15:20–58.

[9] Tom Wright, *Surprised by Hope* (2007).

So let's not settle for experiencing anything less than Paul's true Gospel. If we have forgotten what it means to know God as our Daddy and as the one who will raise both the universe and our bodies to new life, then Paul uses these verses to inform us that the Gospel we are experiencing is far too small.

Two Intercessors
(8:26–27, 34)

*We do not know what we ought to pray for, but the
Spirit himself intercedes for us… Christ Jesus…is at
the right hand of God and is also interceding for us.*

(Romans 8:26, 34)

On 14th January 1878, Alexander Graham Bell gave a telephone
to Queen Victoria. It wasn't much use to her. She had no idea
how to use the as-yet-unknown invention, and she was sceptical
of the idea that a telephone could work at all. How could she use
this wooden box and ivory handset in her summer palace on the
Isle of Wight to speak to her staff in London? Yet the Scottish
inventor was very excited about his present, so she trusted him
enough to give the telephone a try. Picture that scene in your
mind for a moment. It will help you to understand what Paul
says in these three verses.

We are almost at the end of section one of Paul's letter,
and in particular the verses that talk about experiencing
our salvation. Paul tells us that the Gospel gives us intimate
friendship with God, but the truth is that many of us feel a bit
like Queen Victoria. We don't know how to experience this
in practice. To help us, Paul uses a Greek word three times in
these three verses which only occurs in three other places in
the whole of the New Testament.[1] Paul wants this key word to

---

[1] The word is *entunchanō*, which is only used three times outside these
verses, although Paul uses a linked word twice in Romans 11:7 to say that
Israel has failed to "get through" to salvation.

teach us how to experience this relationship, because God has provided us with two *intercessors*.

First, let's look at verse 34, where Paul talks about Jesus as our first intercessor. He *"is at the right hand of God and is also interceding for us"*, because the Gospel isn't just about Jesus dying, but about him being raised to life as well. One of the other three occurrences of this word in the New Testament is when Hebrews 7:24–25 expands on what Paul is trying to say: *"because Jesus lives forever...he is able to save completely those who come to God through him, because he always lives to intercede for them."* The Gospel isn't just the news that Jesus died to save us from death and judgment, but also that he rose to life and ascended to heaven in order to "save us completely" by leading us into full experience of that salvation. It is a promise that at this very moment, Jesus is sitting with the Father and directing his favour towards you and me. He has gone on before us as our great intercessor to ensure that the prayers we pray never fail to get through.[2]

Alexander Graham Bell gave Queen Victoria a wooden box with an ivory handset, but she trusted that what she saw was the evidence of much, much more. She believed that he had also laid cables from her palace across the seabed to the English mainland and then over eighty miles of fields to London. She had to trust him that his gift was not an ornament for display, but a promise that the infrastructure was in place to make her call.

It's very difficult to experience our relationship with God without trusting that Jesus is our constant intercessor. Intercession means influencing someone's attitude towards another, and both Romans 11:2 and Acts 25:24 use the word to describe someone making accusations of guilt. The context of verse 34 is Paul's warning that there are plenty of accusers

---

[2] Some people object that it is the prayer of a *righteous person* which gets through in James 5:16, and that sin cuts our line to the Lord in Isaiah 59:2. Paul's point, however, is precisely that in Jesus we *are* righteous!

whose condemning voices want to cut the line between us and God. *Satan* literally means *Accuser* in Hebrew, and if we listen to his lies then we won't pick up the phone. He specializes in making Christians run away from God's presence by focusing them on their own shortcomings instead of on Christ's intercession. The English Puritan, Thomas Brooks reminds us:

> *God's hearing of our prayers doth not depend upon sanctification, but upon Christ's intercession; not upon what we are in ourselves, but upon what we are in the Lord Jesus; both our persons and our prayers are acceptable in the beloved. When God hears our prayers, it is neither for our own sakes nor yet for our prayers' sake, but it is for his own sake, and his Son's sake, and his glory's sake, and his promise's sake.*[3]

But Paul tells us one intercessor is not enough. How could it be? If Alexander Graham Bell had merely laid the phone line between the Isle of Wight and London, and sent the phone by post to Queen Victoria, she would not have had the first idea how to make her call get through. He needed to travel to her palace and sit with her, and in verses 26 and 27 Paul uses the same Greek word to say God has: *"We do not know what we ought to pray for, but the Spirit himself intercedes for us...the Spirit intercedes for the saints in accordance with God's will."* Don't miss the point and start debating whether "groaning" in these verses is a reference to speaking in tongues.[4] Paul's main point is that we need the Holy Spirit to come alongside us to enable us to pray in the manner which releases our experience of salvation.[5]

---

[3] Thomas Brooks, *The Privy Key of Heaven* (1665).

[4] There are plenty of other passages to encourage us that speaking in tongues is a part of what the Spirit helps us do. See Acts 10:45–47 and 1 Corinthians 14:1–5 and 14:39.

[5] Zechariah 12:10 predicted that this would be a key part of the Gospel when it promised that after the crucifixion God would literally send *"the Spirit of*

Back in the palace on the Isle of Wight, Alexander Graham Bell contravened strict royal protocol. Queen Victoria was struggling to make her telephone work and complained that *"It is rather faint and one must hold the tube rather close to one's ear."* Instinctively, he put his hand on her arm to help, forgetting commoners and royalty were not allowed to touch. Paul breaks royal protocol himself in verse 26 by using the same Greek word to describe the Holy Spirit's help as was used by Martha in Luke 10:40 to request her sister help her with the household chores.[6] It was a servant's word, a word which describes a person rolling up their sleeves to lend a hand. Paul wants us to grasp that it's the humble way our second intercessor works, as he comes alongside us to help us experience the Father. Jesus has paved the way for our calls and is sitting with the Father to ensure our words get through, but the Spirit sits with us at the other end of the line to help us know what we should say.

So take some time today to enjoy your relationship with the Father through the help of the Spirit and the Son. Fix your thoughts on what Jesus says to the Father to bring you near, and not on the voices of condemnation that drive you away. Let the Holy Spirit help you as your assistant as you pray. When you do so, you will find that you have God on the line, fulfilling the promise he made back in Jeremiah 29:12–14:

> *You will call upon me and come and pray to me, and I will listen to you. You will seek me and find me when you seek me with all your heart. I will be found by you.*

Grace and Earnest Prayers".

[6] Romans 8:26 and Luke 10:40 are the only two places the word is used in the New Testament.

Total Assurance (8:28–39)

I am convinced that neither death nor life, neither angels nor demons, neither the present nor the future, nor any powers, neither height nor depth, nor anything else in all creation, will be able to separate us from the love of God that is in Christ Jesus our Lord.

(Romans 8:38–39)

Paul is about to end the first section of Romans, the eight chapters in which he sets out the Christian Gospel. He began it by telling us that *"the gospel of God"* is a personal message *"regarding his Son"*, and now he brings us back full circle. Having talked about the Final Day in verses 18–25, he retrains the spotlight onto Jesus as the only one who can sustain us till we get there. Whereas contemporary Christian culture tends to sing worship songs and tell testimonies mainly in terms of *"I...I...I"*, Paul repeats in verse 30 that the Gospel is really a message about Jesus and about *"he...he...he...he...he...he"*. Only by fixing our gaze on Jesus can we have assurance of God's love and provision in the storms which lie ahead. The Gospel regarding God's Son is not just how we become part of God's People. It is also the hope which sustains us until Jesus finally comes again.

In verse 28, Paul tells us to fix our eyes on Jesus when *in pain*. However difficult the Roman Christians might find their lives at present, Paul suspected that they were going to get worse. That's why verse 28 is one of the greatest statements of comfort and assurance in God's purposes anywhere in the

Bible.[1] Paul tells us that because of the Gospel of Christ, *"we know that in all things God works for the good of those who love him."* In the old days, when we thought the world revolved around ourselves, we got angry with God when trouble came into our lives. Now that we know history revolves around his Son, we trust him to work things for good even in the midst of pain. If God's plan involved his own beloved Son being tortured, crucified and killed, and if he was able to turn *even that* round for good, then we can trust him to do the same in our own lives. Don Carson comments on this passage:

> *In the darkest night of the soul, Christians have something to hold onto that Job never knew – we know Christ crucified. Christians have learned that when there seems to be no other evidence of God's love, they cannot escape the cross. "He who did not spare his own Son but gave him up for us all – how will he not also, along with him, graciously give us all things?"... When we suffer there will sometimes be mystery. Will there also be faith? Yes, if our attention is focused more on the cross and on the God of the cross than on the suffering itself.*[2]

In verses 29 and 30, Paul also tells us to fix our eyes on Jesus when *in doubt*. There will be times when we struggle to hold on to this Gospel, and when we wonder if we will even persevere in our faith at all, but these two verses contain nine *"he"s* and no *"I"s*. Paul reminds us that we were only saved because the Lord foreknew us, the Lord predestined us, the Lord called us, and the Lord justified us.[3] God doesn't call us to hold on to him in the tough times. He promises to hold on to us. If he truly chose us,

---

[1] It follows on from verse 20 which told us that even the Fall was part of God's great plan.

[2] D.A. Carson, *How Long, O Lord?: Reflections on Suffering and Evil* (1990).

[3] The mention of predestination here and election in verse 33 is to prepare us for Paul's theme in chapter 9.

predestined us, called us and justified us, we can trust him to preserve us until the Final Day when he glorifies us.[4]

Sinclair Ferguson observes: *"The evangelical orientation is inward and subjective. We are far better at looking inward than we are at looking outward. Instead, we need to expend our energies admiring, exploring, expositing, and extolling Jesus Christ."*[5] Paul tells us that most of our doubts are caused by too much looking at self and not enough looking at Jesus.

In verses 31 and 32, Paul tells us to fix our eyes on Jesus when *in need*. One of the biggest questions for Christians to settle in their hearts is the question: *Is God on my side?* In financial need, in relationship difficulties, in times when we feel out of our depth in ministry – whatever the need, we must to do as Paul says and keep our steady focus on the cross. If God is "for us" enough to have sent his Son to die in our place when we were still sinful rebels, then how can we doubt that he will also give us everything we need now as his children?! There may be plenty that we want that our loving Father knows better than to give us, but there is nothing we need that he will not provide. Just keep looking at Jesus and come to the Father like Oliver Twist, grateful for what you have but still wanting more. He is not a stingy workhouse master, and he will never turn you away. *"He who did not spare his own Son, but gave him up for us all – how will he not also, along with him, graciously give us all things?"*

In verses 33–38, Paul tells us to fix our eyes on Jesus when *in battle*. This chapter began with a promise that there is no condemnation for those who are in Christ Jesus. How can there be? We didn't deserve our salvation so we cannot undeserve it either! Paul quotes in verse 36 from Psalm 44, which concentrates on God's People being attacked because they are his. Paul is therefore telling us that life as a Christian is tougher

---

[4] This promise links back to 8:17–18 and is linked to other promises in 2 Corinthians 4:17 and Colossians 3:4.

[5] Quoted by C.J. Mahaney in *The Cross-Centred Life* (2002).

than life as a non-Christian, because it means being born into a People who are at war. Yet at the same time, life as a Christian is easier, because we are more than conquerors through his fifth Gospel picture. What we have is a victory which we didn't have to win and which we cannot lose. We can therefore laugh in the face of both death and the Devil. The Christian life isn't easy, but the secret is to keep our eyes focused on *"the love of God that is in Christ Jesus our Lord."*

That's where Paul ends this great first section of Romans, beginning chapter 8 with *no condemnation* and finishing with *no separation*. God does more than justify and sanctify those who believe Paul's message. He also comforts, soothes, provides, protects and glorifies them. He gives them total assurance of his love every day as they keep their eyes focused on the Gospel concerning his Son. This is what it means to respond to the Lord Jesus. It's what it means to believe the good news that there's a new King in town.

Romans 9–11:

The New King Has a Plan

The Proof of the Pudding
(9:1–11:36)

It is not as though God's word had failed. For not all who are descended from Israel are Israel.

(Romans 9:6)

Talk is cheap. What matters is delivery. Everybody knows it's easier to state a plan than turn it into reality. That's why Paul needed to follow up his general teaching about the Gospel in chapters 1–8 with a description of that plan in action in chapters 9–11.

In November 2008, Barack Obama was voted president of the United States by a landslide majority and on a wave of popularity. Voters connected with his promise that *"Nothing can stand in the way of the power of millions of voices calling for change... In the unlikely story that is America, there has never been anything false about hope... Yes, we can heal this nation. Yes, we can repair this world. Yes, we can."* A year later, however, a troubled first year in office and plummeting approval ratings emboldened his opponent Sarah Palin to ask audiences *"How's that hopey-changey stuff working out for ya?"* and to dismiss him as nothing more than *"a professor of law standing at the lectern."*[1] It doesn't matter if you are Republican, Democrat or neither. It's simply a reminder that the proof of the pudding is not in the mixing, the baking or the marketing, but in the eating.

Paul's readers in Rome knew this as well as we do. The

---

[1] Barack Obama spoke these words after the New Hampshire Democratic Primary in January 2008. Sarah Palin spoke hers at the first national Tea Party Convention in February 2010.

Emperor Nero's propaganda in his early years was loud and unrestrained, likening himself to his great predecessor Augustus. Yet his boasting had been undermined within months of his accession by news that the Armenians on the eastern reaches of his empire had overthrown his puppet ruler and installed a local ruler of their own. He knew that his imperial credibility was on the line, and quickly despatched his armies to protect his reputation.

Perhaps Paul's Roman readers were wondering if the same might be true of Jesus. It was one thing for Paul to hail him as the new King in town, always faithful to save, but quite another to demonstrate it against the backdrop of Jewish history. Psalm 2 had promised the Messiah would deliver God's People from their enemies and establish an empire that would eclipse and outlast Caesar's, but this bore little surface resemblance to the current situation in Judea. The Jews were still subject to Emperor Nero, and for all Paul's talk of assurance in chapter 8, it looked as if Israel *had* been separated from the love of God. If the proof of the Gospel pudding was in the eating, then it tasted pretty rotten to the Jewish Christians who lived in Rome.

Paul doesn't shrink back from tackling this question, and seizes it as an opportunity to clarify the Gospel he is preaching. In 9:1–13 he asks the question *Has God failed the Jewish nation?* and delves into the Old Testament to prove the answer is *not at all*. He quotes from the Old Testament four times in thirteen verses, and re-examines Israel's history to prove from the lives of Abraham, Rebekah, Isaac, Jacob and Esau that God never chose every ethnic Israelite to be part of his true Israel. He uses the same Hebrew idiom as 1 Samuel 3:19 when he tells us literally in verse 6 that God's covenant promises to Israel have *"not fallen to the ground"*, and he uses the Jewish Scriptures to flesh out his statement back in 3:1–4 that God has by no means finished in his purposes for the Jewish nation and that Israel's unfaithfulness has not made him unfaithful towards them.

The new King Jesus has a plan, and it is succeeding against the confusing backdrop of Jewish history.

Paul is conscious, however, that this answer raises a second question, and he uses it to clarify his Gospel message still further. In 9:14–29 he asks the question *Is God unjust in judging?*, since God's choice of some and rejection of others provokes a charge that he is therefore unfair to judge the sin of those he has not chosen. Again, Paul quotes seven times from the Old Testament as he re-examines the defining moment in Jewish history when Moses confronted Pharaoh and freed the Israelites from slavery. God's mercy, compassion and justice are beyond reproach, but this doesn't mean that his plan is easy to understand. The whole sweep of Jewish history warns that the opposite is true. The new King Jesus is fulfilling the plan which God revealed through the Jewish prophets many centuries before.

This then launches Paul into 9:30–10:21, where he explains how his teaching in Romans 1–8 applies to ethnic Israel. He quotes thirteen times from the Old Testament as he re-examines the messages of the Lawgiver Moses and of the prophets Joel and Isaiah. He explains that the Jewish nation has misunderstood the Law in general, and in particular how it must be fulfilled in their Messiah. They are zealous yet ignorant, like a man running very fast in the wrong direction. If they confess that Jesus is God's new King in town, there is still time for them to become part of God's true Israel by receiving his gift of righteousness through the one Caesar's soldiers crucified because he claimed to be *"the King of the Jews"*.[2] Yet even if they reject Jesus as their King, they cannot do anything to thwart God's faithful plan for Israel.

Paul explains in chapter 11 that, far from rejecting the Jews, God is working a clever plan to save them in their rebellion. He still saves a remnant of Jews in every generation (11:1–10), and has the remainder in mind as he saves many Gentiles around the world (11:11–24). He is working towards a moment when

---

[2] See Matthew 2:2; 27:11, 29, 37.

Jewish jealousy will boil over into national repentance and revival (11:25–32). When that day comes, all believers will revel in the wisdom of God's plan and in his faithfulness towards Israel (11:33–36).

This was far more than a side issue for Paul's Roman readers. The Gentile Christians needed to hear that the Lord had not given up on Israel, and that they must repent of the anti-Semitic culture of their city. They needed to grasp that the Gospel which had saved them was the message that the Jewish Messiah was now King of all the earth. On the other side of the divided church in Rome, the Jewish Christians needed to hear that their ethnicity could not save them. The God of Israel had not forgotten his covenant promises to their nation, but they would be received by copying the faith of their father Abraham, not by misguided confidence in his family tree. Together, the church at Rome needed to hear that the proof of the Gospel pudding would come in its final eating. The new King Jesus whose salvation Paul proclaimed in chapters 1–8 had a plan to bless the Jewish nation, even as the Gospel spread to the Gentiles.

So get ready for section two of Paul's letter to the Romans. In a world where earthly Caesars look all-powerful and where the God of Israel often looks defeated, we need to hear Paul's Gospel perspective. We need his reassurance that the new King has a plan.

Anathema (9:1–13)

I could wish that I myself were cursed and cut off
from Christ for the sake of my brothers, those of my
own race, the people of Israel.

In around 1406 BC, Joshua and his Israelite army captured the city of Jericho. God destroyed the walls but told the Israelites to destroy everything else. No wicked Canaanite or any ill-gotten treasure must be spared because this bloodbath was a pointer to a greater Judgment Day to come. God stressed this by using the Hebrew word *hērem* five times in Joshua 6:17–18, translated by the Greek Septuagint as *anathema* and by many English Bibles as *devoted to destruction*. God warned them that, if they lusted after a city that was devoted to destruction, the Israelite camp would be devoted to destruction too.

If you've read the book of Joshua then you know what happened next. Joshua's army destroyed the city in 6:21, but a soldier named Achan pocketed some of the silver and gold. A few verses later, the cursed Israelites were defeated in battle and their invasion plans lay in tatters. God used the word *hērem* or *anathema* five times more as he rebuked Joshua in 7:11–13. Far from being unfaithful towards Israel, he tells Joshua that he is simply doing what he promised he would do. They had chosen to hang on to what the wicked world had to offer, and God had decreed that their nation was *anathema*.

Are you wondering what this has to do with Romans 9:1–13? The answer is everything, because Paul has this story in mind when he writes in verse 3 that his Jewish compatriots are *anathema* to God. He deliberately uses the same word as Joshua 6 and 7 to warn his readers that the Jewish nation is cursed and cut off from Christ and hurtling towards destruction, just like Achan.[1] Like Joshua's renegade soldier, they have seen God's glory, received God's covenants, read God's Law, experienced God's presence and heard God's promises. They are descendants of the same patriarchs and members of the same Jewish nation which God adopted in Exodus 4:22 as his firstborn son. But, like Achan, they have succumbed to the glittering treasures of the world. When God's Messiah appeared and called them to renounce their wicked lives, they shouted *"We have no king but Caesar"* and begged the Roman governor to crucify him.[2]

It should come as no surprise, therefore, that Paul tells his readers in verses 6–13 that the Lord has declared many Jews to be *anathema*. Achan was a pure ethnic Jew, but that didn't save him or his family from being cursed and destroyed as proof of Paul's message that *"not all who are descended from Israel are Israel."* If even Isaac's half-brother Ishmael was not counted as a true son of Abraham and Jacob's twin brother Esau was not counted as a true heir of Isaac, then Paul's readers must not expect God's purposes to have suddenly changed.[3] Even though he still saves many "Isaacs" and "Jacobs" from within the Jewish nation, he lets the majority follow the lead of Ishmael and Esau by selling out their birthright for Rome's bowl of lentil stew.[4]

Paul's three quotations from Genesis about Isaac-versus-Ishmael and Jacob-versus-Esau explain why so few Jews embrace Jesus as their Messiah, but they also raise a second,

---

[1] The Greek word *huper* in verse 3 means that Paul wants to be cursed and cut off *instead of* his Jewish brothers, as well as *on behalf of* them. He is saying that the Jewish nation is under God's curse.

[2] John 19:15. Note their motive for crucifying Jesus in John 11:48.

[3] The Lord tells Abraham three times in Genesis 22:2, 12, 16 that Isaac is *"your son, your only son"*.

[4] Israel had copied Esau's contempt for his Hebrew birthright in Genesis 25:29–34.

broader question about God's justice. How can God be fair in judging Ishmael, Esau or any backslidden Jew, if he chooses who to save before people are even born? Paul will answer that question in verses 14–29, but first he teaches us how to respond to Israel's tragedy. Debates about election must not excuse lack of emotion.

First, he tells his readers not to forget that God has elected the entire Jewish nation to privilege, even if he has not elected them all to salvation. He refuses to let us act in verses 4 and 5 as if God has finished with ethnic Israel and replaced it with the Church. He has already told us in 1:16 that the blessings of the Gospel belong first to the Jew and only then to the Gentile, and he will expand on this on chapter 11 by telling us that Gentile believers have been grafted into Israel's tree. There is one People of God, begun in the Old Testament and continuing throughout the New.

Second, he models how we should react to Israel's sin by copying Moses' reaction to the Lord's cursing of Israel for making a Golden Calf in Exodus 32. Moses begged, *"Please forgive their sin – but if not, then blot me out of the book [of life] you have written."*[5] He instinctively offered to become *anathema* instead of the Hebrew nation, if any human sacrifice might somehow atone for sin. Paul explained in Galatians 3:13 that Jesus fulfilled Moses' hope when he died the death of a cursed one upon the cross, and he adds now that he would gladly be *anathema* himself if any extra sacrifice might help the Jewish race respond to Christ. Aided by the Holy Spirit in his intercession in verse 1, he would gladly be destroyed like Achan, if only his beloved Jewish nation might be saved.

Third, as he talks about God saving those who are *anathema* through Jesus' sacrifice, he reminds us of the second part of Joshua 6 and 7. While the Jewish soldier Achan sold his soul for

---

[5] Exodus 32:32. Moses was referring to the same book as Revelation 20:11–15.

Jericho's treasures, a Canaanite prostitute named Rahab was saved through faith in a very basic picture of Jesus' cross. Rahab took money for sex in downtown Jericho and was so used to lying to cover her tracks that she instinctively broke the Ninth Commandment to save the lives of two Hebrew spies. She was about as Jewish as a bacon salesman, but she accepted she was *anathema* to God and obeyed the spies' strange instruction to hang a blood-red cord from the window of her brothel to be saved. This Gentile prostitute was added into the family tree of Abraham, David and Jesus the Messiah,[6] and God promised to do exactly the same for backslidden Israel in Hosea 2:14–15: *"I will lead her into the desert and speak tenderly to her. There I will...make the Valley of Achan a door of hope. There she will sing as in the days of her youth, as in the day she came up out of Egypt."* Paul tells his readers that God's history with Israel isn't over.

The Jewish Christians in Rome needed to stop complaining to God that many of their countrymen had not yet been saved. They needed to believe that God had a plan to turn Israel's desert into a fresh Exodus from Egypt, and that many Jewish Achans would be saved through Rahab's faith. The Gentile Christians in Rome needed to stop pretending that the Gospel message had begun with themselves, and to grasp that God had saved them into Israel, just like sinful Rahab.[7]

We all need to pray with Paul's passion for the Jewish nation. Even if they reject Jesus and become *anathema* to God, the Gospel is the good news that the new King has a plan.

---

[6] Matthew 1:5.

[7] 1 Corinthians 14:36 tells us Paul fought a similar battle with arrogant Gentiles in the church at Corinth.

God Gets to Choose
(9:14–29)

What then shall we say? Is God unjust? Not at all!

(Romans 9:14)

When Hercules fought the dreaded Hydra for his Second Labour, he was dismayed to find that each time he cut off one of the monster's heads two more grew back in its place. Paul finds the same as he deals with the question of God's faithfulness towards Israel, but unlike Hercules he deliberately provokes the two fresh questions which arise. He wants us to express two extreme views about the role of God's choice and human free will in our salvation, so that he can correct both extremes before taking us any further.

Note how he incites us to object in verse 14 that if God chooses to save some people but not others then his judgment is unfair. He starts in 8:29 by telling us that God *foreknows* and *predestines* those he calls to salvation, and takes it further in 9:11 by telling us that God chose Jacob and not his twin brother Esau *"before the twins were born or had done anything good or bad – in order that God's purpose in election might stand."*[1] He completes the job in verse 13 by quoting a prophecy from Malachi 1:2–3 about God's love and hatred for the nations descended from Jacob and Esau, but applying it directly to the

---

[1] Paul's word for *purpose* in Greek is *prothesis*, the very word used by the Septuagint for the twelve loaves of *show-bread* which represented the tribes of Israel in the Temple's Holy Place. Paul therefore uses a key word from self-confident Judaism to warn that Jews have only ever been saved through God's sovereign election.

two brothers themselves.[2] Paul wants to trap us into foolishly overstating people's freedom to choose whether to accept or reject the Gospel, so that he can demonstrate from Scripture that the Gospel means God gets to choose who he will save.

If we overemphasize the role of human choice in our salvation, it means we have *misunderstood God's character*. Paul quotes from God's great revelation of his character to Moses in Exodus 33:19 to remind us that sovereign choice is at the heart of who God is. His great desire is to show mercy and compassion to all people, but he reserves the right to save only those he chooses by his grace. As Jesus explained in John 6:37 and 44: *"Whoever comes to me I will never drive away,"* but *"No one can come to me unless the Father who sent me draws him."*

If we overemphasize the role of human choice in our salvation, it means we have also *misunderstood the essence of the Gospel*. We assume that people are spiritually sick and need to crawl to Jesus as their doctor, when in fact Paul has told us they are spiritually dead and need more than medicine; they need a miracle. He tells us in verse 16 that salvation is not about human desire or human effort, but God's mercy. If we complain that God is unjust to choose some and not others, then we act as if humans have a claim upon God's mercy, which Louis Berkhof reminds us is absolutely not the case:

> *If God owed the forgiveness of sin and eternal life to all men, it would be an injustice if He saved only a limited number of them. But the sinner has absolutely no right or claim on the blessings which flow from divine election. As a matter of fact he has forfeited those blessings. Not only have we no right to call God to account for electing some*

---

[2] Esau's descendants were so hostile towards Israel that the Old Testament prophets used *Edom* as shorthand for the enemies of God (see Isaiah 34:5 and 63:1–6 or Ezekiel 35). Paul treats Malachi's prophecy as a statement about the two brothers themselves in order to provoke us to ask the question of verse 14.

and passing others by, but we must admit that He would
have been perfectly just if He had not saved any.[3]

If we overemphasize the role of human choice in our salvation, we have also *misunderstood the purpose of God's plan.* These three chapters will culminate in a song of praise that God has ordained human history in order to gain maximum glory. To illustrate this, Paul quotes Exodus 9:16 from the Hebrew, instead of from the Greek Septuagint, to emphasize that the Lord did more than *preserve* Pharaoh as king of Egypt; he actually *raised him up* in order to be glorified through his hard-hearted rebellion. If Paul wanted to repeat the message of chapter 1 that God hardens those who first harden their hearts towards him, then he would have quoted from Exodus 7:13 or 9:35 instead. He chooses this verse to emphasize that we are lumps of clay in the hands of a master potter. The more we understand the Gospel, the less we talk about our own choice and the more we talk about God's. Charles Spurgeon observed that:

> *When I was coming to Christ, I thought I was doing it all*
> *myself... One week-night...the thought struck me "How*
> *did you come to be a Christian?" I sought the Lord. "But*
> *how did you come to seek the Lord?" The truth flashed*
> *through my mind in a moment – I should not have sought*
> *him unless there had been some previous influence in my*
> *mind to make me seek him. I prayed, thought I; but then*
> *I asked myself, "How came I to pray?" I was induced to*
> *pray by reading the Scriptures. "How came I to read the*
> *Scriptures?" I did read them but what led me to do so?*
> *Then, in a moment, I saw that God was at the bottom of*
> *it all, and that he was the author of my faith; and so the*
> *whole doctrine of grace opened up to me, and from that*
> *doctrine I have not departed to this day, and I desire to*

---

[3] Louis Berkhof, *Systematic Theology* (1938).

> *make this my constant confession, "I ascribe my change*
> *wholly to God."*[4]

But there is another extreme which we can fall into, and Paul
tricks us so he can deal with this second error like the first. He
wants us to nod in verses 22 and 23 when he divides the world
into *objects of God's wrath* and *objects of his mercy*, so that he
can then surprise us with four quotations from Hosea and Isaiah
which demonstrate that none of us can second guess to which
category any individual belongs. Any ancient observer would
have jumped to the conclusion that the Jews would be saved
and the Gentiles would not, but God explicitly warned them that
such speculation was misguided. We cannot use Paul's teaching
about God's sovereign choice and predestination as an excuse
to write anyone off for salvation. If we do, then we haven't
understood the Gospel at all.

If we truly understand the Gospel, then *we will pray more
and not less*. We will lay hold of God with Paul's passionate
emotion in verses 1–5, and give God no rest until he has saved
even those who show zero interest yet in Christ. If salvation
depends more on God's choice than our own, then it means that
no one is beyond his power to save.

If we truly understand the Gospel, then *we will work
harder to share it*. We will act like Paul, who stayed in Corinth
for eighteen months after Jesus appeared to him in Acts 18:9–
11 with a promise that *"I have many people in this city"*. God's
election is not an excuse for evangelistic laziness, as Paul insists
in chapter 10. It is a reason to be confident that our mission
cannot fail, and that God will make us fruitful if we lay down our
lives to save the lost.

So don't fall for either of these two false extremes. Paul
deliberately provokes us into stating them so that he can clarify
the Gospel and stir us to pray and work much harder on its

---

[4] Quoted by William Fullerton in *C.H. Spurgeon: A Biography* (1920).

behalf. The Gospel means that God gets to choose the vast crowd that he will save, and it ensures that when he does so all of the glory goes to him alone forever.

The End of the Law
(9:30–10:13)

Christ is the end of the law so that there may be righteousness for everyone who believes.

(Romans 10:4)

Paul has gone and done it again. He has answered his readers' questions about election and free will, but only at the expense of raising yet another question. He quoted four times from Hosea and Isaiah to prove that God's predestination is no excuse for prayerlessness or passivity, and he chose verses which he knew would provoke an explosive reaction from the Jewish Christians in Rome. If Hosea predicted that God would save many Gentiles who were not even looking for salvation, and if Isaiah warned that God would save about as many Jews in some generations as he did from wicked Sodom and Gomorrah, then isn't God's plan for Israel terribly unfair?![1]

Paul knows what he is doing. He deliberately chose those verses to clarify his Gospel message. He states his readers' question in 9:30–31 to reassure them that he fully understands their objection, and then gives a response from 9:32–10:13. The Jews have not failed to be saved because they care little about the Law or about being righteous before God. They are passionate about the Law in a way which shames the Gentiles. The issue is that God sent his Messiah to the Jewish nation in order to reveal how ignorant and rebellious they actually were.

---

[1] God only saved three people from Sodom and Gomorrah in Genesis 19, and by the end of the chapter even those three had backslidden. Isaiah's comparison was completely outrageous!

Jesus was the "stumbling stone" which God had promised to send in Isaiah 8:14 and 28:16. *"Christ is the end of the Law,"* Paul explains in 10:4, and if the Jews had truly understood the Law then they would have received him with open arms. The fact that they didn't was simply proof that their passion was for self-righteousness instead of for the Gospel.

Jesus is the end of the Law because *the Law points to our need for a Saviour.* The Hebrew word *Torah* means literally *instruction*, and God gave it to Moses to instruct Israel about their need. Paul quotes in 10:5 from Leviticus 18:5 where God told Israel that the Law would only save them if they obeyed its requirements to the letter.[2] They quickly discovered when they made the Golden Calf that they couldn't even keep the Ten Commandments long enough for Moses to pick them up on tablets from Mount Sinai, which was a warning to Jewish readers that they would not fare any better. A true understanding of Moses' Law leads to the conclusion Paul delivers in Galatians 3:24: *"the law was put in charge to lead us to Christ that we might be justified by faith."* When Jesus came as Israel's Messiah, his arrival exposed the fact that the Jewish nation was pursuing a false gospel of self-righteous works, which had turned Moses' Gospel into Jewish-flavoured pagan idolatry.

Jesus is also the end of the Law because *the Law points to his coming on every page.* In Genesis he is the seed of Eve, the true heir of Abraham, and the ram caught in the thicket as a substitute for Isaac. In Exodus he is the Passover lamb and the rock which was struck so that Israel could drink from his life-giving water. In Leviticus he is the one prefigured in each blood sacrifice offered at the Tabernacle, and in Numbers he is the bronze snake which saved Israel in the desert. In Deuteronomy he is the true King of Israel and the Prophet greater than Moses who brings more complete revelation of the Gospel. The Law

---

[2] The Old Testament used this verse in Ezekiel 20:11 and Nehemiah 9:29 as a summary of Moses' Law. Paul also quotes it in Galatians 3:12 alongside Deuteronomy 27:26 to prove that in practice nobody fulfils the Law.

didn't just tell the Jewish nation that they needed a Saviour. It also promised that God was about to send one in the form of a bleeding and suffering Messiah.

Note that Paul's quotation from Leviticus in 10:5 can be read in two ways and not just one. Jesus is the end of the Law because *he alone has obeyed it to the letter. "The man who does these things will live by them"* tells us that we need a Saviour, but *"**The Man** who does these things will live by them"* tells us how he is able to save. Jesus fulfilled every command of the Law and enacted the promise of Leviticus 18:5 for those who don't. He died under God's curse for the Law-breaker in Deuteronomy 21, but he was raised to new life because God would not abandon his Law-abiding Messiah to the grave. If we receive him as the new King in town, then God will count his Law-abiding as if it were our own, just as Paul promised us back in 4:25: *"he was delivered over to death for our sins and was raised to life for our justification."*

Jesus is therefore also the end of the Law because *God's New Covenant through his blood supersedes the old one*. This was so difficult for the Jewish Christians at Rome to hear that Paul quotes in 10:6–8 from Deuteronomy 30:12–14 in order to clarify exactly what he means. He is *not* saying that the Old Covenant promised to save people through human effort, as if anyone could ever become righteous through willpower and New Year's resolutions. These verses come from the end of the Torah and state that the Old Covenant reveals God's Gospel of grace through faith in the Messiah who will come. The Law always promised to save people through Jesus *coming down* from heaven to be crucified and *coming up* from the grave in victorious resurrection.[3] The New Covenant reveals this message more fully, and *"by calling this covenant 'new', he has*

---

[3] The word *abussos*, or *the deep*, is used on eight other occasions in the New Testament and each time it refers to *hell*. Moses only talked about going down into *the sea*, but Paul changes his words to amplify their meaning.

made the first one obsolete."[4] The problem was therefore not that the Jews loved the Law instead of the Gospel. The Law was God's great revelation of his Gospel, and their rejection of the Messiah simply revealed how ignorant of the Law they actually were.

This enables Paul to go back to his initial question, and to explain in no uncertain terms why so few Jews have been saved. Although they have all been given a privileged position in God's plan, when it comes to responding in faith to the Gospel, *"there is no difference between Jew and Gentile."*[5] Paul quotes from the prophets Isaiah and Joel in 10:11–13, who promised that *anyone* and *everyone* who puts their faith in God's Messiah will be saved. God has not let down the Jewish nation. They have fallen down of their own accord over the stumbling stone of Jesus, the new King in town.

If you are Jewish, Paul wants to add knowledge to your passion, so that God can save you from destruction through the death and resurrection of your Messiah. He wants you to recognize that Jesus is the end of Moses' Law, and that you are included in God's *anyone* and *everyone*.

If you are a Gentile, then Paul wants you to grasp that if human effort could not save ethnic Israel, then it certainly isn't going to save you. He wants you to recognize that Jesus the Jewish Messiah is the King of the whole earth. You are included in God's *anyone* and *everyone* because Jesus, God's stumbling stone, is the new King in town.

---

[4] Hebrews 8:13.

[5] Paul already said as much in 2:11, and the Jews should have known this from Old Testament passages such as Psalm 22:27–31, Isaiah 11:9–10 and Jonah 4:11.

How Can I Be Saved?
(10:9)

*If you confess with your mouth, "Jesus is Lord," and
believe in your heart that God raised him from the
dead, you will be saved.*

(Romans 10:9)

Paul isn't about to let these three chapters become an academic
discussion. At the heart of his argument about God's plan
for ethnic Israel, he throws in the answer to a very practical
question. Although he painted five Gospel pictures in the first
section of his letter, he didn't explicitly teach us how to respond
to the Gospel. Now, as he contrasts Christian Gentiles with
unsaved Jews, he finally tells us what we must do to be saved.
It's both disarmingly simple and incredibly difficult.

Paul tells us that we need to confess Jesus is Lord. That
made conversion very difficult for a Jew. Paul's word for *Lord*
is *kurios*, which was the word used throughout the Septuagint
to refer to *Yahweh*. Jews could only be saved by confessing
that there was more to the character of Israel's God than was
contained in the "Shema", the Jewish national creed which was
taken from Deuteronomy 6:4: *"Hear, O Israel: the Lord our God,
the Lord is one."* Confessing Jesus as Lord meant accepting he
is God, and that the Lord is not just one, but three-in-one. On
the surface, that might sound easy, since Isaiah 9:6 had already
prophesied that the Messiah's name would be *"Wonderful
Counsellor, Mighty God, Everlasting Father"*, but in practice the
Jews found this message so offensive that they mistranslated
that verse in the Septuagint to read that the Messiah would

be merely the *"Messenger of the Mighty Counsellor... Health to him!"*

We need to understand this background to see that Paul is deliberately raising the stakes for his Jewish readers. He is telling them that they cannot be saved unless they admit that their leaders have got it wrong. They must confess that their Sanhedrin was no more in tune with God's purposes than the translators of the Septuagint when they executed Jesus *"for blasphemy, because you, a mere man, claim to be God."*[1] There was nothing easy for a Jew in responding to the Gospel. It meant facing up to the fact that their nation had rejected and murdered the Messiah, the Son of God.

But conversion to Christ was no easier for a Gentile Roman. Their emperor had already laid claim to the title *Kurios*, starting with Augustus and increasing as time went on. Nero's subjects were expected to prove their loyalty by confessing Caesar as *Kurios*, like Governor Festus in Acts 25:26. In our world of constitutional monarchs and fixed-term presidents, it is easy to treat "Jesus is Lord" as little more than a throwaway line in a worship chorus, but in the first-century Roman Empire it was viewed as tantamount to treason. If Jesus was Lord then it meant that Caesar wasn't. Conversion to Christ meant stepping out on a collision course with the world.

Only seven years after Paul wrote this letter, the Roman Empire made its move. Nero began executing Christians in 64 AD, and many of his successors forced them to confess that Caesar was *Kurios* or else face execution. One of their most famous victims was Polycarp of Smyrna in modern-day Turkey, who was told he would be burned at the stake unless he confessed that the emperor was *Kurios*. *"What harm is there in saying that Caesar is Lord?... Swear the oath and I will set you free,"* his prosecutor pleaded, but Polycarp had read what Paul says in Romans 10:9. *"I have served Jesus for eighty-six years and*

---

[1] John 10:33.

he has never done me any wrong. How can I blaspheme my King who saved me?... I am a Christian."[2] The martyrdom of Polycarp in 156 AD is a reminder of what it meant for a Roman to confess that there's a new King in town.

Conversion may sound easier in our own, less savage culture, but Paul warns you not to be fooled. Conversion is never easy because it costs you all you have. If Jesus is *Kurios* then we are sinful rebels, as Paul argued so passionately in chapters 1–3. If he is *Kurios* then we must abandon self-rule and offer him complete obedience. The American preacher Gardiner Spring explained to his nineteenth-century hearers that no one can be saved unless

> *he sees that he has broken God's holy law, and resisted the claim of his rightful Sovereign. The thought which most deeply affects him, is that he has sinned against God... There is no genuine repentance where there is no forsaking of sin. Still to go on in sin...is incompatible with the nature of that sorrow which is unto salvation.*[3]

Paul doesn't tell us to respond to the Gospel by confessing Jesus as our Saviour, but by going one step further and confessing him as our Lord.

Because conversion is so difficult, Paul tells us that a second indispensable aspect to being saved is believing in our heart that Jesus rose from the dead. If we are convinced that Jesus truly defeated Satan's generals Sin and Death, the cost of following him suddenly seems a puny price to pay. The resurrection means that Paul's five Gospel pictures in chapters 3–5 are all true: Christ exonerates the guilty, frees the enslaved, takes the place of the death-row prisoner and absorbs God's wrath against our sin to make us his friends. Augustus, Tiberius,

---

[2] Recorded by the church at Smyrna shortly after his death in *The Martyrdom of Polycarp* (chapters 8–11).

[3] Gardiner Spring, *Essays on Christian Character* (1813).

Caligula and Claudius had all claimed to be *Kurios*, but Death had spoken the last word. Jesus claimed to be *Kurios* and then proved it by rising from the dead to back up his royal claim. This is what made Polycarp laugh at the threat of being burned at the stake:

> *You threaten me with fire which burns for a season and is quickly quenched, for you are ignorant of the judgment fire which is coming, and of the eternal punishment which awaits the ungodly. Why are you taking so long? Bring it on. Do what you wish.*

It is what helps us to laugh at the cost of conversion too.

Paul therefore asks you to check you have received Jesus as Lord in your *heart*, by believing the Gospel message he lays out for you in Romans. Do you believe in your heart that God raised him from the dead and that Paul's five Gospel pictures are worth giving your life to own? If so, he asks you to confess with your *mouth* that Jesus is Lord, since there is no such thing as a secret believer. Although it is counter-intuitive, Paul puts verbal confession ahead of the heart faith which makes it possible, because he does not want us to fool ourselves that conversion is something private. Genuine conversion involves a person being baptized in water and declaring publicly that Jesus is Lord.[4]

So whatever your religious background; whatever your long-held beliefs or your deeply cherished sins; whatever it may cost you that Jesus is the new King in town – Paul writes these words for you as the only way you can be saved: *"If you confess with your mouth, 'Jesus is Lord,' and believe in your heart that God raised him from the dead, you will be saved."*

---

[4] If you have not yet been baptized in water as Paul instructed in 6:1–4, then Paul reminds you a second time. He insists in Galatians 3:27 and 1 Corinthians 12:13 that baptism is a key aspect of Christian conversion.

God Still Loves Israel
(10:14–11:32)

I do not want you to be ignorant of this mystery,
brothers, so that you may not be conceited:…all
Israel will be saved.

(Romans 11:25–26)

Paul has finished delivering bad news to the Jewish Christians in Rome. Now it is time for him to move on to the good. The Jews had reaped a spiritual disaster of their own making, but they hadn't stopped God from loving them and they hadn't spoilt his plan. Even in their darkest hour, Paul tells them that Israel's history will have a happy ending.

First, he argues in 10:14–21 that the Jewish nation still has a chance to confess Jesus as Lord. The Old Testament predicted that the Jews would hear and reject the Gospel (verses 18 and 21), and that Gentiles would gladly receive it instead (verses 19–20), but it also predicted this would not be the end of the Jewish story. Don't miss the way Paul changes God's prophecy about the Messiah in Isaiah 52:7. The Hebrew and Greek Old Testaments both use the masculine singular form of the verb to say *"How beautiful on the mountains are the feet of **him** who brings good news"* (that is, Jesus), but Paul changes it to read *"How beautiful are the feet of **those** who bring good news"* (that is, us).[1] This is no mere slip of the pen. Paul is saying that when we tell a Jew that Jesus is Lord, they can respond to him afresh

---

[1] He quotes from this same prophecy in verse 16 when it predicts that Israel will initially reject its Messiah.

through his Gospel-preaching People. Israel's history isn't over, and we are the ones who get to write its next chapter.[2]

Paul encourages us in 11:1–6 by pointing out that even now God is saving many Jews. He reminds us that when Elijah complained that God saved a Gentile widow but not the Israelites, the Lord rebuked him in 1 Kings 19 by pointing out that he had saved 7,000 as a faithful remnant. Paul tells his readers that he is part of God's first-century Jewish remnant and so are the Jewish Christians who are questioning God's master plan. We need to open our eyes like Elijah to see what God is doing. As Paul was told by James in Acts 21:20, when he visited his church at Jerusalem a few weeks after writing Romans: *"See, brother, how many thousands of Jews have believed!"*

What's more, Paul continues in 11:7–24, this present-day remnant is nothing compared to what God has planned for Israel in the future. He didn't just prophesy that the Jews would reject his Messiah. He also promised they would change their minds and turn back to him en masse as a nation.

In verses 7–10, Paul quotes from three Old Testament passages that foretold the very tragedy that his readers found confusing. Deuteronomy 29:4 and Isaiah 29:10 both predicted that Israel would become spiritually deaf and blind, and so did the Messiah in Psalm 69:22–23 when he cursed them as false friends who would betray him.[3] The Jews liked to cast themselves in the role of the Messiah's righteous friends in the Psalms, but he warned them they would blindly trip over the Gospel feast he came to spread.

Paul then sets this curse in context in verses 11 and 12 by referring us back to his quotation from Deuteronomy 32:21 earlier in 10:19, where God promised that this curse would yield

---

[2] Since the word for *send* in 10:15 is the root of the word *apostle* in 11:13, Paul is telling the Romans to do for the Jews what he himself is planning to do for Rome, Italy and the western Mediterranean.

[3] Psalm 69 is the second most quoted psalm in the New Testament, and each time it refers to the Messiah.

even greater blessing for them in the end. Moses' prophetic song contained a pledge that God would make the Jews jealous by saving large numbers of Gentiles, which meant the current situation didn't mean God was unfaithful at all. It was proof he hadn't finished with the Jewish nation and was faithfully continuing to deliver on his plan. The nations of the earth were eating their fill at the Messiah's table so that the Jews would be stirred to spiritual envy and push their way back to the table in order to eat their share.

This leads into verses 13–24, where Paul tells the Gentile Christians how to respond to God's great plan. They must not fool themselves that the Lord has replaced Israel with the Church, preferring to work out his purposes with cultured Romans like themselves. Jesus called his Church the *ekklēsia*, which was the Septuagint word for the congregation of Israel, because the Church is the continuation and not replacement of God's Old Testament People. Gentiles can only be saved in AD history if God grafts them as branches into the same tree which he planted during BC history.[4] They must not boast as if Jewish Christians were an add-on to the Church, but recognize that they themselves were an add-on to God's Old Testament People. They should work hard like him to save as many Gentiles as possible so that Jews would become jealous and be added back into the patriarchs' tree, as Moses had predicted.

Paul now moves in 11:25–32 into his crescendo, which will finally answer the main question posed in section two of Romans. He is still talking to ignorant and conceited Gentile Christians in verse 25 when he says that the Jews' violent enmity towards the Gospel is no reason to assume that they are outside God's great plan. The Gentiles were once pagan enemies of God themselves and had only been saved through unwarranted mercy, so they should not be surprised that God will do the

---

[4] Paul picks up on the fact that the Lord called Israel his *olive tree* in Jeremiah 11:16–17.

same to the descendants of his beloved patriarchs. God's gifts and his calling towards Israel are irrevocable, so there will come a day when *"all Israel will be saved"*.[5] Paul expects us to know Scripture well enough to grasp that in verse 26 he does not mean every single Jew. The Old Testament writers, echoed by Matthew 3:5 and Mark 1:5, used *"all Israel"* as a stock phrase to mean *a vast number from every tribe and clan within Israel.* The Gentile Christians must not write off the Jewish race like other Romans. God will end world history by saving them in unprecedented numbers. The King of the Jews is still finishing his plan.

Paul therefore tells us how we must respond by making another crucial change to an Old Testament quotation. In verses 26 and 27, he combines three separate prophecies, the first of which comes from Isaiah 59:20–21. Isaiah wrote in Hebrew that *"the Deliverer will come **to** Zion"*, and the Septuagint translated it as *"the Deliverer will come **for the sake of** Zion"*. Paul updates it with his own God-inspired perspective and quotes it as *"the Deliverer will come **out of** Zion"*. Jesus came to Israel with the Gospel *for the sake of* their salvation, but their rejection propelled the Gospel *out of* Israel towards the Gentiles, who in turn will pray and preach the Gospel back to sinful Israel. Only a fool would judge the flight of a boomerang based on the first half of its trajectory, and only a fool would judge God's faithfulness towards Israel while his Messiah's plan is still in full flow.

That's why Paul spends three chapters explaining why God has as yet saved so many Gentiles and so few Jews. If the proof of the Gospel pudding is in the eating, then AD history will prove that all Paul preached in chapters 1–8 is true. As we believe the Gospel and preach it back to the Jews, we write the final pages of the new King Jesus' plan.

---

[5] The debate over whether Paul can actually mean ethnic Israel rather than the Church in verse 26 is aggravated if we render the Greek word *houtos* at the start of the verse *so* or *therefore*. It actually means *in this way* and therefore refers back to *Israel* in verse 25. God will fulfil the prophecy of Zechariah 12–14 by saving a vast number of Jews *in this way* through the Messiah.

Kindness and Severity (11:22)

Consider therefore the kindness and sternness of God: sternness to those who fell, but kindness to you, provided that you continue in his kindness.

(Romans 11:22)

There won't be anything boring or repetitive about praising Jesus throughout eternity. The more we understand the Gospel and God's plan to make it known, the more it stirs us with new ways to worship Jesus, God's new King.

Paul has almost finished section two of Romans and wants to help us respond to these eleven chapters about the Gospel. William Tyndale, who lost his life because he defied the authorities to translate the Bible into English, called them

> the principal and most excellent part of the New Testament... No man verily can read it too oft or study it too well; for the more it is studied, the easier it is; the more it is chewed, the pleasanter it is; and the more groundly it is searched, the preciouser things are found in it, so great treasure of spiritual things lieth hid therein.[1]

Let's therefore linger a few moments in 11:22 to examine two reasons why Paul's Gospel means we can never tire of worshipping Jesus.

Paul's first reason is that the Gospel focuses our worship on

---

[1] William Tyndale in the 1534 edition of his New Testament. He was executed in 1536.

the kindness of God. We may have been respectable or degenerate when we confessed Jesus as Lord, but Romans 1:18–3:20 convinces us we were all guilty rebels, dead in sin and hurtling towards a judgment we deserved. Richard Dawkins speaks for our present culture when he asks, *"What kind of ethical philosophy is it that condemns every child, even before it is born, to inherit the sin of a remote ancestor?"*[2] The Gospel silences such self-flattery by telling us that we were born into Adam but adopted into Christ through the unfathomable kindness of the God against whom we had rebelled. What is more, it tells those of us who are Gentile believers to sing loudest of all. Paul's main thrust in this verse is that we had no share in Israel's Gospel, but that God's kindness has included us in a message which was not ours.

We find fresh reasons to worship Jesus for God's kindness in Romans 3:21–5:21, since those five Gospel pictures tell us that Jesus died and rose again to justify us, free us, save us, reconcile us and raise us to new life. Again, Richard Dawkins speaks for our present age when he angrily objects that *"The creator of the universe, sublime inventor of mathematics, of relativistic space-time, of quarks and quanta, of life itself, Almighty God, who reads our every thought and hears our every prayer, omniscient, omnipotent, omnipresent God couldn't think of a better way to forgive us than to have himself tortured and executed."*[3] On the day that Jesus returns to end world history, nobody – not even Richard Dawkins – will be looking at his wounds and raising any such objection. Paul invites us to worship Jesus in advance of that day, by telling us that those five pictures will fuel our worship for endless days.

There are still more reasons to worship Jesus for God's kindness in Romans 6–8. We will not simply praise him for saving us from hell, but that we get to experience his salvation

---

[2] Richard Dawkins, *The God Delusion* (2006).

[3] Richard Dawkins writing in *The Guardian* newspaper on 24th December 2010.

straight away. When the nineteenth-century preacher Samuel Logan Brengle discovered the baptism in the Holy Spirit for the first time as described in Romans 8, he wrote

> *Jesus gave me such a blessing as I never had dreamed a man could have this side of Heaven. It was a Heaven of love that came into my heart. I walked out over Boston Common before breakfast, weeping for joy and praising God. Oh, how I loved! In that hour I knew Jesus, and I loved Him till it seemed my heart would break with love... I loved the dogs, I loved the horses, I loved the little urchins on the street, I loved the strangers who hurried past me, I loved the Heathen – I loved the whole world.*[4]

When we truly experience God's salvation as explained in Romans 6–8, and when we grasp in Romans 9–11 that it is only God's kindness that has included us in this Jewish hope at all, it stirs in us a similar passion to worship Jesus for all eternity.

But Paul hasn't finished with his reasons why we will worship. That was only the first half, and the second half is that the Gospel focuses our worship on *the sternness* or *severity of God*. We have been brought up in a culture, once more captured by Richard Dawkins, which complains that *"The total amount of suffering per year in the natural world is beyond all decent contemplation... The universe that we observe has precisely the properties we should expect if there is, at bottom, no design, no purpose, no evil, no good, nothing but pitiless indifference."*[5] This means we find the suffering of the present world hard to bear, let alone the news that Jesus is coming back for Judgment Day. These eleven chapters help us to see why God's severity is such good news that it will evoke our praise forever.

Romans 1:18–3:20 convinces us that it is only right and

---

[4] Samuel Logan Brengle describing his 1885 experience in his book *Helps to Holiness* (1896).

[5] Richard Dawkins, *River Out of Eden* (1995).

proper for God to judge people for their sin. We instinctively want war criminals and terrorists to face justice, and the Gospel tells us humans are both of those things and worse. It makes us grateful that God is not a pushover in the courtroom, like the spineless high-court judges that our newspapers despise. Romans 3:21–5:21 reminds us how unfair it is to complain about God's judgment, when he has personally tasted the worst of this earth's suffering in order to save us from the hell about which we complain. Even Israel, which bears the brunt of God's severity in this verse, can still receive his mercy by confessing Christ as Lord. Romans 6–8 helps us to see why God's fierce judgment is such brilliant news. Richard Dawkins is merely groaning with the rest of the fallen universe in 8:20–22, and fails to realize that God's severity in judging is the answer to its pain. Our only hope is for the Lord to fumigate our sinful world with the ruthlessness of a Rentokil employee and to rid it of everything which would contaminate the new.

The book of Revelation tells us that we will worship God for his severity as much as for his kindness throughout eternity. We will remember the old world and sing, *"True and just are your judgments... Hallelujah! The smoke from her goes up for ever and ever."*[6] So if the past eleven chapters haven't stirred you to worship God for both his kindness and his severity, then Paul tells you that you haven't understood them and you need to go back and re-read them.

William Tyndale, who so loved these chapters, died at the stake crying out, *"Lord, open the King of England's eyes."* My prayer is that God will open your eyes to worship Jesus in the light of the words which you have read in Romans 1–11. When you grasp what Paul means by God's kindness and severity, it will be enough to fuel your worship, both now and forevermore.

---

[6] See Revelation 16:5–7; 18:20; 19:1–3.

The Ultimate A-Lister
(11:33–36)

From him and through him and to him are all things.
To him be the glory for ever! Amen.

(Romans 11:36)

Paul hasn't finished giving us reasons in these eleven chapters to praise God for the Gospel. In fact, he is only just getting started. This second section of Romans is not primarily about Jews or Gentiles or predestination. It is about God deserving our never-ending worship for the all-surpassing greatness of his plan.

We live in a culture which worships A-list celebrities, and first-century Rome was every bit as bad. Paul's explanation of God's strategy in chapters 9–11 is meant to convince us that he is far wiser, far more knowledgeable and far wealthier than any of our earthly celebrities. It is meant to stir us to worship Jesus as the ultimate A-lister.

The Emperor Nero wanted to be worshipped for his wisdom, so he tried to bask in the reflected glory of the A-list Julius Caesar. Even before he came to the throne, he renounced his surname, Ahenobarbus, to take the surname of his hero. Julius Caesar's conquest of Gaul and Britain, coupled with his flair for political machinations back in Rome, had made his name so proverbial for consummate human wisdom that every emperor adopted it as a title of great praise. That's why Paul ends his second section with a song which praises God for his far greater wisdom revealed in the Gospel. It begins by exclaiming in verse 33, *"Oh, the depth of the riches of the wisdom and knowledge of God!"*

Rome was a city which worshipped wisdom but it was praising the wrong man. Julius Caesar hadn't even been wise enough to foresee his own assassination in 44 BC, and had been duped into thinking that Brutus and the other senators were his friends. Jesus, on the other hand, knew exactly what he had to do to save the human race, and was perfectly fulfilling the master plan of Romans 9–11 in order to save people from every nation while remaining faithful to the Jews. Paul's five Gospel pictures all begin with such confusing brushstrokes that any human artist would have thrown the canvasses away. Jesus, however, knows exactly what he is doing – condemned and murdered to defeat every enemy and break down every obstacle between us and salvation. No wonder Paul tells us that God's wisdom will fuel our worship throughout eternity. He makes the wisest A-listers of this world look like a troupe of circus clowns.

The Emperor Nero also wanted to be worshipped for his knowledge, so his mother paid the A-list philosopher Seneca to become his personal tutor.[1] He promoted him to chief adviser in the early years of his reign, but Nero's faith in human knowledge was as misplaced as his faith in human wisdom. Seneca had outstanding knowledge for his day, but he didn't have the character to put his own words into practice. He flattered Nero, gave in to him and turned a blind eye to his murders. In the end, Nero tired of his knowledge altogether and scared him into committing suicide.

Paul therefore carries on his song of praise by asking in verse 34, *"Who has known the mind of the Lord? Or who has been his counsellor?"* King Jesus needs no Seneca or any other celebrity philosopher, because nobody could have second-guessed the genius of his plan in Romans 9–11. Paul reminds us in 9:20–21 that we are mere lumps of clay on God's potter's wheel. We can't understand him, advise him or dare to talk back

---

[1] Seneca was one of the greatest names in Rome, and brother to the Gallio who is mentioned in Acts 18:12.

to him.[2] All we can do is fall down in worship which will last forever.

John Piper explains from verse 34 that,

> *Paul says that God's knowledge is unfathomably deep. He knows all recorded facts – all the facts stored in all the computers and all the books in all the libraries in the world. But vastly more than that, he knows all events at the macro level – all that happens on earth and in the atmosphere and in all the farthest reaches of space in every galaxy and star and planet. And all events at the micro level – all that happens in molecules and atoms and electrons and protons and neutrons and quarks. He knows all their movements and every location and every condition of every particle of the universe at every nanosecond of time. And he knows...how all facts and all events, of every kind, relate to each other and affect each other. When one event happens, he not only sees it, but he sees the eternal chain of effects that flow from it and from all the billions of events that are unleashed by every other event. He knows all this without the slightest strain on his mind. That is what it means to be God.[3]*

It's why Paul expects chapters 9–11 to give us endless fuel to worship him.

The Emperor Nero also wanted to be worshipped for his riches, like Julius Caesar's ally and financier Marcus Crassus. The equivalent of a modern-day trillionaire, Crassus was easily the richest man in Roman history, but Pliny lists two officials of Claudius who came pretty close to rivalling that claim. One

---

[2] Paul quotes verse 34 from Isaiah 40:13, which told Israel to stop trying to talk back to the Lord. He quotes the same verse again in 1 Corinthians 2:16 and promises that the Holy Spirit tells us Jesus' mind.

[3] John Piper preaching on Romans 11:33–36 at Bethlehem Baptist Church, Minneapolis, on 21st March 2004.

was Narcissus, whom Nero forced to commit suicide in the early weeks of his reign so he could appropriate his Forbes-rich-list fortune. The other was Pallas, whom Nero later murdered as a ploy to confiscate his wealth as well.[4] Nero longed to be worshipped for his wealth, but Paul tells us in verses 35 and 36 that he didn't even come close to God's real A-lister. Jesus is the Son of God, who doesn't need to borrow, steal or confiscate because *"From him and through him and to him are all things."*

John Piper adds:

Not only does God own the earth and all that is in it, including you, but he also owns the reaches of space and the heavens beyond the heavens with all their angelic armies. In other words, nothing exists outside God that is not God's. He owns it, and, as his possession, he may do with it as he pleases. Human wealth compared to God's wealth is ridiculously tiny and laughable to boast in. Bill Gates is a pauper and has nothing compared to the poorest heir of God... God is infinitely rich because he owns all that is, and because he can make more of anything that he pleases out of nothing.

Paul therefore ends his eleven chapters about the Gospel and God's plan to make it known by calling us to worship the Lord forever. He tells us to turn our back on this world's empty worship of A-list celebrities, and to shift all our worship onto the new King Jesus and his glorious master plan. Far wiser than Caesar, far more knowledgeable than Seneca and far, far richer than Crassus ever was – Jesus is simply the one that Paul's first two sections of Romans give us ample fuel to worship. Let's start praising him now with a song which will last throughout eternity: *"To him be the glory for ever! Amen."*

---

[4] Tacitus, *Annals* (13.1, 14.65); Pliny the Elder, *Natural History* (33.47).

Romans 12:1–15:13:

The New King Is Lord

Therefore (12:1–15:13)

Therefore, I urge you, brothers, in view of God's mercy, to offer your bodies as living sacrifices, holy and pleasing to God – this is your spiritual act of worship.

(Romans 12:1)

It doesn't matter how massive the door frame, it only takes a tiny hinge to open a mighty door.

After eight chapters of detailed teaching about the Gospel in section one, and three chapters about God's glorious master plan in section two, Paul opens the door to three and a half chapters of practical application by starting section three with the tiny Greek word *oun*. He hasn't darted back and forth between theology and application in his first two sections – like Peter, James and John do in their letters – but has taken time to build a doorframe of theology through which he now invites us to step inside. The hinge which opens the door is this tiny Greek word for *therefore*, and it opens a section of practical application about how we must live *"in view of God's mercy"*. If there truly is a new King in town, then nothing about the way we live our lives can stay the same.

We desperately need the message of section three of Romans. Three-quarters of the population of many Western countries describe themselves as "Christian", but only a small fraction of them make any effort to live their lives as if Jesus is Lord. On the afternoon of Sunday 27th June 2010, five times as many English people watched their football team lose to Germany in the World Cup as went to church that morning to celebrate Jesus' win.[1] Even church-going Christians need a constant reminder that confessing Jesus as Lord means signing up for revolution, and that worship means more than singing songs together on one morning of the week. Paul tells us that there is only one true *"spiritual act of worship"*, and it is offering our bodies to the Lord as living sacrifices every day.

The Gospel and God's master plan must change the way we act towards God and each other. Paul tells the Jewish and Gentile Christians at Rome to bury their differences and start seeing themselves as Jesus' single, multiracial Body. They must live out the Gospel towards each other in 12:3–8, towards God in 12:11–12, and towards unbelievers in 12:13 – even when those unbelievers persecute them in 12:14–21. The Greek word translated *spiritual* in 12:1 is *logikos*, from which we get the English word *logical*, so Paul is saying that these things are the only *reasonable* act of worship for us to offer in response to the news that Jesus is Lord. If the Gospel hasn't made you live very differently towards God and other people, then Paul tells you that you haven't truly responded to it at all.

The Gospel and God's master plan must also change the way we act towards the world's authority. In 13:1–7, Paul tells the Romans to submit even to Emperor Nero because, if God is as sovereign as section two explained, he didn't become emperor through his wicked schemes and murder. He only succeeded Claudius because King Jesus chose him as the right candidate to serve as his viceroy in Rome.[2] *"There is no authority except that which God has established."*

At the same time, there is plenty of man-made authority, which tries to steal our obedience away from Christ as Lord. In 13:8, Paul addresses the suffocating Roman system of patronage, and in 13:8–14 he tells us to reject the reign of Sin

---

[1] 17.4 million English people watched the match with Germany. Only 3.5 million went to church.

[2] However evil Nero might be, Paul insists in 13:4 that he is the *servant* of King Jesus.

and Death which have lost their authority but constantly try to woo us back onto their team. Confessing Jesus as Lord means honouring Caesar and resisting Sin. If we don't, Paul tells us once again, we haven't truly responded to the Gospel.

The Gospel and God's master plan must also change the way we live when we disagree with one another. Paul ends this section in 14:1–15:13 by returning to the issue of Moses' Law and what it means for Jewish–Gentile race relations. He devotes one and a half chapters – almost half of all his practical application – to teaching Gentile Christians how to exercise their freedom without offending Jews, and Jewish Christians how to keep their cultural traditions without looking down on Gentile Christians. Paul doesn't believe that preaching the door frame of the Gospel is enough on its own to solve the problems in the church at Rome. They need to walk through the door which he swings open with his *therefore*, and start working out in practice what it means for Jesus to be the new King in town.

So do we. We saw in the previous chapter that Nero's tutor Seneca was a much-respected teacher who failed to practise what he preached. He excused his sins through his Stoic philosophy, which taught that the body matters little and that *"You are a little soul, burdened with a corpse."*[3] Paul contradicted this in 3:13–18 when he told us that sin expresses itself through our throats, tongues, lips, mouths, feet and eyes, and he begins this new section by insisting that devotion to Jesus as Lord must also be expressed through our bodies. We must offer God our bodies as a *thusia*, the Septuagint word for the sacrifices at the Temple, and we must offer him our minds so he can transform and renew them to know his *"good, pleasing and perfect will"*.[4]

---

[3] Quoted from the Stoic philosopher Epictetus (Fragment 26), who lived in Rome just after Seneca.

[4] *Be transformed* is a passive command in Greek. We are to offer our minds to God and let him change them through the Holy Spirit as we read Scripture together and submit to what it says. Paul says that is the key to receiving God's daily guidance for our lives, and not clever techniques.

If Jesus is Lord, we must worship him every day through everything that we do with our body, mind and spirit.

Rick Warren, best-selling author of *The Purpose-Driven Life*, asked tens of thousands of Christians at the Anaheim Angels sports stadium in January 2005:

> *In 1939, in a stadium much like this in Munich, Germany, they packed it out with young men and women in brown shirts for a fanatical man standing behind a podium named Adolf Hitler, the personification of evil. And in that stadium, those in brown shirts formed with their bodies a sign that said in the whole stadium, "Hitler, we are yours." And they nearly took the world...*
>
> *What would happen if American Christians, if world Christians, if just the Christians in this stadium, followers of Christ, would say, "Jesus, we are yours"? What kind of spiritual awakening would we have?*

Paul asks the same question in section three of Romans to people living under a dictator as murderous as Hitler, and tells us that being a Christian means declaring *"Jesus, we are yours"* through every aspect of our lives. In the light of the Gospel he has outlined in Romans 1–11, we must live to sound the message that the new King Jesus is Lord.

Live It Towards the Church (12:3–10)

In Christ we who are many form one body, and each member belongs to all the others.

(Romans 12:5)

Rome was a city obsessed with social status. The patricians looked down on the equestrians, the equestrians looked down on the plebeians, the plebeians looked down on the freedmen and the freedmen looked down on the slaves. Men looked down on women, the old looked down on the young and together they all looked down on the Jews and barbarians. Every Roman knew his station in society, and those above him made sure that he never forgot it.

That's why Paul begins applying the Gospel by telling them their status games have got to stop. *"Do not think of yourself more highly than you ought,"* he warns in verse 3, and a few verses later, *"Do not be proud, but be willing to associate with people of low position."*[1] If the Gospel which Paul laid out in chapters 1–11 is true, it has to change our attitude towards the Church and everyone in it.

If we believe what Paul says in 1:18–3:20 about our need for salvation, then we can no longer think *too highly of ourselves.* Even if we were born the equivalent of a Roman senator, our status was that of a sinner until the moment God came and found us with the Gospel. If we accept Paul's teaching in chapter 9 that we only responded because God chose us before the beginning

---

[1] *Hoi tapeinoi* in verse 16 means literally *the lowly*. It could either refer to menial chores or to the slaves and workers who were forced to do them.

of time, then even our new-found status as children of God gives no grounds for boasting. God deliberately designed the Gospel to rule out any cause for human boasting at all. The glory goes to Jesus alone, not to his subjects who have been levelled by the message of his cross.

If we believe what Paul says in 3:21–5:21 about the way in which God has granted us salvation, we can no longer think *too little of others*. Jesus laid down his life in those five Gospel pictures because God loved them, chose them and counted it worth giving his Son's life to purchase them. How can we not love them and lay down our own lives for them as well? *"Honour one another above yourselves,"* Paul urges us in verse 10. A few weeks ago somebody asked me if they really needed to go to church to be a Christian. I hope you can see that that is a very Roman question. Paul tells us there is nothing me-centred about following Jesus as Lord. We are not truly following him at all unless we take care of his Body and take our place within his Bride.[2]

If we believe what Paul says in chapters 6–8 about experiencing our salvation, we can no longer act as if we *do not need other Christians*. Verses 4–8 are meant to echo 1 Corinthians 12 and its call to build up Jesus' Body through exercising spiritual gifts, and verses 9–10 are meant to echo 1 Corinthians 13 and its call to do so with self-sacrificial love. Paul warned the church at Corinth, and he does the same for Rome, that there is no such thing as a Christian loner. God makes us all different and incomplete by ourselves until we are knitted into a local church body, just as our physical organs and limbs are of little use unless they are joined to the rest of our bodies. We may be busy, but the Gospel tells us that no Christian is too busy to get plugged into church.

If we believe what Paul tells us in chapters 6–8, we cannot

---

[2] In fact, Paul says literally in verse 1: *"present your **bodies** as **a** living sacrifice"*.

act as if *other Christians don't need us*. Although Paul starts by warning the Romans in verse 3 not to think too highly of themselves, he ends the verse by warning them not to think too little of themselves either. *"Think of yourself with sober judgment, in accordance with the measure of faith God has given you,"* he urges, perhaps thinking of the slaves who might discount their usefulness to others. *"Each member belongs to all the others,"* he insists in verse 5, using similar language to 1 Corinthians 7:4–5, which literally calls holding back our debt a form of *swindling*. Believers who fail to give themselves as completely to a local church as Jesus did when he died to save it are therefore spiritual swindlers and Christian crooks. Paul could hardly be clearer in his application of chapters 1–11. If you have not been transformed in your attitude towards the Church, you haven't understood the Gospel.

If we believe what Paul tells us in chapters 9–11 about God's sovereign plan to save all nations including Israel, we no longer act as if our response to this truth can wait until tomorrow. If God has filled us with his Holy Spirit to empower some of us to prophesy, some of us to serve, some of us to teach, some of us to encourage, some of us to give financially, some of us to lead and some of us to express acts of Christian mercy, we cannot rest until we have discharged our role in his master plan.[3] Paul told us in 10:15 that we continue Jesus' incarnate ministry, and he clarifies here in verse 5 that we cannot truly make Jesus incarnate unless we unite with the local expression of his Body. He has formulated his plan so that enlightened self-interest alone should be enough to devote us to one another with the brotherly love Paul commands in verse 10. Love and unity and shared lives and co-operation lead as surely to successful Christian living as strife and separatism lead to failure.

Some years after Paul wrote Romans, the Christian

---

[3] There is some overlap between Paul's list of spiritual gifts here and the two lists in 1 Corinthians 12, but they are different enough to make it clear that they only serve as a sample of many other gifts.

philosopher Aristides was able to tell the emperor to look at the church in his city as a proof that the Gospel must be true:

> *They walk in all humility and kindness, falsehood is not found among them, and they love one another. They do not despise the widow or grieve the orphan. He that has, distributes liberally to him that has not. If they see a stranger they bring him under their roof, and rejoice over him as if he were their own brother; for they call themselves brothers, not after the flesh, but after the Spirit and in God. When one of their poor passes away from the world and one of them sees him, he provides for his burial according to his ability; and if they hear that any of their number is imprisoned or oppressed for the name of their Messiah, all of them provide for his needs, and if it is possible that he may be delivered, they deliver him. And if there is among them any man who is poor and needy, and they have not an abundance of necessaries, they fast two or three days so that they may supply the needy with the food they need. And they observe scrupulously the commandments of their Messiah.[4]*

Paul applied the Gospel by shaping a revolutionary community of devoted followers of Jesus at the heart of status-obsessed Rome. In time, the whole culture of the city would be changed. That's just what happens when people live together as the Church of Jesus, the new King in town.

---

[4] Aristides wrote these words to the Emperor Hadrian in c.125 AD in his *Apology* (chapter 15).

Live It Towards God (12:11–12)

Keep your spiritual fervour, serving the Lord. Be joyful in hope, patient in affliction, faithful in prayer.

(Romans 12:11–12)

Let me confess to you how stupid I can be. It might help you to understand what Paul is saying in these two verses.

A few months ago, I got a new laptop. It worked fine for several weeks but then suddenly lost all broadband connection. I checked the lights on my wireless router and moved my laptop closer, but in the end I took my laptop back and complained that there was either a problem with my router or I had been sold a faulty product. Imagine how embarrassed I felt when the man flicked a switch on the side of the laptop, which I must have inadvertently knocked into the off position. I hadn't realized there was a switch to turn off my new machine's ability to pick up a Wi-Fi signal. There was nothing wrong with the laptop or the router. It was just the laptop's owner who needed a bit more RAM.

That story makes me sound pretty stupid, but Paul is concerned that you will be just the same in applying the Gospel. It's all too easy to complain that our Christian lives feel dry and lifeless, or that the Gospel hasn't delivered the experiences Paul describes in chapters 6–8. I was preaching to a large group of Christians recently and asked them all to close their eyes and put up their hand if they felt disappointed with how following Jesus stacked up against their initial hopes and expectations. A frightening number of hands went in the air. It seems that many of us have got used to the fact that our daily connection with God feels rather faulty.

Paul tells us in verse 12 that part of our challenge is to remain *joyful in hope*. We are not just saved through believing Paul's message in 1:18–3:20 that we are wretched sinners. We are saved through believing the Gospel message of 3:21–5:21, which tells us we have been transformed into forgiven children of God. The Holy Spirit convicts us that we are sinners who need saving, but once we are saved it is the Devil who condemns us by whispering that we are nothing more than sinners. One of the reasons why many Christians feel far more distant from the Lord than Paul describes is that they spend too much time listening to the lie instead of preaching Gospel truth afresh to themselves every time they sin. We can even fool ourselves that beating ourselves up over sin is pleasing to God and the way to know him more and more.

I find C.J. Mahaney very helpful on this point:

> *Don't buy the lie that cultivating condemnation and wallowing in your shame is somehow pleasing to God, or that a constant, low-grade guilt will somehow promote holiness and spiritual maturity. It's just the opposite! Some of us have been carrying so much, for so long, that we think it's normal to go through life weighted down. And the truth is that, apart from the cross, condemnation **is** normal. Without Jesus, we all deserve to be condemned and punished for sin. But in Romans 8:1 the Bible tells us, "There is now no condemnation for those who are in Christ Jesus."*[1]

If your connection to God feels weak or non-existent, start drowning out Satan's guilty whispers by preaching to yourself the Gospel of hope in the sacrifice of Jesus.

---

[1] C.J. Mahaney, *The Cross-Centred Life* (2002).

Paul also warns in verse 12 that our challenge is to remain *faithful in prayer.* We must never forget that Paul's close friendship with the Lord was firmly grounded in his testimony in 1:8–10 that *"I thank my God...constantly I remember you in my prayers at all times... I pray."* Don't be as foolish as I was when I blamed my router and my laptop for my lack of internet connection. Do you want to know the intimacy with God that Paul describes in Romans 8? Then let James 4:8 teach you how to flick the switch to get connection: *"Come near to God and he will come near to you."* The Gospel teaches us that we do not need to earn merit through our prayers in order to be rewarded with relationship with God. But we have such promises in Christ that we mustn't be slow in taking up God's free invitation to spend time alone with him.

Linked to this is Paul's encouragement in verse 11 to *"keep your spiritual fervour."* He uses a Greek phrase that can be translated in either of two ways, which is usually what Paul does when he wants us to understand it both ways. It could mean *"keep fervent in [your] spirit"* or it could equally mean *"keep fervent by the [Holy] Spirit".* Paul's clarity in 8:9–17 that God wants to fill us with his Spirit must be coupled to his clarity in Acts 19:1–6 and 1 Thessalonians 5:19 that we can resist being filled and stifle his work when he comes. Even I wasn't stupid enough to assume that wireless routers are not for today or that my laptop had picked up a signal without realizing it – but that is precisely what large numbers of Christians do today when they consign baptism in the Spirit to the history books or believe they have already received it, albeit imperceptibly. Since John 3:34 promises that *"God gives the Spirit without limit,"* the problem is on our side. Let's flip the switch by praying for God to fill us with his Spirit and put fervour in our spirits.

Paul tells us in verse 12 that a final challenge comes in the area of being *patient in affliction.* It is all too easy to let past disappointments and confusion distort God's signal to us.

Resentment against God is like drinking spiritual cyanide. Paul expects his explanation of God's master plan in chapters 9–11 to prepare us for suffering and confusion in our Christian lives, and to convince us that God is wise enough to turn those setbacks into blessings in the end. He reminds us of his teaching in 8:28 that *"in all things God works for the good of those who love him."* This alone can keep us patient in affliction, and ensure we know the close relationship with God which Paul describes.

So if your daily experience of God doesn't always match up with what Paul tells you to expect in Romans, it may well be that the problem is fixed by a proper application of the Gospel. If we are joyful in hope, faithful in prayer, full of the Spirit and patient in affliction, we will find there's nothing wrong with God's signal to us at all. If you struggle to flick the switch yourself, ask someone you trust at your church to help you. This is what it means to apply the Gospel in our lives towards God.

Live It Towards Unbelievers
(12:13)

Share with God's people who are in need and pursue love towards outsiders.

(Romans 12:13)[1]

PepsiCo ran into problems when they translated their advertising slogan for commercials shown in China. What they thought read *"Come Alive! You're in the Pepsi Generation"* had been mistranslated *"Pepsi brings your ancestors back from the grave!"*

Several other American companies have fared no better in Latin America. The Parker Pen Company thought the Spanish word for "embarrass" was "embarazar", and was embarrassed itself when its sales slogan read, *"It won't leak in your pocket or make you pregnant."* Coors mistranslated their beer slogan, *"Turn it loose!"*, and told Spanish-speakers to *"Suffer from Diarrhoea!"* Translation is a tricky business, which is why it sometimes helps to know the Greek words that Paul used in writing Romans.

Most English translators render the Greek word *philoxenia* in verse 13 as a command to offer *hospitality*. There is some justification for this. It is linked to the words that are used in Acts 10:6, Acts 21:16, 1 Peter 4:9 and 3 John 5 to refer to believers giving lodgings to Christians from out of town.[2] A similar word is even used in Hebrews 13:2 to describe Lot offering bed and

---

[1] Literal translation.
[2] Paul uses a similar word in Romans 16:23 to describe Gaius hosting him and many open church meetings.

breakfast to some disguised angels who wanted to sleep rough in the city square at Sodom. But while *hospitality* isn't a wrong translation of the Pepsi Cola variety, it fails to capture what Paul is actually telling us to do here. The word conjures up pictures of Christians entertaining other Christians from their churches, whereas Paul is telling us that responding to the Gospel means doing something far more radical.

The Jews used the word *xenos* to refer to pagan foreigners, for example in Matthew 27:7 when looking for a separate burial ground for Gentiles to avoid contaminating Jewish graves. Paul used the word in Ephesians 2:12 and 19 to describe what Gentile Christians used to be before they were adopted into the family of God. Therefore note Paul's progression here in verses 10 and 13. He tells the Romans in verse 10 to pursue *philadelphia* and *philostorgia*, meaning *love for [Christian] brothers* and *love for [God's] family*. He stresses care for God's People again in the first half of verse 13, but then contrasts these two former kinds of love with a further call to pursue *philoxenia*.[3] Paul is telling us that the Gospel should make us love sinful unbelievers. If we don't receive them gladly into our homes, we are fooling ourselves we have understood Romans 1–11.

The Roman Christians desperately needed to hear this message. The pagans in their city were so depraved that many Christians wanted to disassociate themselves from their company altogether. Even Tacitus complained that *"All degraded and shameful practices flourish in the capital."*[4] The Christians were in danger of denying the Gospel through a misguided policy of splendid isolation.

Paul insists that no one who truly understands the Gospel can turn their back on unbelievers, however vile they may be.

---

[3] Hebrews 13:1–2 makes exactly the same contrast. It tells believers in verse 1 to pursue *philadelphia* towards fellow Christians, and tells them in verse 2 to pursue *philoxenia* towards unbelievers.

[4] Tacitus, *Annals* (15.44). Ironically, one of the main things he identified as filthy was the Christian Gospel!

Are they wicked and degenerate? So were you until God sought you out with the Gospel. Do their lives offend you, repulse you and make you want to run the other way? Excellent. Then you are ready to imitate Jesus, the friend of sinners. I love the way that William Tyndale translated this verse a few years before his execution. He pictures non-Christians as battered vessels close to shipwreck on stormy seas, and has Paul telling the Romans that their role is to "harbour people diligently". The Roman church was at a fork in the road. Would they become an inward-looking club for the perfect, or let the new King Jesus use them to spread his love throughout their city?

Paul's letter stopped the Roman church from acting like the priest and the Levite on the road to Jericho. It taught them to act like the Good Samaritan towards their city, so that Tertullian was able to tell Roman officials in the second century that,

> We have filled every place among you – cities, islands, fortresses, towns, market-places, even the camps, tribes, companies, palace, senate, forum – we have left nothing to you but the temples of your gods... We are not Indian Brahmins or fakirs living in woods and exiling themselves from ordinary life. We do not forget the debt of gratitude we owe to God, our Lord and Creator. We reject nothing and no one he has made... Our compassion spends more in the streets than yours does in the temples.[5]

The Roman church went out to find the neediest unbelievers, and turned their homes into welcoming harbours which gave them shelter through the Gospel.

We need to hear this message as desperately as the Romans. A good Christian friend told me recently that he wants to quit his work because his colleagues are so ungodly in their chatter. Another explained he has no non-Christian

---

[5] Tertullian wrote this to the Roman governors in c.197 AD in his *Apology* (chapters 37 and 42).

friends because he finds so much more in common with the average believer. The interesting thing about both of those conversations was that my friends saw their attitude as a sign of increasing Christian maturity. We tend to assume that the more we experience our salvation, the more we will find ourselves retreating from the world.

That's the kind of thinking which Paul tells us must die as part of our response to the Gospel. Later, he will tell Timothy and Titus not even to consider anyone for church leadership unless they have a consistent track record in *philoxenia*. If they do not routinely share their lives with sinners, how can they teach other people to follow Jesus? He will also tell Timothy that the church should not give financial help to any widow who professes faith in Christ but does not prove it by welcoming non-Christians into her home.[6] Paul says that no one can truly respond to the Gospel without it making them want to welcome sinners as Jesus did. *"It is not the healthy who need a doctor, but the sick,"* Jesus said. *"I desire mercy, not sacrifice. For I have not come to call the righteous, but sinners."*[7]

That's why Paul uses a strange word here to describe the importance of *philoxenia* in the normal Christian life. The word he uses in verse 13 to describe Christians *pursuing* love for unbelievers is deliberately the same as the word he uses in verse 14 for unbelievers *persecuting* them. Do you find their lives offensive? Then be equally offensive in your love. Do they deliberately hunt you down to taunt you with their sin? Then hunt them down in the same way to bless them with your kindness. Do they rub your face in their lifestyle as rebels against God's Word? Then rub their face in your lifestyle as a follower of Jesus, the new King in town.

---

[6] 1 Timothy 3:2; 5:10; Titus 1:8.
[7] Matthew 9:12–13.

Live It When You Are Wronged (12:14–21)

Bless those who persecute you; bless and do not curse.

(Romans 12:14)

Ordinary Romans hated the Christians living in their city. Suetonius saw their faith as a *"new and dangerous superstition"*, and Tacitus railed against *"the notoriously depraved Christians"* and their *"deadly superstition"*. Although they both wrote some years after Paul, Tacitus tells us that even in the 50s AD the whole *"human race detested them"*.[1] So when Paul wrote to the Romans and told them to apply the Gospel by blessing those who persecuted them, he wasn't merely talking about abstract Christian theory.

Paul was pointing out that the Christian message is about God sending his Son to people who hated and crucified him. It is the news that while Roman soldiers nailed him to a cross and the Jewish crowd mocked him, he cried out *"Father, forgive them, for they do not know what they are doing."* Paul began to take this message seriously himself when he saw the young Christian Stephen react the same way when he was stoned to death, crying out, *"Lord, do not hold this sin against them"*.[2] Roman persecution of Christians had not yet escalated to the shedding of blood, but Paul knew that the day would surely come. Now he tells his readers that responding to the Gospel must transform the way they deal with being wronged in matters great and small.

---

[1] Suetonius, *The Life of Nero* (16); Tacitus, *Annals* (15.44).
[2] Luke 23:34; Acts 7:60.

Paul, no stranger to being persecuted himself, says that in view of his teaching in 8:28 and chapters 9–11, we can have faith that God will turn injustice into blessing. When those who confess Jesus as Lord are wounded unfairly, they are to love and forgive and keep blessing in return. If that sounds impossible, Paul gives three great encouragements to help us. Since he warns in 2 Timothy 3:12–13 that *"everyone who wants to live a godly life in Christ Jesus will be persecuted, while evil men and impostors will go from bad to worse,"* we all need to pay attention to what he says.

In verses 15 and 16, Paul promises that *being wronged will unify us as Christ's Body*. Nothing levels and unites Christians quite as effectively as being forced to grovel together in the dirt under enemy fire. Just as the warring British tribes forgot their differences at the sight of Caesar's legions, petty differences within the Church are often silenced by a greater foe. The rich and powerful Roman Christians would obey Paul's command to mix with commoners and slaves when they saw their fellow patricians persecuting them for Christ.[3] Paul had seen churches under pressure in the Eastern Mediterranean rejoicing together, mourning together and eventually triumphing together. He reassures the church at Rome that persecution is part of God's great master plan.

In verse 17, Paul promises that *being wronged will result in Jesus being noticed*. When Jesus forgave his crucifiers, the entire squad of Roman soldiers was converted.[4] When Stephen forgave his killers, the young Pharisee who held their coats – Paul himself! – was challenged by what he saw.[5] Even Tacitus

---

[3] Perhaps Paul is remembering Nehemiah 3:5. James 2:6–7 makes a similar point in the face of persecution.

[4] Matthew 27:54 indicates that all of them were converted as thoroughly as described in John 19:34–35.

[5] Jesus was probably referring to this as one of his "goads" in Acts 26:14. See *Straight to the Heart of Acts*.

admits that when Nero started persecuting Christians, *"there arose a feeling of compassion"* among the pagans towards them.

In verses 18–21, Paul promises that *being wronged will result in our persecutors being shamed into conversion.* Since the Jews were the main persecutors of the Church until 64 AD, Paul quotes in verse 19 from Deuteronomy 32:35, the same song of Moses that he cited in 10:19 as a reminder that God has promised to make Israel jealous by saving many Gentiles. Paul quotes this same song again as a promise that when Jews see godlier character among the persecuted Christians than is found in their own synagogues, some of them will take notice and be saved. It had happened to Sosthenes, the Corinthian synagogue ruler, and Paul promises his readers it will happen in Rome as well.[6]

Paul expands the scope of this promise in verse 20 to reassure them that the same will be true when persecution starts to come from their own government. Paul quotes God's command in Proverbs 25:21–22 to feed and nourish the one who wrongs us because *"in doing this, you will heap burning coals on his head."* The best revenge on persecutors is to love them into repentance.[7] Paul didn't know it yet, but soon he would be demonstrating how to do this, when he was arrested a few weeks later in Jerusalem and preached grace and forgiveness to every Roman official in Judea through the way that he handled his unjust imprisonment. He would arrive in Rome under house arrest and Roman guard, but would react so graciously that he could write to friends that *"What has happened to me has really served to advance the gospel. As a result, it has become clear throughout the whole palace guard and to everyone else that I am in chains for Christ."* Soon he could write that he had even made converts *"who belong to Caesar's household."*[8]

---

[6] Acts 18:17; 1 Corinthians 1:1. Luke only mentions persecutors by name in Acts when he has good reason.

[7] The prophet Elisha had demonstrated this in 2 Kings 6:21–23.

[8] Acts 25:23; Philippians 1:12–13; 4:22.

Paul is very convincing in these verses, but if you are actually experiencing persecution you are bound to ask: *Is Paul saying we should pretend that their injustice doesn't matter?!* That's why Paul adds verse 19 at the heart of these three encouragements, because the reason we refuse to repay evil with evil is that we want to make room for a far greater Avenger. Jesus told Paul on the road to Damascus that he treats persecution as an attack upon *himself*. Paul therefore urges victims of injustice to *"leave room for God's wrath"*, because our puny acts of retaliation actually get in the way of God's own vengeance in due time.

Seven years after Paul wrote this letter, the Emperor Nero launched a violent persecution against the church at Rome. They responded as Paul commanded by making room for the Avenger, and returned blessing and forgiveness even as their loved ones died. Sure enough, less than four years later, the Roman Senate and the emperor's bodyguard turned against their persecutor. He was forced to flee and committed suicide in abject misery. Suetonius tells us that *"Nero stabbed himself in the throat"* and that *"in the widespread rejoicing, citizens ran through the city wearing caps of liberty."*[9]

So let's trust the Lord to be our Avenger, and make room for his wrath when we are wronged and persecuted. When we apply the Gospel to our lives by blessing those who persecute us, we overcome their evil through our message of greater good.

---

[9] Suetonius, *The Life of Nero* (49 and 57).

Live It Towards Caesar (13:1–7)

Everyone must submit himself to the governing authorities, for there is no authority except that which God has established.

(Romans 13:1)

Jesus is Lord and Caesar is not, so is the Gospel a call to political revolution? The fact that this question is so surprising to most of us is simply proof of how far from Paul's message we have strayed. We treat *"Jesus is Lord"* as a spiritual pleasantry, while both his disciples and his enemies understood that it meant far more.[1] How could the Christians at Rome continue to live under Caesar in light of the fact that Jesus is the new King in town? Paul answers their question at the start of chapter 13, because if the Gospel doesn't change our politics we haven't understood it.

In verses 1–6, Paul insists that *the Gospel makes Christians the most loyal of subjects.* Unlike unbelievers, who submit to their rulers out of fear, the Gospel teaches us to submit to them out of conscience towards God. It tells us that even the Emperor Nero's reign did not begin with his mother's murder of Claudius. It began with the Lord, who planned his accession and established him as emperor to be *"God's servant to do you good"*. Astonishingly, since Nero would order Paul's beheading, Paul tells the Romans that Nero only *"bears the sword"* because God entrusted it to his hand.[2] Perhaps inspired by David's

---

[1] Luke 23:1–2; John 19:12–16; Acts 1:6.

[2] Partly for this reason, supporters of capital punishment use this as a key verse.

refusal to lay a hand on King Saul because he was the Lord's anointed ruler,[3] Paul tells his readers to honour their rulers and be more loyal to them than any of their unbelieving courtiers. Paul's fellow martyr, Peter, gave similar instructions: *"Submit yourselves for the Lord's sake to every authority instituted among men: whether to the king, as the supreme authority, or to governors... Fear God, honour the king."*[4]

In verse 7, Paul adds that *the Gospel makes Christians the most courageous of subjects*. They pay their rulers honour and taxes and everything else that they are owed, but they are not afraid to point out where that obligation ends.[5] The Hebrew midwives refused Pharaoh's wicked command in Exodus 1:15–21. Peter did the same in Acts 4:19 and 5:29 when he saw rulers overstepping their God-given authority: *"Judge for yourselves whether it is right in God's sight to obey you rather than God... We must obey God rather than men!"* The Romans did as Paul commanded and were able to tell Caesar that *"We pray without ceasing for all our emperors. We pray for long life, for security to the empire, for protection to the imperial house, for brave armies, a faithful senate, a virtuous people, the world at rest, whatever an emperor would wish...but we refuse to swear by the Caesars as gods."*[6]

How you apply these two principles to the politics of your nation will vary depending on the country you live in. But to help you do so, let me tell you about three people who have tried to apply them under difficult conditions in Germany.

We have already seen that Martin Luther loved the book of Romans, so he was thrown hard against these verses when the Holy Roman Emperor and the Pope commanded him to stop preaching its message. When they put him on trial at the Diet

---

[3] 1 Samuel 24:6–15; 26:9–11; 2 Samuel 1:14–16.

[4] 1 Peter 2:13–17.

[5] Paul uses two Greek words, which in modern terms refer to *direct income tax* and *indirect sales tax*.

[6] Tertullian in c.197 AD in his *Apology* (chapters 30 and 32).

of Worms in 1521, he remembered verse 7 and told his rulers that *"Unless I am convicted by Scripture and plain reason – I do not accept the authority of popes and councils, for they have contradicted each other – my conscience is captive to the Word of God. I cannot and I will not recant anything, for to go against conscience is neither right nor safe. Here I stand. I cannot do otherwise. God help me."*[7]

Four years later, however, Martin Luther panicked. The German peasants had rebelled against the princes who had power to undo the Reformation and restore the Church to Rome. He grasped at the fact that Pilate found Jesus innocent of rebellion when he told him that *"My kingdom is not of this world"*, and used it to separate the world into two distinct realms: the spiritual Church and the secular State.[8] So long as rulers didn't meddle in spiritual affairs, he taught believers that Romans 13:1–6 meant silent submission towards political injustice. He wrote a pamphlet against the peasants in 1525, arguing that *"Nothing can be more poisonous, hurtful or demonic than a rebel... Fine Christians they are! I think there is not a demon left in hell; they have all gone into the peasants!"*[9]

This was Dietrich Bonhoeffer's view initially, as a Lutheran pastor in early 1930s Germany. Yet he came to believe that this Christian withdrawal from the political arena was effectively condoning Adolf Hitler. He led the Christian opposition to the Nazi regime, arguing that the Church must not just *"bandage the victims under the wheel, but jam a spoke in the wheel itself"*. He submitted to Hitler's government but became its most vocal critic. This led to his being hanged naked, using piano wire, in

---

[7] Roland Bainton, *Here I Stand: A Life of Martin Luther* (1950).

[8] John 18:33–38; Luke 23:3–4. Luther's "doctrine of two kingdoms" and of the "divine right of rulers" dominated Christian thought well into the nineteenth century.

[9] Luther carefully entitled the pamphlet *Against the Rioting Peasants*, but his printers changed the title without his permission to *Against the Murderous, Thieving Hordes of Peasants*.

one of the Nazi concentration camps in the last days of the war. The medic who witnessed his death testified later that *"In the almost fifty years that I worked as a doctor, I have hardly ever seen a man die so entirely submissive to the will of God."*[10]

Christian Fuehrer drew inspiration from Bonhoeffer as pastor of the St Nicholas Church in Leipzig, East Germany. He was sickened by the injustice of his Communist rulers, and decided to apply Paul's teaching in Romans 13. He refused to treat secular politics as a no-go area for Christians, and in 1982 started "peace prayers" every Monday evening at his church. For seven years he led ever-growing numbers of East Germans in prayer that the Lord would save their land. Finally, on Monday 9th October 1989, a crowd of 70,000 gathered at his church to demand that the injustice end. Their placards bore Christian Fuehrer's message of *"No Violence!"* and, as the protest quickly spread to other cities, one month later the Berlin Wall came down. One protester was asked who had planned this revolution, and replied that *"There was only one leadership: Monday, 5pm, St Nicholas Church."* Horst Sindermann, the former Prime Minister of East Germany, agreed: *"We were prepared for everything. But not for candles and prayers."*[11]

The political situations around the world are very different, but my prayer is that these three examples will help you to apply these seven verses to your own. Paul tells us in his first six verses that the Gospel means we are to be more loyal to our rulers than anyone else in the land. Then he tells us in his seventh verse that we must also be courageous enough to point it out whenever they overstep the line. If we render to Caesar what is Caesar's, while remembering he is *"God's servant to do you good"*, then we can be the best of citizens because Jesus is the new King in town.

[10] See Eric Metaxas, *Bonhoeffer: Pastor, Martyr, Prophet, Spy* (2010).

[11] See Mike Dennis, *The Rise and Fall of the German Democratic Republic, 1945–1990* (2000).

Live It Towards Sin
(13:8–14)

Clothe yourselves with the Lord Jesus Christ, and do not think about how to gratify the desires of the sinful nature.

(Romans 13:14)

The British government was faced with a terrible dilemma. France had fallen to the Nazis with very little fight, and its navy was about to fall into German hands. The most senior French naval officer was the descendant of a sailor who had been killed by the British at Trafalgar, so he refused to hand his battleships to the British to fight on. If Prime Minister Winston Churchill allowed the vessels to remain in harbour, very soon they would be refitted under the German ensign, but to sink them would mean opening fire on sailors who were friends and allies. When their final ultimatum was rejected, the British fleet sailed into Mers-el-Kébir harbour and opened fire. Within fifteen minutes the French fleet was destroyed.

Winston Churchill looked back on that evening as a turning point in the war:

The elimination of the French Navy as an important factor almost at a single stroke by violent action produced a profound impression in every country. Here was this Britain which so many had counted down and out, which strangers had supposed to be quivering on the brink of surrender to the mighty power arrayed against her, striking ruthlessly at her dearest friends of yesterday and

*securing for a while to herself the undisputed command
of the sea. It was made plain that the British War Cabinet
feared nothing and would stop at nothing… Henceforth
there was no more talk about Britain giving in. The only
question was, would she be invaded and conquered?*[1]

As Paul turns to apply the Gospel to how we act towards sin,
he tells us to be as ruthless as Winston Churchill and his navy.
He calls us to commit a *decisive act of war*, waking up to the
spiritual "night time" and the battle raging for our souls. He fills
verses 8–14 with words and phrases that point us back to his
teaching on sanctification in chapters 6–8.[2] Just as he told us
in 6:11 to *"count yourselves dead to sin but alive to God in Christ
Jesus"*, so he tells us now to *"put aside the deeds of darkness…
put on the armour of light…clothe yourselves with the Lord Jesus
Christ."* These three commands are all "aorists", which speak
of decisive one-off actions. In view of the Gospel, Paul tells us
we need to be as ruthless with our cherished sins as Winston
Churchill was in war.

Note that this also means that we must positively make
a *decisive act of commitment*. Only one of those aorists is
about declaring war on sin. The other two are about giving
ourselves completely to the Lord. One of the main proofs of true
conversion is our willingness to commit ourselves entirely to
our new King's way of life. This doesn't mean returning to the
"dos" and "don'ts" of Moses' Law, which Paul lists in verse 9. He
picks out Leviticus 19:18 – *"Love your neighbour as yourself"* –
as Law enough for anyone who follows Christ.[3] Paul described

---

[1] Winston Churchill in volume two of his World War Two memoirs, *Their Finest Hour* (1949).

[2] For example, although translators do not always faithfully reflect this, the word *hopla*, or *weapons*, is used twice in 6:13 and once in 13:12.

[3] The New Testament also teaches that love is the fulfilment of Moses' Law in Matthew 22:35–40; Galatians 5:13–14; 6:2; 1 Timothy 1:5; James 2:8; 1 Peter 4:8; 1 John 3:23.

Jesus as the end of the Law in 10:4, so St Augustine was right to say that we can *"Love and do whatever you like... If love is the root within, nothing but good can spring out of that root."*[4] This radical freedom is simply the natural conclusion of Paul's Gospel in chapters 1–11, but it is worth us clarifying what this love of Jesus looks like.

The love that characterizes true Christian lifestyle is not weak. Paul told us back in 12:9 that sincere love means hating what is evil. Paul lists wicked "night-time" deeds in a way that tricks his readers in order to prepare them for chapter 14. He gets them nodding about the seriousness of orgies, drunkenness, sexual immorality and debauchery, then commands them to display a similar hatred towards *dissension* and *jealousy* – the very issues at the forefront of the conflict between the returning Jewish Christians and the Gentiles they had left behind. Paul tells us that we need to torpedo even cherished sins, because these former friends have become enemy vessels now that there is a new King in our lives. The call to love does not mean becoming soft on sin. It is a call to hate wickedness as implacably as Jesus does.[5]

The love that characterizes true Christian lifestyle is not man-made. Don't misunderstand Paul's command in verse 14 to clothe ourselves with Jesus. It may sound like something we need to do to ourselves, but Paul expects us to know Scripture well enough to understand his meaning. The word he uses is the Greek word that described Old Testament warriors being *clothed with the Holy Spirit* in Judges 6:34, 1 Chronicles 12:18 and 2 Chronicles 24:20. It is the same word that Jesus used in Luke 24:49 when he told his disciples to *"stay in the city until you have been clothed with power from on high."* It is the word Paul used in Galatians 3:27 to describe Christians being filled

---

[4] Augustine of Hippo's *Seventh Sermon on 1 John*, preached in the early fifth century.

[5] Hebrews 1:8–9, quoting Psalm 45:6–7, tells us Jesus' hatred of wickedness greatly pleased his Father.

with the Holy Spirit, and he uses it again here in verse 14 to tell the Romans to do the same. *"God has poured out his love into our hearts by the Holy Spirit"* because *"it is God who works in you to will and to act according to his good purpose."*[6] Paul warns us not to forget the message of chapters 6–8. We can never produce godly character through grit and New Year's resolutions. We must ask the Lord to fill us with his Spirit and change us from the inside out.

The love that characterizes true Christian lifestyle is not produced in a day. If you hoped that you could be made perfect from day one, Paul tells you to think again. You were justified – *declared* righteous – the moment you were converted, but you are sanctified – *made* righteous – as you apply the Gospel to your life every day. Although Paul uses three "aorist" commands in verses 12 and 14 to demand we make a decisive, one-off declaration of war against sin, he finishes verse 14 with a "present imperative", which means literally *"do not go on thinking about how to gratify the desires of the sinful nature."* Winston Churchill made a decisive commitment to fight tooth and nail when he sent his ships into Mers-el-Kébir harbour, but it took four more years of daily resolve before the war was finally won.

So count your old life dead once and for all, and offer your life to the Lord from this day forward. Ask him to fill you with his Holy Spirit to fight the war you have declared. Make no mistake: Those who do not deal ruthlessly with sin have not yet grasped the Gospel, but God's Spirit will sanctify you every day if you torpedo your old life and tell sin you have joined Christ's war.

---

[6] Romans 5:5; Philippians 2:13. See also Galatians 5:22–25.

Live It When You Disagree
(14:1–15:13)

Who are you to judge someone else's servant? To his own master he stands or falls.

(Romans 14:4)

In 167 BC, King Antiochus IV Epiphanes launched a fierce persecution against the Jews in Jerusalem. He forced them to contravene Moses' Law, and was amazed at their determination to die rather than do so. Eleazar, a ninety-year-old teacher of the law, chose to be beaten to death rather than obey the king's command. *"It is clear to the Lord in his holy knowledge,"* he cried. *"I am glad to suffer these things because I fear him."* A mother and her seven sons refused the same command, so Antiochus scalped them, amputated their tongues, hands and feet, and finished them off by frying what was left of them in pans. *"The King of the universe will raise us up to an everlasting renewal of life, because we have died for his laws,"* one of them declared before he lost his tongue.[1] So what exactly was this terrible crime which they would rather be tortured for than commit? King Antiochus was trying to force his Jewish subjects to eat pork.

It's important that we understand the strength of feeling which the Jewish Christians in Rome still felt towards the detail of Moses' Law. Otherwise, we will find it hard to grasp why Paul devotes almost half of his section of application of the Gospel to their conflict with the pork-eating Gentile Christians. Unless we grasp that they cherished their food laws so dearly that Peter

---

[1] 2 Maccabees 6:18–30 and 7:1–42 in the Old Testament Apocrypha.

argued with the Lord to defend them in Acts 10:14, and that they viewed breaking them as seriously in Acts 15:29 as committing sexual immorality, we cannot understand these verses. The Jewish Christians despised the half-converted Gentile Christians they found leading their old church when Nero finally allowed them back to Rome.

But this judgmental attitude was by no means one-way. The Gentile Christians had been brought up in a culture that despised the Jews, and they considered the squeamish returnees to be half-converted too. Couldn't they see that Jesus' death and resurrection had superseded the detail of Moses' Law? They would not share church leadership with the returning Jewish Christians if it meant changing its culture to be more like the city's synagogues. The Christian Jews and Gentiles were at loggerheads in the Roman church. It was time for Paul to make his final application of the Gospel.

He tells the Jews to accept the fact that they are carrying cultural baggage which is inessential to the Christian faith. The more their faith grows in the new King Jesus, the more they will surrender to his teaching that all foods are clean.[2] In the meantime, they can observe their Jewish food laws and feast days, but they must not foist them on the Gentiles who grasp the Gospel better than themselves.

At the same time, Paul tells the Gentiles that their disregard for Jewish sensibilities is itself a denial of the Gospel. Each believer is God's servant (14:4) who is judged by God alone (14:10), and he will judge them based on whether or not they act out of *good conscience* and *sincere faith* (14:14 and 23). If a Jew grasps with the Gentiles that Jesus is the end of the Law, eating with strong faith and a well-trained conscience, his action is not sin. But if he lets peer pressure goad him into

---

[2] Romans 14:14, 20 echo Mark 7:18–23. Although Romans 14:1–15:13 has similarities with 1 Corinthians 8:1–11:1, the crunch issue here is "unclean" meat as opposed to meat sacrificed to idols in 1 Corinthians.

eating what he thinks is wrong, his action is a sinful violation of his conscience.

Let me try to put this in a modern context, for there are still plenty of *"disputable matters"* like the ones Paul mentions in 14:1. When I was a young Christian, I misunderstood Acts 15:29. I thought it was a command for Christians not to consume blood out of reverence for the cross. I lived in France, where most beef is eaten rare, and then in England where the traditional breakfast includes black pudding, which is made from pig's blood (it's nicer than it sounds!). Paul is saying that if I had eaten rare beef or black pudding in those early days, I would actually have been sinning against the Lord. If you had laughed at my misunderstanding and goaded me into eating it against my conscience, then Paul is saying that you would have been sinning as well. Of course, later I came to understand that Acts 15:29 was a first-century concession to help Jewish Christians cope with the salvation of the Gentiles. My conscience and faith in the Gospel are now mature enough to thank God for his provision of rare beef and black pudding, so Paul says I can eat them now without sinning.

Another example. Some years ago, I watched the Brad Pitt movie, *Fight Club*. I found it so disturbing that I promised the Lord as I went to sleep that I would not watch it again. Nowadays, I'm quite convinced that it is no worse than many other films, but the point is that for *me* it would be a sin to watch it. I still take my old prayer seriously and could not watch it out of faith. We haven't space to apply these verses to alcohol, parties, fashion, music and how we observe Sundays, but I think you have already got the picture. Paul is telling us that this is how to preserve unity in the church wherever Scripture is silent and people hold different positions over side issues. Those with strong faith should not abuse their freedom by goading those with weaker faith to copy them (14:13, 15 and 22). In the world, the strong dominate the weak. Through the Gospel, the Church is a place where the weak are nurtured by the strong.

Paul therefore tells the Gentiles to express more grace towards the returning Jewish Christians. They are still entitled to honour their ethnic Jewish culture,[3] and so must the Gentiles if they are to fulfil Jesus' desire to use them to save many more Jews (15:8).[4] Given time, the Jews will no doubt grasp their Christian freedom, but until then the Gentiles should hold their tongues and give them all the time they need (14:22).[5]

If they do so, Paul promises that peace will reign in their divided church. The Jews will love them for their gracious tactfulness, and they will learn to love the Jews for their passion for holiness and obedience to their consciences. Together, they will please the Lord and glorify him as the new King in town. As they apply the Gospel within their multiracial church, it will be noticed by the world. Paul promises in 15:5–6 that God will *"give you a spirit of unity among yourselves as you follow Christ Jesus, so that with one heart and mouth you may glorify the God and Father of our Lord Jesus Christ"*.

Jesus wants to foster that same unity in our own churches too, so that our divided world will see the glory of the Gospel in us, his loving Body.

---

[3] Paul fought hard to secure Gentiles their spiritual freedom, but he chose to celebrate his Jewish culture personally in Acts 16:3; 18:18; 20:16; 21:26. See also Acts 21:20.

[4] Paul ends this passage in 15:8–13 with a reminder that Jesus is saving Gentiles in order to save Jews.

[5] This verse also applies to church leaders! We are to teach people to think disputed issues through for themselves, rather than insisting they adhere to our own particular conclusion. The German theologian Peter Meiderlin expressed this in 1626 as: *"In essentials, unity; in non-essentials, liberty; in all things, charity."*

Debt Repayment (15:1)

*We who are strong ought to bear with the failings of
the weak and not to please ourselves.*

(Romans 15:1)

Ancient Rome had a complex welfare system. Reliance on
patronage was as old as the city itself. The poor looked to rich
plebeians, who looked to the equestrians, who looked to the
senators, who looked to the emperor in turn. Patrons gave their
clients money, food, advancement and protection, which obliged
clients to serve at their every beck and call. Almost everyone in
Rome had obligations towards somebody, which is why some
historians refer to patronage as a moderate form of slavery.[1]
Christopher Francese observes that *"More democratic societies
find this sort of semi-permanent dependency uncomfortable."*[2] But,
more to the point, so did the Roman citizen Paul. That's why he
ended his seven verses on submission to the government with
a command in 13:8 to *"Let no debt remain outstanding, except
the continuing debt to love one another."* Paul wants to take a
moment to talk to us about the true debt we owe in light of our
salvation.

First, Paul tells us *we are indebted to the Lord*. He isn't just
the new King in town. He is the new and better Patron too. If
Roman clients had to present themselves before their patrons
each morning to ask how they could serve them, then Christians
can be no less eager to start each day by offering themselves

---

[1] Interestingly, in the light of 6:15–23, many freedmen were so dependent on
their former masters as patrons that their experience of freedom was little
better than their former lives as slaves.

[2] Christopher Francese, *Ancient Rome in So Many Words* (2007).

to the Lord. *"We have an obligation,"* Paul warned back in 8:12, using the same word for *debt* which described the patron–client links throughout the city. It is not to the sinful nature, the old patron who abused us, but to the Spirit and to turn our back on sin to walk with him every day.

Second, Paul tells us *we are indebted to the Church.* He tells us literally here in 15:1 that *"we who are strong have an obligation to bear with the failings of the weak and not to please ourselves."* The Gentile and Jewish Romans were in need of that message, but it hasn't become any less important for us today. Two of the top three reasons routinely given in surveys of Christians who no longer attend a local church are *"I don't need to go to church to be a Christian"* and *"I have other things I prefer doing"*. It seems the Romans weren't the only ones who attempted to confess Jesus as Lord while carrying on pleasing themselves. That's why Paul insisted so strongly in 13:8 that confessing Jesus as Lord means taking on a *"continuing debt to love one another"*. Unlike Roman clients, who served the strong in the hope of gifts and favour in return, Christians serve the weak out of gratitude for the gifts and favour they have already received through the Gospel.[3]

Third, Paul tells us *we are indebted to our nation.* Churches are not to be parasites, using their cities merely as a platform to increase the size of their tribe. They are to obey the command of Jeremiah 29:7 to *"Seek the peace and prosperity of the city to which I have carried you... Pray to the Lord for it, because if it prospers, you too will prosper."* They are to behave like the first believers in Samaria, who produced *"great joy in that city"* in Acts 8:8. Paul says the Gospel means the Romans must not turn their backs on their city, even when its government tries to kill them. They must do as he commanded in 13:7, and *"Give everyone what you owe him: If you owe taxes, pay taxes; if revenue, then*

---

[3] See also 1 Corinthians 12:24. This was as counter-cultural for the Romans as it is for us today.

revenue; if respect, then respect; if honour, then honour." After all, if King Jesus is truly our new Patron, we need to represent him in our cities as well as Roman clients did their own.

Fourth, Paul tells us *we are indebted to unbelievers*. He began his letter in 1:14–15 by explaining literally that the Gospel means *"I am in debt both to Greeks and to non-Greeks, both to the wise and the foolish. That is why I am so eager to preach the gospel also to you who are at Rome."* Back in 2 Kings 7, when the city of Samaria was starving under siege, four lepers went to beg food from the enemy and found the camp deserted because God had worked deliverance for his People. For a while, they ate and drank and revelled in their treasures, but soon they realized that *"We're not doing right. This is a day of good news and we are keeping it to ourselves. If we wait until daylight, punishment will overtake us. Let's go at once and report this."* Paul tells the Romans that their city is under spiritual siege, and that they owe it to their neighbours to tell them that the Lord has worked another mighty deliverance. Later on in chapter 15, he will add that they must also help him to move west with the Gospel to the unreached cities of Spain and Gaul.

Fifth, and perhaps surprisingly, Paul tells us *we are indebted to the Jews*. Perhaps this shouldn't surprise us in the light of chapters 1–11, but Paul tells us in 15:27 that when Christians invest money in evangelism and mercy ministry among the Jews, *"they owe it to them. For if the Gentiles have shared in the Jews' spiritual blessings, they owe it to the Jews to share with them their material blessings."* Paul does not miss another chance to reiterate to his readers that God still loves Israel, and that he still has a plan to save the Jews through Gentile Christians. As he put it in 1:16, our obligation with the Gospel is *"first for the Jew, then for the Gentile."*

Therefore it doesn't appear that Paul is forbidding his Roman readers to serve human patrons, any more than he is forbidding them to honour Caesar's rule. What he means is simply that the Gospel gives us all a greater Patron, who demands we repay the great debt we owe to him, to his Church, to our nation, to unbelievers and to the Jews. Paul encourages us as we do so by ending this third section of Romans with a wonderful promise to all of Jesus' clients.

Every Roman client hoped to receive enough favours to gather clients of their own. Paul therefore promises in 15:13 that when we follow our new Patron, he will *"fill you with all joy and peace as you trust in him, so that you may overflow with hope by the power of the Holy Spirit."* Discharging our debt in the light of the Gospel will never result in us living impoverished lives. The Lord promises to give us all we need as his clients, so that we can respond to our fivefold debt even more.

Julius Caesar was one of Rome's mightiest patrons, and claimed *"One cannot abandon one's clients without incurring the greatest disgrace."*[4] Therefore we can rest assured that our own great Patron will never fail us, for we are the clients of Jesus Christ the Lord.

---

[4] Aulus Gellius, *Attic Nights* (5.13), quoting from Caesar defending some of his clients in court.

Christian Means Like Christ (15:1–13)

Accept one another, then, just as Christ accepted you, in order to bring praise to God.

(Romans 15:7)

Paul is about to finish his third section of practical Gospel application. He only needed three and a half chapters – less than a third of what it took him to explain the Gospel in Romans 1–11 – because when we lay good Gospel foundations for believers, we don't have to shout at them to make them want to live that Gospel out. Paul expects his readers to be eager to live with passion for their new King, so he ends this section with thirteen verses which serve as a closing summary. Whatever else you may forget from Paul's third section, don't forget this: he says being a Christian means imitating Christ.

In verses 1–3, Paul tells us that being a Christian means *loving other people like Jesus*. That would put an end to the conflict within the church at Rome, and it will also resolve whatever conflicts harm our own. If at the heart of Jesus' ministry was his willingness to fulfil the Messianic prophecy in Psalm 69:9 – *"The insults of those who insult you have fallen on me"* – then how can we, his followers, live to please ourselves any longer? On an individual level, confessing Jesus as Lord means bearing with the weak and preferring other people in their need. On a corporate level, the other half of that verse is Jesus' cry that *"Zeal for your house consumes me"*.[1] If Jesus was insulted on behalf of the Father because he loves his People (the word for *you* in

---

[1] John 2:17 quotes this part of the verse and applies it to Jesus.

Psalm 69:9 is singular), we cannot complain when we are also wronged if it allows him to continue to love them through us. If you have been wounded by Christians or even by your church, Paul tells you to apply the Gospel by keeping on loving them like Jesus.

In verse 4, Paul tells us that being a Christian means *loving Scripture like Jesus*. Jesus studied Deuteronomy and it prepared him for his temptation in the desert, where he quoted lessons from Israel's time in the desert each time the Devil came to tempt him. He studied the prophecies in the Psalms and they prepared him for the cross, where he buoyed his spirit in death by quoting its promises about the Messiah.[2] We must not therefore neglect the Scriptures which our King prized so dearly. Paul tells us that *"everything that was written in the past was written to teach us, so that through endurance and the encouragement of the Scriptures we might have hope."* It's not that following Jesus means that we need to add Bible reading to our to-do lists. It's that Christian means like Christ, and so we love the Word of God like him.

In verses 5 and 6, Paul tells us that being a Christian means *loving the Church like Jesus*. Paul repeats that God's plan is to save a People who follow Christ together, and that the endurance and encouragement which come from reading Scripture in verse 4 will always lead us to a similar passion for his plan. God wants to give us *"a spirit of unity"* which turns us from a collection of individuals into his Son's Body on the earth. No person can glorify God as much on their own as they can as part of a united, multiracial congregation.[3] When we praise the Lord *"with one heart and mouth"*, we are truly Jesus' Body and fulfil God's plan as Paul described it in chapters 9–11.

In verse 7, Paul tells us that being a Christian means *loving the Gospel like Jesus*. It means looking at people who offend us and

[2] See Jesus' quotations in Matthew 4:4, 7, 10, as well as in Matthew 21:16; 21:42; 22:44; 23:39; 27:46; Luke 23:46; John 13:18; 15:25.

[3] This is why Paul addresses the Jewish and Gentile Christians as *brothers* together in 15:14, 30 and 16:17.

annoy us, and loving them with the same mercy Jesus showed to us. Unlike the Parable of the Unmerciful Servant in Matthew 18:21–35, we are to imitate the way that Jesus accepted us, and to bring God praise by welcoming outcasts and sinners as new-found friends. We are not to reject even the vilest unbeliever because of their pre-conversion sin, and we are not to reject one another because of ongoing post-conversion weaknesses and failure. If we fail to extend God's grace towards people who don't deserve it, then Paul tells us we haven't grasped God's grace towards ourselves.

In verses 8–12, Paul tells us that being a Christian means *loving God's mission like Jesus*. He reiterates the message of Romans 9–11 through four Old Testament quotations. The first reminds us that 2 Samuel 22:50 and Psalm 18:49 promised that the Messiah would make God's glory known to the Gentiles. He backs this up with yet another quotation from Moses' song about jealous Israel in Deuteronomy 32:43, and also by quoting from Psalm 117:1. This paves the way for a final, climactic quotation from Isaiah 11:10, which promised the Messiah would not just *conquer* the nations, but also be the object of their *hope*.[4] Paul intends to convince us through this cross-section of quotations from the Law, the History, the Psalms and the Prophets that God's desire to save the Gentiles was always at the heart of the Old Testament.[5] His grace towards the pork-eating Gentiles should not offend the Jewish Christians at Rome. It should cause them to rejoice and to commit themselves afresh to playing their role in his mission.

In verse 13, Paul rounds off his application of the Gospel with a call to Jew and Gentile to let God fill them with his *hope*, his *joy*, his *peace* and his *power*. The Gentiles should trust in Jesus, just as Isaiah prophesied, and the Jews should trust that

---

[4] Jesse was the father of King David, so the *"Root of Jesse"* was an Old Testament name for the Messiah.

[5] Jesus summarizes the entire Old Testament in the same way in Luke 24:44–49. See also Ephesians 2:15–20.

each new convert from the nations was a worker whose hope could overflow back to their nation by the power of the Holy Spirit. As Paul reminds us in verses 8 and 9, Jesus came as the servant of the Jews to display God's faithfulness to Israel, and he continues to do so by spreading mercy to the Gentiles so that the Messiah-rejecting Jews will eventually grow jealous and come back en masse to receive their salvation.

The Gospel affects every area of life, resolving the present conflict in the church at Rome and preparing them for greater conflict when Nero's persecution began. Since *Christian* means a person who is becoming more like Christ, Paul tells us to imitate Jesus in everything we do. Then those around us will not fail to see that there's a new King in town.

Romans 15:14–16:27

The New King Is Advancing

The Western Front
(15:14–16:27)

Since I have been longing for many years to see you,
I plan to do so when I go to Spain. I hope to visit you
while passing through and to have you assist me on
my journey there.

(Romans 15:23–24)

Rome. The mother city. All roads led there because that's where everybody wanted to be. Its streets were crowded, its housing oversubscribed, and it stood head and shoulders above every other city. Its population of over a million made it history's largest city until the growth of London in the nineteenth century. As a result, the Roman Christians can't have been the least bit surprised when Paul wrote in 1:13 and 15:23 that *"I have been longing for many years to see you."* Of course the apostle wanted to come to the wealthiest, most influential, most exciting city in the world. But they must have been surprised by what Paul went on to say in the rest of section four of Romans.

For a start, he told them that the reason for his delay was that he had been busy preaching the Gospel *"from Jerusalem all the way round to Illyricum"*. Although the journey from Judea to modern-day Croatia took in major cities such as Ephesus and Corinth, it also meant that Paul had been prioritizing backwater villages such as Lystra instead of rushing on to Rome. Imagine a news report about the president of the United States calling off a trade summit with the Chinese in Beijing in order to discuss rising mineral water prices with the prime minister of

Andorra. That's how the Romans must have felt when they read that Paul's focus was decidedly different from their own. Even now, he told them that he would not sail to Rome from Corinth because he wanted to deliver a special offering from the Greeks and Macedonians to the struggling church in Jerusalem.[1]

As they read on, their eyes must have widened still further. Paul tells them that he has not merely been detained against his wishes, as they might have assumed from 1:13. He was obeying one of the key verses which the Lord had placed on his life. In the same passage that he quoted from in 10:15 to say that our *"beautiful feet"* carry on Jesus' mission, it also reads in Isaiah 52:15 that *"Those who were not told about him will see, and those who have not heard will understand."*[2] Paul tells the Romans that God spoke to him through this chapter soon after his conversion, and gave him an *"ambition to preach the gospel where Christ was not known, so that I would not be building on someone else's foundation"*. Although he pointed out in 10:14 that this meant him going to the pagans to preach Christ to them, they still can't have been prepared for what he tells them now. He is eager to come to Rome, but not as a final destination. He simply wants to use them as a sending base for planting churches in Spain and the rest of the unreached Western Mediterranean!

Paul's attitude must have shocked the Roman Christians who thought they lived at the centre of the world, but it is largely ignored by most modern students of the book of Romans. Most commentaries devote the bulk of their attention to Paul's teaching on the Gospel in chapters 1–11, and the better ones also focus on his application of the Gospel in 12:1–15:13. Then they tend to rattle very quickly through Paul's fourth section as

---

[1] The Christians in Jerusalem lived in a poorer region of the Empire, but Hebrews 10:34 tells us their poverty was exacerbated by the Jewish authorities confiscating their goods because they were believers.

[2] Paul also applies prophecies about Jesus' own mission to himself in Acts 13:46–47. Jesus does the same in Revelation 2:26–27, telling us that he fulfils these promises through his missionary People.

little more than a list of travel plans and personal greetings. For Paul, however, this final section is the climax of his letter. It is the natural outworking of all the chapters which go before.

Paul tells the Romans in 15:22 that he has not yet come to Rome because he needed to plant churches in the unreached cities of Cyprus, Asia Minor, Macedonia and Greece. They might despise those lands for being inhabited not just by Roman citizens and educated Greeks but by barbarians as well, but he has already told them literally in 1:14 that *"I am in debt both to Greeks and barbarians, both to the wise and the foolish."* After nine years of missionary journeys, he can now finally announce in 15:23 that *"there is no more place for me to work in these regions"*,[3] but this does not mean that he intends to settle down as a celebrity church leader in Rome. He tells them in 15:24 that there is already a church in their city, so he must take the Gospel to the Western Mediterranean where the Spaniards and other barbarians have yet to hear it.[4] He has longed for years to preach the Gospel in Rome, but as a means to an end, not as an end in itself. He is convinced in 15:14 that they are a missionary congregation who can reach their city without his long-term help. What he wants is to catch them up in what the Gospel means for unreached nations, and to yield better fruit in Spain and southern Gaul by enlisting them onto his team.

So don't expect this fourth section of Romans to be a wind down from the Gospel heights of sections one and two, and from the Gospel application of section three. Paul wants to catch you up, as he did the Romans, in the greatness of God's plan, and to make you more than a student and practitioner of the Gospel. He wants to enlist you in Jesus' missionary army, as you see him open up a Western Front and declare that the new King is advancing.

---

[3] 2 Corinthians 10:14–16 tells us that Paul was in Corinth to resolve issues so as to be free to head west.

[4] These were *barbarians* too. Cicero famously called Sardinia *"a land of barbarians"*, and Luke calls the Maltese islanders barbarians in Acts 28:2, 4.

In a world where 340 million people are still without the Bible in their own language;[5] where over 40 per cent of people groups are considered unreached and a further 20 per cent are considered only nominally reached; where several of those people groups are over 50 million strong; and where 2.7 billion individuals have no indigenous church to tell them the Good News of Jesus[6] we need to listen to what Paul says.

Because if Jesus truly is the new King in town; if there truly is no salvation outside of him; if God's plan truly is to save people from every tribe and tongue, making the Jews so jealous that they also believe in his Son, then we must turn our Romes from comfy homes into springboards for world mission. We must carry on the task that Paul began.

How can they call on the one they have not believed in? How can they believe in the one of whom they have not heard? Paul's answer is to fire a starting pistol through this final section and to call us to play our own part in God's great plan. The book of Romans ends with a cry to rally the nations of the world to Jesus. Paul announces in his fourth section that the new King is advancing.

---

[5] 2011 data from the website of Wycliffe Bible Translators.

[6] These other figures are all 2011 data from the website of the Joshua Project.

Missionaries Need the Gospel Too (15:14–18)

...because of the grace God gave me to be a minister of Christ Jesus to the Gentiles...

(Romans 15:15–16)

Thanks for the pep talk, but let's get real. It's one thing for you to tell me that Paul opened up a Western Front, but quite another thing to tell me that I can carry on the battle too. I find it hard enough to share the Gospel with the people from next door!

If that's how you are tempted to respond to section four of Romans, don't switch off yet because Paul has anticipated your objection. He begins section four by explaining how he was able to win people to Christ and plant churches in each city. If you have ever felt that God's missionary call is meant for someone more talented than yourself, you will find his explanation very encouraging indeed.

The reason for Paul's missionary success was *not his own innate ability*. He was writing from Corinth, where his enemies sneered that *"His letters are weighty and forceful, but in person he is unimpressive and his speaking amounts to nothing."* He had expected to be a natural evangelist among the Jews because of his background as a Pharisee and persecutor of the Church, but he was so unsuccessful in his early attempts that growth only resumed in the Jerusalem church after the apostles sent him back home to Tarsus![1] Paul refuses to let you opt out of God's mission because you think that he has any ability which is unavailable to you. He confesses in 2 Corinthians 3:5: *"We are*

---

[1] 2 Corinthians 10:10; Acts 9:28–31; 22:17–21.

not competent in ourselves to claim anything for ourselves, but our competence comes from God."

The reason for Paul's missionary success was *not his fervent passion*. When he told the Romans in 10:2 that the Jews *"are zealous for God, but their zeal is not based on knowledge"*, he knew what he was talking about because that was once his own story. Paul didn't lack passion before his conversion to Christ, but ignorance directed his passion towards persecuting the Church. Once converted, his ignorance made him argue with Jesus in a vision at the Temple, insisting adamantly that the best strategy was for God to make him an apostle to the Jews, not to direct his passion towards the Gentiles.[2] Of course knowledge without passion is of little use either, but Paul wants us to understand that his fervent passion was actually a handicap until God harnessed it with clear revelation.

The reason for Paul's missionary success was *not his own charm and connections*. It is tempting to think of Paul as the perfect Gospel-sharer, since he could connect with Jews as a former Pharisee and with pagans as an apostle to the Gentiles.[3] The reality, however, was very different. We find in Acts 21:21–29 and 22:21–22 that the Jews found him far too Gentile, and in Acts 16:19–22 and 19:30–34 that the Gentiles found him far too Jewish. Paul's connections proved useful in all of his travels, but only because the Lord opened doors for him by his grace.

The reason for Paul's missionary success was *not even his diligent prayers*. Although he wears his active prayer life on his sleeve in 1:8–10 and 10:1, he makes it clear in 1:11 that every answer was a *gift of grace* from God.[4] Paul's prayers did not

---

[2] Acts 22:17–21. Romans 11:13 and Galatians 2:8 show us that Paul eventually backed down.

[3] Note the significance of Paul calling himself literally *an apostle* rather than *the apostle* to the Gentiles in Romans 11:13. He goes out of his way to convince us that we are included in God's mission.

[4] The word *charisma* in 1:11 comes from *charis*, meaning *grace*, and means literally a *grace gift*.

wrestle fruitfulness from a reluctant God, as if human effort can ever build a successful Gospel ministry. Prayers no more oblige God to grant us fruitfulness than good works oblige him to grant us forgiveness. No, the secret of Paul's ministry is something that is available to each one of us, no matter how spiritually weak and useless we may feel.

Paul begins this fourth section, which promises that the new King is advancing, with an explanation of how he has been able to win converts and plant churches across the Eastern Mediterranean. *"We received grace,"* he told us in 1:5, and now he adds that he only succeeded *"because of the grace God gave me"*.[5] Paul tells each one of us that we can all advance God's Kingdom, because the Gospel is God's message towards missionaries too.

It may help you to see this message echoed in Luke's account of Paul's ministry in Acts, as one of his closest team members and co-workers. Luke stresses that Paul was a man just like any of us (14:15), and tells us three times that his First Missionary Journey was successful due to *"the grace of God"* and *"all that God had done through them"* (14:26–27; 15:4; 15:12). He says Paul's Second Missionary Journey was similarly successful due *"to the grace of the Lord"* (15:40; 18:27). We may feel tempted to place Paul on a pedestal and to worship him as a hero, but the New Testament refuses to let us do so because this plays into Satan's hands.

Unlike us, Satan never doubts that the new King is advancing. He knows he is defeated and that the nations will all fall one by one to Jesus' rule. He therefore falls back on two strategies to stop us joining in the fight: he tries to convince us that Paul was a Christian superhero, whose example is so inimitable that we might as well not try, or else he tries to convince us that we should strive to become Christian

---

[5] Paul says similar things in Galatians 2:9; Ephesians 3:2, 7; 1 Corinthians 3:10; 15:10; 2 Corinthians 4:1.

superheroes too, and therefore start ministering out of pride. Paul teaches us not to forget that Gospel fruitfulness only comes through relying, like him, on the Lord's power through his grace. As Jesus taught him in a vision before he catapulted him out on mission: *"My grace is sufficient for you, for my power is made perfect in weakness."*[6]

Let's therefore set out on God's mission by preaching the Gospel first and foremost to ourselves. If we are saved by confessing that we cannot justify ourselves but Jesus can, and if we break free from sin by confessing that we cannot sanctify ourselves but Jesus can, then we must share the Gospel and plant new churches by confessing that we cannot minister successfully but Jesus can. When we leave our own strength in the tomb and let God raise us to life with his own strength instead, there is no limit to what we can achieve for the increase of his Kingdom.

When we grasp this, we see that any success which God gives us with the Gospel makes us even more indebted to him. When we confess that our past triumphs are all *"because of the grace God gave me"*, we give him the glory and enable him to trust us with even more. This in turn means we can look to future challenges with the same confidence as Paul in 15:29: *"I know that when I come... I will come in the full measure of the blessing of Christ."*

---

[6] 2 Corinthians 12:9. This could also be translated: *"When you admit your complete weakness, my complete power is given you."*

Gentiles in the Temple
(15:16)

*...a minister of Christ Jesus to the Gentiles with
the priestly duty of proclaiming the gospel of God,
so that the Gentiles might become an offering
acceptable to God.*

(Romans 15:16)

Paul's travel plans were about to change. In a big way.

It is early 57 AD, and Paul tells the Romans that *"by God's will"* he will come to their city in the summer, after travelling to Jerusalem to deliver the gift he has collected from the churches in Greece and Macedonia. In the final eight chapters of Acts we discover what actually happened. Paul was almost lynched at the Temple and was imprisoned by the Roman governor of Judea for two frustrating years. He only got his ticket to Rome by appealing to Caesar, and arrived in February 60 AD as a prisoner in chains. What crime did Paul commit which made the Jewish mob try to kill him? They believed a rumour that he was bringing Gentiles into the Temple. This serves as a window onto just how far the Jewish mindset had strayed from what Paul says was always God's intention for his People.

The Jews thought that being part of God's People simply meant that *God wants to bless us*. This was partly true, but when they treated it as the whole truth it became a lie. When they memorized verses like the one Paul quoted in 9:13 – *"Jacob I loved, but Esau I hated"* – they forgot that two verses later Malachi continued, *"Great is the Lord – even beyond the borders of Israel!"* When they talked about God's promises to the patriarch

Abraham, they remembered his promise in Genesis 12:2 that *"I will bless you"*, but not in 12:3 which added *"and all peoples on earth will be blessed through you."* When they looked back on God forging their nation at Mount Sinai in Exodus 19:6, they stressed *"you will be for me...a holy nation"*, and not the rest of the verse in which the Lord commissioned them as *"a kingdom of priests"*. In fact, the Jews had strayed so far from their calling to be God's missionaries that Josephus tells us they even put up a sign at the Temple telling Gentiles that they would kill them if they entered the inner courtyard.[1]

That's why Paul restates what it means to be part of God's People by telling us in verse 16 that God has called him to be a *priest* to the Gentiles. The word he uses is a sister word to the one used in the Greek Septuagint of Exodus 19:6, as Paul tells his readers that God has always called his People to be a *"kingdom of priests"* representing him to the world. Paul also calls himself a *minister*, using the common Greek word for a priest in one of Rome's pagan temples, because he wants to make sure that both Jewish and Gentile believers understand that churches are missionary or they are not churches at all. God calls his People to say what Moses said to Hobab the Midianite: *"If you come with us, we will share with you all the blessings that the Lord gives us."*[2]

The Jews also thought being part of God's People simply meant trusting that *unbelievers know where we stand*. They kept themselves to themselves on the assumption that non-Jews would ask them if they wanted to know about Yahweh. That's why Paul reminds his readers in verse 16 that one of the main roles of a priest was to preach the Gospel verbally. They had forgotten that Malachi went on to say that *"the lips of a priest ought to preserve knowledge, and from his mouth men should seek*

---

[1] The first-century Jewish historian Josephus in *Antiquities of the Jews* (15.11.5).

[2] Numbers 10:32 (Good News Bible).

instruction – because he is the messenger of the Lord Almighty."[3]
When God told his People that they were a kingdom of priests, he did not mean they were to hide themselves away in their Temple. He meant for them to go to the nations with the news about Yahweh, whose Messiah is the only one who saves. Paul says he has been freshly commissioned to *"the priestly duty of proclaiming the gospel of God."* He says that we share this same commission too.

The Jews also thought being part of God's People simply meant that they could *celebrate the Lord and unbelievers will come.* The power of this lie is that once again it is partly true – after all, who wants to hear about a God who makes his People miserable? – but the activity of a priest should have been a constant reminder that God's People needed to go and gather unbelievers in. Every day, the priests brought grain and animal offerings to the Lord. Somebody needed to harvest the grain and rear the animals, and then somebody had to bring them from the fields to the altar. Therefore when Paul tells his readers in verse 16 that God has called him to make the Gentiles *"an offering acceptable to God"*, he is saying that going out to gather unbelievers to the altar was always at the heart of what it meant to be God's People. That's why the Lord described the revival of his self-centred People in Isaiah 66:19–21 by saying *"they will proclaim my glory among the nations... They will bring them, as the Israelites bring their grain offerings, to the temple of the Lord in ceremonially clean vessels. And I will select some of them also to be priests and Levites."* Now Paul tells his readers it is time to rediscover what it means to be God's People and to bring that prophecy to pass as the Lord's priests to the nations.

Finally, the Jews thought being part of God's People simply meant *pleasing the Lord through worship songs.* They sang psalms in their synagogues and at their Temple, and thought

---

[3] Malachi 2:1–8. See also Leviticus 10:8–11; 2 Chronicles 17:8–9; Nehemiah 8:2–12.

that they had done enough to make God glorified. Paul corrects his readers in verse 17 by reminding them that priestly service as God's missionary People is one of the primary ways in which we worship him. Paul is simply repeating what Jesus taught in Luke 15 when he said that God will gladly leave ninety-nine Christians in a worship meeting in order to go and find a single lost unbeliever. He said that the salvation of sinners triggers *"rejoicing in the presence of the angels of God"*, because quiet witness gives God more pleasure than deafening inward-looking worship. It's not that God doesn't like our worship meetings; it's just that he wants us to treat them as times of spiritual refreshing that recharge us to head back into our daily mission field.[4]

Let's face it. This isn't just a first-century Jewish problem. Churches can easily forget that the new King is advancing. We need to hear Paul's statement that he is one of Jesus' priests to the nations, and see the last eight chapters of Acts as proof of the price he was willing to pay. We need to grasp afresh that God has also commissioned us to be priests to the unbelieving nations of today.[5] Let's express our delight in the first three sections of Romans by accepting the commission described in its fourth. God is recommissioning his People to be his priests to the entire world. Make sure you play your role in his priestly team.

---

[4] This was always God's intention in verses such as Psalm 9:11, 96:8–10 and 105:1.

[5] 1 Peter 2:9 repeats the commission of Exodus 19:6 and applies it to us. He adds that God saved us in order that we might declare his greatness to the world.

Jesus Heals (15:18–19)

...by the power of signs and miracles, through the power of the Spirit... I have fully proclaimed the Gospel of Christ.

(Romans 15:19)

To tell you the truth, I used not to like what Paul says in these two verses. Ironically, it was because I love the rest of his Gospel. I want to share with you frankly some of the problems I had with these verses, because it may help you to move forward in your own journey.

My first concern with Paul's teaching that *"signs and miracles"* are an essential part of our missionary arsenal was caused by the fact that *I love the Bible*. I had been taught that spiritual gifts such as healing were given as "the signs of an apostle" in order to authenticate a small group of Scripture writers in the first century.[1] If modern-day miracle-workers were right and I was wrong, then I was concerned that the authority of the Bible would be compromised. Their teaching might be treated with the same authority as Paul's, in which case we were better off without their signs and miracles.

Eventually, true love for the Bible changed my mind. If Jesus was not restrictive over who could perform miracles in Mark 9:38–40, and if he empowered the muddled Corinthian and Galatian churches to perform miracles, then I probably didn't need to be so protective either. If many Scripture writers performed no recorded miracles (Mark, Luke, James, Jude), and

---

[1] This view originated with an English mistranslation of what 2 Corinthians 12:12 actually says. See *Straight to the Heart of 1 & 2 Corinthians*.

Paul insists elsewhere that such spiritual gifts will endure till Jesus comes again, it was hardly defending the Bible to claim otherwise.[2] Most of all, I accepted Paul's teaching in these two verses that unless he had preached the Gospel including *"the power of signs and miracles"*, he would not *"have fully proclaimed the Gospel of Christ."* I became convinced that if I truly loved the Bible, I would have to submit to what it actually says.

My second concern with Paul's teaching was caused by the fact that *I love Church history*. I lead a church that was planted by one of Charles Spurgeon's students in the midst of a Victorian revival, so I respected Spurgeon's teaching that *"Miracles were the great bell of the universe which was rung in order to call the attention of all men all over the world to the fact that the Gospel feast was spread. We do not need the bell now."*[3] I knew that large portions of Church history had seen very few miracles, so perhaps Paul was teaching something specific to the first century? Yet my love for Church history also showed me examples of signs and wonders throughout the centuries, from Augustine to Francis of Assisi to Martin Luther to the Scottish Covenanters. If I really loved Church history, I needed to stop explaining away the evidence and face up to the fact that Peter promised in Acts 2 that *"signs on the earth below"* are available to *"all whom the Lord our God will call."* Besides, as I looked at the struggling Western Church, I felt we might need the "bell" more than Spurgeon had imagined.

My third concern with Paul's teaching was caused by the fact that *I love seeing people saved*. If Paul really meant us to tell unbelievers that Jesus both forgives sin and heals sickness, then I was worried that when they failed to be healed they would also doubt his more important offer of salvation. I still struggle with this one, but I find the best answer in these two verses

---

[2] For example, in 1 Corinthians 1:7 and 13:8–12. *"Face to face"* refers to Jesus' Second Coming.

[3] Charles Spurgeon preached this in a sermon entitled "Sheep Among Wolves" on 19th August 1877.

where Paul warns us not to be so hasty. In only nine years, Paul had planted thriving churches in the cities of modern-day Cyprus, Turkey, Greece and the Balkans, and he attributes his remarkable feat to *"the power of signs and miracles, through the power of the Spirit"*. If we truly love to see people saved, then we ought to listen to someone with such a great track record.

My fourth concern with Paul's teaching was caused by the fact that *I love honesty*. It didn't seem right, in the light of our setbacks and failures, to claim that God still empowers us to perform the same signs and wonders as Paul. Paul healed everyone who came to him on Malta in Acts 28:9 and raised a young man from the dead in Acts 20:7–12. Nobody I knew healed even a majority of people, and they often failed to heal even relatively minor conditions. On top of this, I was offended by some of the character flaws I saw in many healing evangelists. However, I needed to be more honest about the other passages of Scripture which tell us that the apostles often failed to heal people,[4] and that perhaps one of the reasons why some modern healers display poor character is that Paul tells us in 11:29 that *"God's gifts and his call are irrevocable."*[5]

But most of all, I discovered I needed to be honest with myself. My main concern with Paul's teaching was actually that *I didn't want to look stupid*. If signs and miracles were no longer available today, I could share the Gospel, safe in the knowledge that if people failed to respond then it was their fault, not mine. If Paul really meant, however, that we share an incomplete Gospel unless we fully proclaim it with signs and miracles, then my task was far scarier. I needed to be honest with myself that the Gospel meant Jesus looking foolish on the cross and the apostles looking foolish all around the Roman Empire, so I must run the risk of looking pretty foolish too. If the new King

---

[4] For example, Matthew 17:14–20; Galatians 4:13–15; Philippians 2:25–27; 2 Timothy 4:20.

[5] The word Paul uses is *charismata*, from which we get the phrase *charismatic gifts*.

is advancing and he has called us to be his soldiers, we mustn't run away from the thought of enemy fire.

Things came to a head one weekend a few years ago when a friend challenged me that it was time to take Paul at his word. I was due to preach the Gospel at a guest service in another town, and I was persuaded to pray for healing during the worship time before I spoke. I think I was the most surprised person in the room when two people were miraculously healed, and again a little later when more people responded to the Gospel after my sermon than had responded in my previous three years of preaching put together. That's what Paul means when he attributes his success at winning converts and planting churches to signs and miracles through the Holy Spirit.

I still have questions, and I still leave more people unhealed than healed. But more people are being healed now than they were when I fed my concerns instead of my faith in the teaching of these two verses. Time is running out, and the new King Jesus is still advancing his reign. I encourage you to do the same as me and risk looking foolish by preaching the Gospel in all its fullness, so that he can look great in the eyes of the entire world.

Ambition (15:20)

It has always been my ambition to preach the gospel where Christ was not known.

(Romans 15:20)

Ambition gets a bad press in Christian circles. We remember Paul's warnings against selfish ambition, but somehow we forget that he commends ambition too.[1] In fact, he does more than just commend it here in verse 20. He uses his own example as a challenge that lack of ambition for Jesus' name is a terrible sin.

Let me illustrate. A few years ago, I took a trip deep into rural India to see tigers in one of their few remaining hunting grounds. To get there, I had to take a plane, a train, a bus, a boat, a rickshaw and finally hitch a ride on the back of a bicycle. I was excited to be so far away from the Western world that crowds of children gathered round me to look at a white man. Then I walked past a clump of makeshift huts and came face to face with a sign which told me I should be drinking Coca-Cola! I don't know which bright executive created the famous 1970s advert, *"I'd like to buy the world a Coke"*, but thirty years later the dream has certainly come true. On the same trip, I chatted with a local who spoke English and tried to challenge him about his need to respond to Jesus. At first I thought his blank stare was due to lack of language skills, until I suddenly realized that this man was drinking Coke but had never heard the name of Jesus.

That's the kind of scene Paul has in mind when he tells

---

[1] The word *selfish ambition* in English New Testaments is actually an interpretation of the Greek word for *strife*. The Greek word Paul uses here for *showing ambition* is only ever used positively.

the Romans literally that *"It has always been my ambition to proclaim the gospel where Christ's name has not been uttered."* Caesar and Coca-Cola may be ambitious for their own names, but Paul outdoes their passion. In a world where marketeers move faster than missionaries to tap into emerging geographies, we must not read the letter to the Romans without catching Paul's contagious ambition to make Jesus known.

This ambition compelled him to leave his comfortable life in Antioch to start his First Missionary Journey. When he was stoned so severely by the citizens of Lystra that they dragged his body outside their city walls thinking he was dead, this ambition made him struggle to his feet and follow them back into the city.[2] When the Philippians flogged him and imprisoned him on his Second Missionary Journey, this ambition stopped him from freeing himself instantly by revealing that he was a Roman citizen. He considered it well worth silently enduring their torture so that he could teach the city magistrates not to dare to mess again with the infant church in their city.

When the Ephesians rioted during his Third Missionary Journey and searched the city in order to lynch him, this ambition made him want to rush out to preach to the crowd as soon as he heard the noise. It was what made him say to the Ephesian elders in Acts 20:24 that *"I consider my life worth nothing to me, if only I may finish the race and complete the task the Lord Jesus has given me."*

Paul wants to impart this same ambition to us as he describes his ministry here in verse 20. He wants some of us to become pioneers like him, leaving our own Rome or Antioch to go to far-off lands.[3] He calls others to stay and become missionaries at home, obeying the two other commands in which he uses this same Greek word. He tells us all in 1 Thessalonians

---

[2] Acts 14:19–20. Paul's three missionary journeys are in Acts 13–20.

[3] One of the spiritual gifts Paul lists in Romans 12:8 is literally the gift of *going ahead as a leader*. This doesn't just mean prominent position in the church, but also scouting out fresh lands beyond existing battle-lines.

4:11–12 to *"Make it your ambition…that your daily life may win the respect of outsiders"*, and in 2 Corinthians 5:9–11 that we should literally *"Make it our ambition to please him… Therefore… we try to persuade people."* Regardless of whether you are called to be a missionary abroad or a missionary at home, you cannot read the letter to the Romans and remain unchanged.

A twenty-five-year-old working-class Englishman named William Carey caught Paul's ambition in 1786. The population of the world was almost 750 million, and he calculated that three quarters had never heard the Gospel of Christ. He brought the issue before a gathering of church leaders but was told, *"Young man, sit down, sit down! You're an enthusiast. When God pleases to convert the heathen, He'll do it without consulting you or me."* In response, he penned a tract that stirred his nation and preached a sermon a year before sailing to pagan India in 1793 in which he took Isaiah 54:2 – *"Enlarge the place of your tent, stretch your tent curtains wide, do not hold back"* – and gave a repeated call for his listeners to *"Expect great things from God. Attempt great things for God."* William Carey caught such a strong dose of ambition for Jesus' name that by the time he died after four decades of foreign mission, he had so stirred Western Christians to action that he is still known as "the father of modern missions".[4]

A fourteen-year-old boy named James Chalmers caught the same ambition in 1856, when he heard a letter read in church from an explorer in far-away Fiji. When the preacher asked, *"I wonder if there is a boy here who will by and by bring the Gospel to the cannibals?"*, all his friends laughed off the challenge. But as he grew to be a man, he found, *"The nearer I get to Christ and his cross, the more do I long for direct contact with unsaved people."* At last the day came when he sailed with his young wife for islands which even greedy British traders were too frightened to explore. His wife died of a tropical disease but he ignored

---

[4] These quotes come from S. Pearce Carey's book *William Carey* (1923).

the letters from friends and family who urged him to give up and come home. *"Let me bury my sorrow in work for Christ,"* he replied. *"I cannot rest with so many thousands of heathen without a knowledge of Christ."*[5] On 7th April 1901, he went to preach the Gospel to cannibals on the remote island of Goaribari. He was surrounded by their warriors, beaten with stone clubs, decapitated, boiled and eaten. The London newspapers responded with a defiant headline: *"James Chalmers is dead, but others will carry on his work."*

Paul's question to us is, *Will we? Will we really?* Will we rediscover death-defying ambition for Jesus' name? If Paul's heart broke for Spanish cities with fewer than 100,000 people in them, will we feel less ambition for a world in which Bangladesh alone has an unreached population twice as big the entire first-century Roman Empire? William Carey wept and prayed for an eighteenth-century world which was barely 10 percent as populous as our own, and James Chalmers gave his life for islands with fewer people on them than live on the housing estates around many of our homes. Will we pray and sacrifice less than those who have gone before?

Paul says it's time for us to feel godly ambition for Jesus' name. It's time to pick up the baton from these dead missionaries' hands, and to let nothing steal our attention away from our own role in God's plan.

---

[5] These quotes come from Galen Brown Royer's book *Christian Heroism in Heathen Lands* (1914).

Everyone Has a Role to Play (15:23–16:24)

I urge you, brothers, by our Lord Jesus Christ and by the love of the Spirit, to join me in my struggle.

(Romans 15:30)

One of my favourite TV programmes is *Dragons' Den*.[1] If you haven't seen it, you are missing a great show in which inventors and start-up businesses make a pitch to five entrepreneurs to invest in their idea. The dragons, as their name suggests, are vicious in their frank assessment of what they see. Sitting next to coffee tables piled high with money, they break products, poke holes in business plans and find fault with the sales pitches which the nervous contestants deliver. Finally, having found a fatal flaw in the business proposition, each of the dragons smugly declares: *"And for that reason, I'm out."*

The first three sections of Romans bear the wonderful message that God is not like one of the dragons in the den. He looks at our broken lives in section one and paints five Gospel pictures which all declare: *"And for that reason, I'm in."* Paul tells us in chapters 6–8 that God wants to fill us with his Spirit as a powerful proof that he definitely wants in. Section two reveals his master plan and section three his will for our daily lives, completing fourteen and a half chapters in which God lovingly says to us again and again: *"And for that reason, I'm in."*

But in section four Paul tells us it's our turn. In 15:14–16:27, it is God who presents his unstoppable proposition to take the Gospel to the ends of the earth through his People. Unlike a

---

[1] American readers will know this as *Shark Tank* on US television.

contestant on *Dragons' Den*, he doesn't need our resources to make his plan successful, but as Paul brings his letter to a close he is nevertheless asking us to make a decision. He wants us to invest all we have in the advancement of his Kingdom, and to tell him resoundingly, *"For that reason, I'm in."* Sadly, far too many Christians get to the end of Paul's letter and disqualify themselves. Whether actively or passively, they read about God's mission and tell him, *"For that reason, I'm out."*

Some people write themselves off because of *challenging life circumstances.* They may be long-term sick, old and infirm, or restricted to the home as a parent or a carer. If that's you, then take note of Paul's final verses, because he goes out of his way to show you that you still have a role to play in God's world mission.

First, he tells you in 15:26–28 that you can be part of the team by contributing *money*, even if you can't personally go. There are workers to support, mercy ministries to fund and new church plants which need start-up money to get off the ground. The believers in Greece and Macedonia might never personally travel to Judea, but they could be part of God's plan to bless the Jews by giving some of their money to those who did.

Second, Paul tells you in 15:30–32 that you can be part of the team by contributing *prayer.* In the ancient world, believers could receive letters with information on how to partner with overseas missionaries in prayer. Nowadays, with instant emails and websites and Facebook and phones, it has never been easier to play a role in world mission without leaving your front door.[2]

Third, Paul tells you that you can play your part in his mission by opening up your *home.* It may be to host a Christian worker, as in 16:2 and 23, or it may be to host a church meeting, as in 16:5 and 23. Either way, Paul tells you not to count yourself

---

[2] Note in 15:30 the seriousness of Paul's charge *"by our Lord Jesus Christ and by the love of the Spirit"* for us to pray. Prayer is by no means a second-best role for us to play.

out of God's mission because you cannot leave your home. He tells you to trust that everyone has a role to play, and he urges you to tell the Lord, *"For that reason, I'm in."*

Other people write themselves off because of *who they are*, but Paul anticipates that objection and fills these verses with reasons not do so.

If you think you are somehow less able to serve in the church because you are a *woman*, then note that over a quarter of the names in chapter 16 are female.[3] There is Phoebe, who served as a deaconess in the church at Cenchrea, one of Corinth's ports, and whom Paul appears to have entrusted with carrying this precious letter from Corinth to Rome. There is also Priscilla, the woman who helped Paul to plant churches in Corinth and Ephesus, and who along with her husband discipled the great preacher Apollos.[4] Paul commends many of these women for their hard work in the Lord, and he encourages you to follow their lead.

If you think that you are less able to serve because of your *place in society*, chapter 16 should also make you think again. Paul mentions Erastus who was a senior civil servant in 16:23, but he also mentions Urbanus and Hermes, which were common slave names.[5] He mentions at least eight Jews and around thirty Gentiles.[6] Paul includes Andronicus and Junias, who were so outstanding in their ministry that they stand among the apostles, yet at the same time he commends the mother of Rufus for simply making him feel like part of her family.[7] Paul

---

[3] We are not sure if some of the names are male or female, so well over a quarter may even be women.

[4] Acts 18:2–3; 18:18–28; 1 Corinthians 16:19; 2 Timothy 4:19.

[5] Visitors to the ruins of ancient Corinth can see an inscription which mentions Erastus as *aedile* of the city.

[6] Most scholars assume that when Paul refers to his *relatives* in 16:7, 11, 21, he is talking about *Jews*.

[7] Since Mark uses lots of Latin words in his gospel and tells his Roman readers in Mark 15:21 that Simon of Cyrene was the father of Rufus, this woman may have been the widow of the man who carried Jesus' cross.

is determined to show you that whoever you are, you must not count yourself out of a role in world mission. He wants these final verses to stir you to tell the Lord: *"For that reason, I'm in."*

So if you are a church leader, make sure you value the role which every single person you lead has to play. Don't let your church become like the one about which Shane Claiborne complains: *"I feel like I'm watching professional wrestling. There's a lot of shouting and sweating, but the people seem too superhuman, and I'm not convinced all the moves are real. And as with any sports event, there are tons of spectators, desperately in need of exercise, who sit back and watch a handful of people who could really use a little break."*[8]

If you are a church member, make sure you do as Paul told you back in 12:3 and commit yourself to doing all you can *"in accordance with the measure of faith God has given you"*. Value the church members all around you and invest everything to serve alongside them. As you finish Romans, turn to the Lord and say:

It doesn't matter who I am and it doesn't matter what my circumstances are, because of the Gospel you have made me part of your People. *And for that reason, I'm in.*

[8] Shane Claiborne, *The Irresistible Revolution* (2006).

First-Fruits (16:5)

Greet my beloved Epenetus, who was a first-fruit to Christ in Asia.

(Romans 16:5)[1]

Is Paul losing his Greek marbles? How can he possibly tell the Romans that *"there is no more place for me to work"* in the Eastern Mediterranean, when Acts tells us that in nine years he had only planted a dozen churches? The East had hundreds of towns and millions of inhabitants, so who does Paul think he is trying to fool? Even worse, he claims to have preached the Gospel all the way up to Illyricum in modern-day Croatia, when Acts tells us that the furthest north he ever went was Philippi. How can Paul make such a claim as he leaves the east to plant churches in the west? The answer is found in a little Greek word in 16:5. He refers to one of his converts as his *first-fruit*.

Most modern readers have little clue what this means, so translators tend to render it *first convert*. What this fails to capture is that *aparchē* was a word used in the Septuagint for the early crops which God told the Israelites to offer him in grateful faith that plenty more were definitely on their way.[2] It's the word Paul used in 8:23 to describe our experience of the Holy Spirit as a "first-fruit" of our future glory. It's the word he used in 11:16 to describe the early Jewish converts in Jerusalem as the "first-fruit" which preceded a Gentile harvest around the

---

[1] The Amplified Bible. Some less reliable manuscripts read *Achaia* instead of *Asia*, but this is probably a copyist's error caused by confusion because Paul was writing from Corinth.

[2] For example, in Exodus 23:19 and Proverbs 3:9–10. Jesus applied this to the Gospel in Mark 4:20.

world. It's the word he used in 1 Corinthians 15:20–23 to tell us that Jesus' resurrection is a "first-fruit" of our own to come. So when he tells the Romans that Epenetus was one of his "first-fruits" in Asia, he is explaining how planting twelve churches in nine years was enough to say that he had finished his mission from Jerusalem to Illyricum.

Paul's reference to "first-fruits" should transform *where we plant churches*. It didn't matter that he had only planted a dozen churches in the East, because what really mattered was where he had planted them. He had sped past towns and villages in a hurry to reach the cultural and commercial centres of Ephesus, Philippi, Thessalonica, Berea, Athens and Corinth. The largest of those were Ephesus and Corinth, accounting together for over a million people, so he spent half his nine years in those two cities alone. He went nowhere in Asia but to Ephesus, yet the city received such a constant stream of visitors that in Acts 19:10 *"all the Jews and Greeks who lived in the province of Asia heard the word of the Lord."* That's probably how the Gospel reached Illyricum too, since Corinth was the main port for its Adriatic sailors. Paul wants us to see that God's mission can be completed, just so long as we prioritize planting churches in big cities.

Paul's reference to "first-fruits" should also transform *the kind of churches we plant*. Paul's goal was not to produce dependent daughter churches of a mother church in Antioch. He released local leadership so that he could get out fast, leaving missionary churches with ambition of their own. At Corinth, he offered his "first-fruits" back to God as church elders, and was able to write a letter only three years later to *"all the saints throughout Achaia"*.[3] At Ephesus, he offered his "first-fruits" back to God as church planters, and was delighted to be able to write to new churches in nearby cities such as Colosse and Laodicea.[4]

---

[3] 1 Corinthians 16:15 (literally *first-fruit*) and 2 Corinthians 1:1.

[4] Epaphras was a Colossian who was converted through Paul while in Ephesus. He went home to plant churches in eastern Asia without Paul ever

Vincent Donovan, one of the most successful missionaries to Africa, attributes his success to rediscovering Paul's model:

> *We foreign missionaries have been in East Africa for more than a hundred years... There is something definitely temporary about Paul's missionary stay in any one place. There is something of a deadly permanence in ours... I discovered that the whole area could be divided into twenty-six sections. A different section could be reached every day if one moved out of the mission house and lived in a Landrover and a tent. Instructions in the Christian message would take about a year in any one section visited once a week. Realistically, six sections could be reached in a year. So, the whole Loliondo area of twenty-six sections could be evangelised in five years; less, if others joined me in the task. This struck me as of extreme importance and significance. It would mean I could leave that particular mission after five years, having completed my work.*

He reflects that,

> *I can remember an old missionary telling me that he had spent his life under the snows of Kilimanjaro, and his dream was to die and be buried under the snows of Kilimanjaro. I was deeply impressed at the time. It was a beautiful thought, but looking back on it now I do not think it was a particularly missionary thought. Nor are any involving hundred year plans.[5]*

Paul's reference to "first-fruits" should also transform *our expectations in planting churches*. If we consider it our task to preach to every individual, the fact that the world population

---

needing to go there (Colossians 2:1; 4:12–13, 16).

[5] Vincent Donovan, *Christianity Rediscovered* (1978).

has grown by a billion in the past twelve years is pretty discouraging. But if we see our task as winning "first-fruits" in every people group who can finish what we have started, suddenly our mission becomes achievable by God's grace. The population has grown in the past twelve years, but the number of people groups has slightly declined. Paul says our task is not to convert the ever-growing billions, but to plant 6,918 missionary churches in the 6,918 people groups that still remain unreached as of 2011.[6] He tells us that the new King Jesus is advancing and he will win. We simply need to grasp why Paul calls Epenetus his "first-fruit" and why he says that his work in the East is now complete.

Finally, Paul's reference to "first-fruits" should also give us *patience in planting churches*. Every ancient farmer knew that the first crops took the longest time, and that the rest of the harvest then came very quickly. Paul had spent his early days in Ephesus pastoring an ignorant group of twelve would-be disciples, but after he pushed his way through those early frustrations he found that he soon had a megachurch on his hands.[7] Church planters and missionaries know that the battle for the "first-fruits" is always the hardest. Even William Carey saw no converts from his first seven years in India, but he saw half a million people come to faith in the region in the thirty years after he baptized his "first-fruit".

We have almost come to the end of Romans, so it's time to get specific. How can your church act as God's "first-fruit" by planting new churches in other towns and nations? What can you do to be part of God's plan to plant new "first-fruit" churches in one of those 6,918 unreached people groups? If we take these questions seriously, God gives us a sneak preview in Revelation 7:9 of what will happen:

---

[6] This data comes from the website of the Joshua Project.

[7] Acts 19:1–7, 17–20, 26. The sum mentioned in Acts 19:19, 50,000 drachmas, was the equivalent of £10,000,000, which suggests the church grew quickly to several tens of thousands strong.

After this I looked and there before me was a great multitude that no one could count, from every nation, tribe, people and language, standing before the throne and in front of the Lamb.

He Who Is Able (16:25–27)

Now to him who is able to establish you by my gospel...to the only wise God be glory for ever through Jesus Christ! Amen.

(Romans 16:25, 27)

How do you close a letter like Romans? Should Paul give a last recap of the Gospel? Speak a few final words into the clash between the Jewish and Gentile Christians? Exhort us to live holy lives in view of our salvation? Paul actually chooses to do none of those things, but to end with three verses of assurance and breathless worship. Our only proper response to the message of Romans is to worship the one Paul refers to as *"him who is able"*, and to find that as we worship him our assurance in the Gospel grows.

Perhaps you are still processing the message of 1:18–3:20, because you prefer to think the human race is a bit less sinful than Paul makes out. Paul reminds you in verse 25 that this letter has been about the great *euangelion*, or *Gospel*, that God has sent his Son to live and die and rise again as the new King in town. If any senator who opposed Caesar was swiftly executed, we mustn't fool ourselves that God indulges human rebellion against his Son as King. When we recognize that the Lord's name is *"he who is able"*, we start to worship him even for his justice in judging sin.

Perhaps you are still questioning the message of 3:21–5:21, because you recognize exactly how sinful the human race truly is. Perhaps you are still struggling to believe in those five Gospel pictures, since it sounds too good to be true for the Lord to acquit the wicked and set the guilty free. Paul has already told us in 4:20 that the way to increase our faith in the Gospel is to worship the Lord for what it says,[1] and now he leads us in such worship by reminding us that the Gospel is *"the proclamation of Jesus Christ"*. Of course it would sound too good to be true if God had simply decided on a whim to forgive us, acquit us, free us and raise us to new life. But he hasn't. He has done so by sending his Son to step into our shoes so that we can step into his. Paul tells us in verse 20 where to focus our gaze if we are still struggling to believe the Gospel he shares in Romans. He tells us to worship God for *"the grace of our Lord Jesus"*.

Perhaps you are still processing the message of chapters 6–8, longing to experience your salvation but still feeling as though you are fighting a losing battle against sin. Paul reminds you that you will find your answer in the same truth that *"he is able"*. If you count yourself dead to sin but raised to new life in God's Son,[2] if you ask the Lord to fill you with his Spirit afresh today, and if you cry out to him as Daddy, then you will know the new King's victory. Paul promises you in verse 20 that, *"The God of peace will soon crush Satan under your feet."* There really is a new King in town, and if you lay hold of his Gospel, you will experience his rule.

Perhaps you are still struggling to trust in God's sovereign plan, as Paul describes it in chapters 9–11. Again, the answer is to worship God as *"he who is able"*, as *"the eternal God"* and as *"the only wise God"* in verses 26 and 27. Paul has jam-packed the book of Romans more full of Old Testament quotations than any other book in the New Testament, because he wants to convince you that the new King is accomplishing his perfect plan. Paul uses this to fuel our worship in these three final verses, praising God that he planned the Gospel before

---

[1] Romans 4:20 literally says *"he was strengthened in faith as he gave glory to God."*

[2] Paul points back to his theme in 6:1–8:39 by saying *"in the Lord"* or *"in Christ"* eleven times in this chapter.

the creation of the world, that he made it known through his Prophets and that he has now finally revealed it through the coming of his Son. Paul tells us not to struggle to trust the strategy of *"him who is able"*. His hand is not just on the tiller of history; he has made the new King Jesus what world history is all about.

Perhaps you are still grappling with Paul's application of the Gospel in 12:1–15:13. If so, then note his speed in verse 19 to encourage instead of criticize. He wants you to know that God is delighted with you and with each baby step of fresh obedience which you take. We all need to grow in our obedience, but God is cheering us on, and making himself available to us as *"he who is able"*. He longs to fill us with his Spirit and unite us with other believers who can help us grow into full maturity as disciples of his Son.[3]

Perhaps you still feel daunted by Paul's challenge to world mission in 15:14–16:27, and think the challenge should really be labelled *"Mission: Impossible"*. Yet again, Paul says the answer lies in worshipping the Lord as *"he who is able"*. He reminds us in verse 26 that God has shaped world history *"so that all nations might believe and obey him."*[4] The new King is advancing and he bears the burden of completing his mission, but he invites us by grace to minister at his side. If you can grasp this and step into God's mission as Paul beckons you, grace will teach you to say with Paul in 15:29, *"I know that... I will come in the full measure of the blessing of Christ."* That's what it means for Jesus to be the new King and for his name to be *"he who is able"*.

So with this in mind, don't rush to finish the rest of this commentary without stopping to praise. Take a pause and

---

[3] Note the link between verses 17–18 and verses 19–20. We find that God crushes Satan under our feet when we renounce our petty divisions and unite for our great King's glory.

[4] When Paul talks about the obedience of the nations, he is making a deliberate link back to 1:5 and 15:18.

spend time to worship *"him who is able"*. Praise him as the eternal God, the all-powerful God and the only wise God – and as you worship, start proclaiming that there's a new King in town.

Conclusion: There's a New King in Town

> *The God of peace will soon crush Satan under your*
> *feet.*
>
> (Romans 16:20)

In 64 AD, the Empire struck back. When a great fire swept Rome, Nero seized it as an opportunity to silence the message that there was a new King in town. He pinned the blame on the Christians and devised bizarre executions which would demonstrate once and for all that he alone was Lord. They preached Gospel pictures about their King being crucified to save them, so he nailed them to crosses to show that Jesus hadn't saved them at all. They preached that their King had made them his flock and the light of the world, so he dressed them up as sheep and threw them to packs of dogs, or *"made them into torches to be ignited after dark as substitutes for daylight"*.[1] As Paul, Peter and many other church members died, a sneering Nero asked the world: where is your King Jesus now?

The answer was that Jesus was doing exactly what the book of Romans had promised he would. Paul had warned the church in his letter that persecution was coming, and they responded by blessing their enemies when it came. The emperor's comeback actually stirred the city to feel compassion towards them, and their courage in death made the new King Jesus the talk all over town. While Nero fell from power and committed suicide in 68 AD, and while the Romans got through four new emperors in

---

[1] Tacitus tells us all of this in *Annals* (15.44).

the troubled year which followed, Michael Green explains in contrast that:

> *Here were men and women of every rank and station in life...so convinced that they had discovered the riddle of the universe, so sure of the one true God whom they had come to know, that nothing must stand in the way of their passing on this good news to others... They might be slighted, laughed at, disenfranchised, robbed of their possessions, their homes, even their families, but this would not stop them. They might be reported to the authorities as dangerous atheists, and required to sacrifice to the imperial gods: but they refused to comply. In Christianity they had found something utterly new, authentic and satisfying. They were not prepared to deny Christ even in order to preserve their own lives; and in the manner of their dying they made converts to their faith.[2]*

A few years later, the Emperor Domitian relaunched Nero's failed counter-strike. He made his subjects address him as *"Our Lord and God"*, and executed any Christian who refused to do so.[3] He even killed one of the consuls – his own cousin – for turning to *"atheism"* and *"Jewish ways"* by following the Galilean King.[4] Yet Paul's promise in Romans 16:20, that *"The God of peace will soon crush Satan under your feet"*, was never far away. Domitian was not even powerful enough to prevent his enemies from assassinating him and burning his corpse like that of a common pauper, but King Jesus was able to transform this persecution into the very means by which his Gospel kept advancing. Pliny wrote to Domitian's successor, the Emperor Trajan, and

---

[2] Michael Green, *Evangelism in the Early Church* (1970).

[3] Suetonius, *Life of Domitian* (chapter 13).

[4] Cassius Dio, *Roman History* (67.14). *Atheism* meant refusal to recognize the Roman gods.

complained that *"Great numbers are in danger, currently or imminently, from every rank, every age, and from both sexes. In fact, this contagious superstition is not confined to the cities only, but has spread its infection among the neighbouring villages and country."*[5] Against all odds, just as Paul had promised, the new King was advancing.

The Roman emperors were nothing if not determined to succeed. Septimius Severus, then Maximinus, then Decius, then Valerian – but every time the Empire struck back, the emperor died horribly as proof that there was another, far greater King in town. When they executed the Christians, they gave them such a platform to paint Paul's Gospel pictures with their blood that Tertullian retorted that *"The blood of the martyrs is the seed of the Church."*[6] When they scattered the Christians, they simply forced them to obey section four of Romans and take the Gospel to the world. Eusebius records that,

> *They did the work of evangelists, filled with an ambition to preach Christ to those who had not yet heard the message of faith, and to deliver the holy gospels to them. They simply laid the foundations of the faith in foreign lands, and when they had done so they appointed others as shepherds and trusted them to care for the new growth, while they themselves went on again to other countries and nations with the grace and cooperation of God. A great many miracles were done through them by the power of God's Spirit, so that great crowds eagerly embraced the religion of the Creator of the universe at only their first hearing.*[7]

---

[5] Pliny the Younger in his *Letters* (10.96) in around 112 AD.

[6] Tertullian in his *Apology* (chapter 50) in c.197 AD.

[7] Eusebius of Caesarea, writing about these events in his *Church History* (3.37) just after 300 AD.

I'm giving you this account of what happened next because we have reached the end of reading Romans, but only the beginning of living out what it says. You need to grasp that the message that Jesus is the new King in town seemed utterly destined to fail in 57 AD, but from our perspective the facts are completely on Paul's side. When the Roman church preached the message of chapters 1–11, and applied it to their lives through the message of 12:1–15:13, Jesus rushed to their aid and brought salvation to their city. When they blessed those who persecuted them, they won them over, and 250 years after Paul wrote his letter even Caesar himself hailed Jesus as the King. When they were scattered to the nations – either willingly or because forced to do so – then they planted "first-fruit" churches which went on to reach the world. So don't be fooled into thinking that responding to the book of Romans means little more than signing a statement of doctrinal beliefs. This is a letter that took on an empire and won, with its message that there's a new King in town.

So, what role will you play in the continuing story of Romans? Will you receive Jesus as your King and give your life to him, like these martyrs and missionaries who have gone before? Will you take this message to the houses and schools and workplaces and clubs and gathering places near to where you live? Will you find ways to play your part in God's mission of taking this message to the places where you currently don't live? Or will you let modern-day Caesars – either people or ways of thinking – intimidate you and prevent you from stepping forward into God's plan?

Will you believe Paul's promise that *"The God of peace will soon crush Satan under your feet"*? Will you trust him that the God who helped the Roman Christians will also help you? If you will, then all heaven will rush to your aid, as you start proclaiming to the world that there's a new King in town!

OTHER BOOKS IN THE
STRAIGHT TO THE HEART SERIES:

ISBN 978 0 85721 001 2

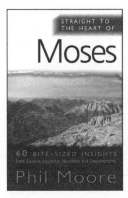

ISBN 978 0 85721 056 2

ISBN 978 1 85424 988 3

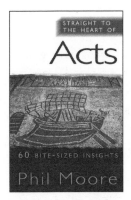

ISBN 978 1 85424 989 0

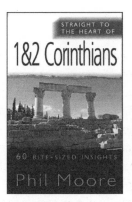

ISBN 978 0 85721 002 9

ISBN 978 1 85424 990 6

For more information please go to **www.philmoorebooks.com** or
www.lionhudson.com.